Sifters

VIEWPOINTS ON AMERICAN CULTURE
Catherine Clinton, Series Editor

Viewpoints on American Culture offers timely reflections for twenty-first century readers. A sensible guide to knowledge in a scholarly field, something one can pick up—literally and figuratively—seems to be facing extinction. Volumes in our series will provide intellectual relief and practical solution.

The series targets topics where debates have flourished and brings together the voices of established and emerging writers to share their own points of view in a compact and compelling format. Our books offer sophisticated, yet accessible, introductions into an array of issues under our broad and expanding banner.

Long Time Gone: Looking Back at Sixties America
Edited by Alexander Bloom

Sifters: Native American Women's Lives
Edited by Theda Perdue

Native American Women's Lives

Edited by Theda Perdue

UNIVERSITY PRESS

2001

OXFORD

UNIVERSITY PRESS

Oxford   New York
Athens   Auckland   Bangkok   Bogotá   Buenos Aires   Calcutta
Cape Town   Chennai   Dar es Salaam   Delhi   Florence   Hong Kong
Istanbul   Karachi   Kuala Lumpur   Madrid   Melbourne   Mexico City
Mumbai   Nairobi   Paris   São Paulo   Shanghai   Singapore   Taipei
Tokyo   Toronto   Warsaw

and associated companies in
Berlin   Ibadan

Copyright © 2001 by Oxford University Press, Inc.

Published by Oxford University Press, Inc.
198 Madison Avenue, New York, New York 10016

Oxford is a registered trademark of Oxford University Press.

Library of Congress Cataloging-in-Publication Data
Sifters : Native American Women's lives / edited by Theda Perdue.
p.   cm. — (Viewpoints on American culture)
Includes bibliographical references.
ISBN 0-19-513080-4; ISBN 0-19-513081-2 (pbk.)
1. Indian women—North America—Biography.   2. Indian women—
North America—History.   3. Indian women—North America—
Social life and customs.   I. Perdue, Theda, 1949–   II. Series.
4. Onomastics.   5. Poetics.   I. Title.
E89.S454   2001
973'.0497'00922—dc21   00-039950
[B]

9 8 7 6 5 4 3 2

Printed in the United States of America
on acid-free paper

PREFACE

The role of individuals in history presents a major challenge for the study of Native American women. The sources are often silent on Native women both because they are Native and because they are women. When Native women do appear in the documentary record, they are usually nameless, and even books devoted to Native history and women's history frequently reflect the sources by condemning their subjects to anonymity. For a few Native women, however, we can ferret out enough information to present outlines and interpretations of their lives. The women whose biographies appear in this volume probably are not representative of all women in Indian societies; only extraordinary behavior created a paper trail that is sufficient to reconstruct their lives. By standing out, they also compromised the corporate ethic that has traditionally governed Native lives. Nevertheless, their stories reflect their cultures and the historical periods in which they lived. They reveal the diversity of Native Americans and the common threads that link their histories. As anomalous as they may be, the lives of these women serve to personalize and feminize the story of Native America.

Readers who would like to know about many other Native women should begin with Gretchen Bataille's *Native American Women: A Biographical Dictionary* (New York: Garland Publishing, 1993), which includes short bibliographies as well as biographical sketches. Like all editors, I had to be selective in terms of subjects and authors, and I relied on my own knowledge of the field and of the research that the contributors to this volume were conducting. I tried to achieve geographical, cultural, and chronological balance, and I sought to present a variety of women's experiences. Readers must remember, however, that this volume only scratches the surface. Scholars should consider its brevity to be a challenge to expand further our understanding of women in Native cultures and histories.

The contributors to this collection represent the diversity of scholarship on Native Americans. Our fields include history, anthropology, English, and American Studies. Our experience ranges from positions as museum curators, professional writers, and journal editors to university professors and administrators, and many of us have worked for the Indian people about whom we write. Two contributors are Native themselves, while some others are honorary members of tribes. We represent three generations of scholarship. The work of the most senior was required reading in the graduate programs of most others. Three contributors have been the students of other contributors. Most of us have attended the same conferences, served on panels together, and read each other's work. Despite our diversity, we truly form a community of scholars.

Of the many members of the broader scholarly community who have shaped my ideas over the years, I would particularly like to thank those who helped directly with this book. Catherine Clinton had the original idea for this collection, and Susan Ferber made it far better through her careful editing. Rosalie Radcliffe provided both clerical assistance and the intangible support that comes from someone who is *really* interested in your work. Rose Stremlau served as my research assistant and reminded me of the enthusiasm I had brought to graduate school when I enrolled nearly thirty years ago. I retain much of that enthusiasm largely because of graduate students. And so for their conversations, ideas, and friendships while I worked on this book, I would like to thank Joe Anoatubby, Victor Blue, Karl Davis, Cary Miller, Anna Smith, and Felicia Wiley. Finally, my husband, Michael D. Green, has been my best sounding board, critic, and cheerleader, but most important, he has been a wonderful distraction who always reminds me that one cannot live by books alone.

Chapel Hill, North Carolina   T. P.
March 2000

CONTENTS

CONTRIBUTORS

DONNA BARBIE is professor of humanities at Embry-Riddle University in Daytona Beach, Florida. She received her Ph.D. in American Studies at Emory University. Her North Dakota upbringing shaped her interest in Native women and the West, which ultimately led to her major work, *The Making of Sacagawea: A Euro-American Legend* (1996). Other publications and presentations centered on Native women have included "Disney's *Pocahontas*: Mythic Revision or Reinforcement?" "Perpetuating the 'Myth of Male Dominance': The Work of Contemporary Lakota Women," and "The Impact of Colonization upon Traditional Lakota Women." Her research interests include popular culture, advertising, and nonverbal communication.

JAMES TAYLOR CARSON is assistant professor of history at Queens University in Kingston, Ontario. He received his Ph.D. from the University of Kentucky, and he is author of *Searching for the Bright Path: The Mississippi Choctaws from Prehistory to Removal* (1999). The recipient of a Pew Foundation Fellowship, Carson has published essays in *Ethnohistory*, *Agricultural History*, and other journals and anthologies.

DEE GARCEAU holds a Ph.D. in American civilization from Brown University and currently serves on the history faculty at Rhodes College in Memphis, Tennessee. She teaches courses on the American West, Native American history, and American women's history. She is author of *The Important Things of Life: Women, Work, and Family in Sweetwater County, Wyoming, 1880–1929* (1997) and articles on women in postwar western literature and on the gendered subculture of cowboys.

MICHAEL D. GREEN is professor of American studies and history at the University of North Carolina. A Fellow of the D'Arcy McNickle Center for the History of the American Indian at the Newberry Library, Chicago, he previously taught at the University of Kentucky and chaired the Native American studies program at Dartmouth College. He is author of *The Creeks: A Critical Bibliography* (1979), *The Politics of Indian Removal: Creek Government and Society in Crisis* (1985), and *The Creeks* (1990), and coeditor of *The Cherokee Removal* (1995).

P. JANE HAFEN (Taos Pueblo) is an associate professor of English at the University of Nevada, Las Vegas. Her work on Zitkala Ša began with a Francis C. Allen Fellowship at the D'Arcy McNickle Center for History of the American Indian at the Newberry Library.

LAURENCE M. HAUPTMAN is SUNY Distinguished Professor of History and SUNY Faculty Exchange Scholar at State University of New York at New Paltz. He has written or edited twelve books, most recently *Conspiracy of Interests: Iroquois Dispossession and the Rise of New York State* (1999), which won Syracuse University's John Ben Snow Prize, and *The Oneida Indian Journey: From New York to Wisconsin, 1784–1860* (1999). *Choice* named two of his works, *The Iroquois Struggle for Survival* (1996) and *Between Two Fires: American Indians in the Civil War* (1995), outstanding academic books. He has worked for the Oneida Nation of Indians of Wisconsin, the Seneca Nation of Indians, and the Mashantucket Pequot Tribal Nation, and twice he has received the Peter Doctor (Iroquois) Memorial Foundation Award for goodwill bestowed on Indian people.

NANCY OESTREICH LURIE retired as head curator of anthropology at the Milwaukee Public Museum in 1979. She received her Ph.D. from Northwestern University in 1952. She has held faculty appointments at the universities of Michigan, Wisconsin-Milwaukee, and Aarhus, Denmark; has served as an expert witness before the U.S. Claims Commission; and was president of the American Anthropological Association, 1983–85. Her publications cover theoretical concerns as well as field research among the Ho-Chunk, also known as Winnebago, and Dogrib Indians. Her most recent book is *Women and the Invention of American Anthropology* (1999).

BUNNY MCBRIDE is a writer with a masters degree in anthropology from Columbia University. She is author of *Women of the Dawn* (1999), *Molly Spotted Elk: A Penobscot in Paris* (1995), and *Our Lives in Our Hands: Micmac Indian Basketmakers* (1990), and coauthor of *The Audubon Society Field Guide to African Wildlife* (1995). From 1978 to 1988 she wrote regularly for *The Christian Science Monitor*, and she has contributed to many other newspapers, magazines, and books. McBride is an adjunct lecturer in anthropology at Kansas State University. From 1981 to 1991 she and her husband, anthropologist Harald Prins, did historical research and community development work for the Aroostook Band of Micmacs in Maine resulting in federal legislation granting the band recognition and funds to buy back aboriginal land. In 1999 the Maine legislature gave McBride a special commendation for her research and writing on the history of Native women in the state, an honor initiated by tribal representatives in the legislature.

DEVON A. MIHESUAH is professor of history at Northern Arizona University in Flagstaff. An enrolled member of the Choctaw Nation of Oklahoma, she is the editor of the *American Indian Quarterly*. Her publications include *Cultivating the Rosebuds: The Education of Women at the Cherokee Female Seminary, 1851–1909* (1993), *American Indians: Stereotypes and Realities* (1996), and *Natives and Academics: Researching and Writing about American Indians* (1998), as well as many articles.

LAURA MOORE received her Ph.D. in 1999 from the University of North Carolina at Chapel Hill, with a dissertation entitled "The Navajo Rug Trade: Gender, Art, Work, and Modernity in the American Southwest, 1870s–1930s." Her research and writing focuses on the intersections of gender and race, with a particular interest in the western United States and Native American women. She currently teaches women's history and United States history at Vanderbilt University.

THEDA PERDUE is professor of history at the University of North Carolina at Chapel Hill. She is author of *Slavery and the Evolution of Cherokee Society, 1540–1865* (1979), *Native Carolinians* (1985), *The Cherokee* (1988), and, most recently, *Cherokee Women: Gender and Culture Change, 1700–1835* (1998). She is editor of *Nations Remembered: An Oral History of the Five Civilized Tribes* (1980) and *Cherokee Editor* (1983), and coeditor of *Southern Women: Histories and Identities* (1992), *Hidden Histories of Women of the New South* (1994), and *The Cherokee Removal* (1995). She is a fellow of the D'Arcy McNickle Center for the Study of the American Indian at the Newberry Library and the Rockefeller Foundation. She serves on the editorial boards of the *Journal of Women's History* and *Southern Cultures*.

TERRY REYNOLDS is the curator of collections and exhibits at New Mexico State University Museum. She is an anthropologist who has done extensive research on southwestern peoples, history, arts, and crafts. She received her Ph.D. from the University of British Columbia and was Director of the University of Denver Graduate Museums Studies Program before arriving at NMSU in 1998.

PHILLIP ROUND earned his Ph.D. in English from UCLA and is the author of *By Nature and by Custom Cursed: Transatlantic Civil Discourse and New England Cultural Production, 1620–1660* (1999). He has written several articles on American literature and culture for *American Indian Quarterly*, *Early American Literature*, and other journals and collections. He is associate professor of English at the University of Iowa.

HELEN C. ROUNTREE received all her degrees in anthropology, including her doctorate, from the University of Wisconsin, Milwaukee, under the direction of Nancy O. Lurie. She joined the faculty of Old Dominion University in Norfolk, Virginia, in 1968 and began researching the historical and modern Powhatan Indians the following year, a project that so far has resulted in four books, including *Pocahontas's People: The Powhatan Indians of Virginia Through Four Centuries* (1990), and many shorter pieces. She is an honorary member of two of the modern Virginia Indian tribes and is the unofficial recording-secretary-for-life of one of them. After retiring from the classroom in 2000, she became a full-time researcher, writer, and consultant with tribes and museums in Virginia.

Sifters

INTRODUCTION

Theda Perdue

"Is it a bow or a sifter?" inquired nineteenth-century Cherokees upon the birth of a child.[1] A bow, the weapon of war and implement of hunting for centuries, epitomized masculinity; the sifter, essential to making bread, was a woman's most important tool. While Cherokee women used sifters in a variety of ways, from seeding fruit to straining the oil they made from crushed nuts, the primary function of these loosely woven baskets was processing corn. Women were intimately associated with corn—the same Cherokee word, *selu*, means both woman and corn—which they planted, tended, and harvested. Sifters sorted out the largest kernels of corn for seed, guaranteeing next year's crop. To make dried corn palatable, women soaked kernels in a mixture of wood ashes sifted into water. Sifters drained off the liquid, and when the dried kernels had been pounded into meal, sifters separated large pieces from finer meal. Each went into different dishes that the women prepared. For the Cherokees, sifters, like women, represented both production and sustenance.[2]

Throughout Native North America, women acted as sifters, giving life and sustaining life. Native peoples honored mothers, not through empty sentimentality, but by recognizing the social, economic, and political importance of their reproductive role. Many Native peoples attributed the earth's creation and peopling to women, not men. Mothers nurtured small children and exercised enormous influence over their adult offspring. In some societies, such as the Iroquois, motherhood conveyed political power to women through clan mothers who chose chiefs and had the authority to depose them.

The status of women also rested on their economic role. Native women, whether they lived in the hunting and gathering societies of the Great Basin or the agricultural societies of the Southeast, provided much of the food for their communities. In various places in North America, they gathered nuts, berries, wild onions and greens, roots, bark, and seeds, and they grew crops of corn, beans, and squash. Women in most societies built and owned dwellings, and they furnished their houses with baskets, pottery, benches, mats, and finely worked skins.

Women controlled their own labor and the goods they produced. Feminist anthropologists have referred to "arenas of power" and "complementary" roles in describing the relationship between Native women and men: each gender had its own responsibilities, and Native societies recognized that the contributions of each were essential to survival.[3] Similarly, each gender had access to spiritual power, although perhaps in different forms. Women, for example, had songs and rituals that made the corn grow, while men's ceremonies brought success in hunting and war. Gender, therefore, distinguished in profound ways the kind of life—from work to prayer—that a person would live.

Sifting out women's historical experiences from the voluminous documents that chronicle Indian-white relations has not been easy.[4] European men largely controlled the historical record, and they were interested in trade, war, and land acquisition rather than in women's roles. Because men and women led remarkably separate lives in most Native societies, male foreigners who visited their communities rarely encountered women on anything other than a superficial or sometimes sexual level. Furthermore, men had little knowledge of or access to women's work and ritual; even if foreigners inquired about women's lives, Native men had scant information to offer.

Ignorance, however, did not keep Euro-Americans from incorporating Native women into their myths about nation building, as Helen Rountree and Donna Barbie demonstrate in their essays on Pocahontas and Sacajawea. Pocahontas, a Powhatan woman, has become a heroine in the national pantheon for saving both John Smith and the Jamestown colony, but the real story of her upbringing, kidnapping, and early death provides a lens through which to view more sharply this early encounter between Native people and Englishmen. We have even less evidence for the life of Sacajawea, the Shoshone woman who supposedly guided Lewis and Clark to the Pacific and thereby opened the continent to U.S. expansion. Instead of contributing to the myth, Barbie has explored the ways in which the myth has been used to accomplish goals ranging from the dispossession of Native people to women's suffrage and racial toleration.[5]

Women's culture in all Native societies tended to emphasize the community over the individual. Native people usually lived in large, extended households where women worked together, delivered and cared for each other's children, shared rituals and celebrations, and socialized and trained the next generation. Sorting out the lives of individual women is not only enormously difficult but the process also belies the very nature of Native society in general and women's culture in particular. Biography and autobiography are alien genres, and an emphasis on individual lives runs the risk of distorting Native values.[6] Nevertheless, the details that we can tease from historical sources about individual lives humanize Native people for a modern audience that too often regards Indians as homogeneous, one-dimensional relicts of the past. Biographies can, in fact, serve as sifters that both separate individual women's lives and distinguish women's experiences from those of men.

Most Native women who appear as individuals in the documentary record do so, as Michael D. Green and James Taylor Carson illustrate in their essays, because they behaved in exceptional ways. Mary Musgrove, daughter of a Creek mother and an English father, moved in the highest circles of Native and colonial government. Crucial to the survival of the struggling Georgia colony, Musgrove also helped the Creeks deal diplomatically with the English presence in the southeast. Her actions reflected her innermost self in which she mediated a dual heritage to construct a successful and powerful persona. The English presented opportunities to Mary Musgrove and to the Mohawk woman, Molly Brant, which these women exploited. After the death of her husband, the British superintendent of Indian affairs, Brant used her status as his widow to expand her role as Iroquois clan mother and assume many of the responsibilities and obligations of Iroquois chiefs. Both Musgrove and Brant present exceptions to the general decline in the status of women that many scholars have chronicled.[7] Their experiences suggest that Native culture equipped at least some women to adapt to the European presence and to act imaginatively and creatively for their people as well as for themselves.

Despite the centrality of community to most Native women's lives, cultural norms did not force women into social straitjackets from which Euro-American contact released them. Many Native societies institutionalized exceptionalism. Women warriors, like Lozen, about whom Laura Jane Moore has written, provide perhaps the best example of the flexibility of Native gender roles.[8] Lozen, an Apache woman, fought alongside the warriors Victorio and Geronimo in their struggle against the United States. Military skill and participation in battles were far more customary for men than women in Apache society, but Lozen's people respected her for being different from most women and regarded her as providing an essential link between the very disparate worlds of men and women.

Although Lozen militarily resisted U.S. domination, most Native women did not have the resources or inclination to take up arms. Furthermore, American imperialism often took more surreptitious forms than military aggression. Since its inception, the United States government has formulated a variety of policies intended to solve the "Indian problem."[9] These policies have vacillated between separation and assimilation, but until the twentieth century, no official seriously considered incorporating Native Americans into the body politic as peoples with cultures and interests that differed from those of other Americans. The first policy, developed in George Washington's administration, focused on "civilization" and assimilation. By "civilization," policy makers meant that Native people needed to learn to dress, work, speak, worship, and think like Anglo-Americans. They also insisted that Native families be nuclear and patriarchal rather than extended and egalitarian, as were families in most Native cultures, and that women's roles be submissive rather than complementary to those of men. Missionaries and government agents descended on Indian populations in the eastern United States in order to implement these changes.

Many Native people selectively adopted European beliefs and practices, but few totally abandoned their culture. As my essay on Catharine Brown suggests, the appearance of total transformation often obscured the persistence of deeply held values and beliefs. A nineteenth-century convert to Protestantism, Catharine Brown lived a pious life of service to others. She taught her fellow Cherokees in mission schools and sought to convert them to Christianity. But the only version of Catharine's life that we have is one constructed by missionaries after her death in order to demonstrate the feasibility of their work among Indians. Even so, careful reading suggests that the cultural transformation was not as complete as missionaries supposed. The failure of most Native peoples to embrace "civilization" immediately and completely sparked doubts about whether they ever could be assimilated.

The "civilization" program had a relatively brief life, but the basic premise on which it was based—that Indians should be assimilated—endured in various forms throughout the nineteenth century. Nevertheless, in the early nineteenth century, Indian policy moved toward separating Natives and non-Natives, a policy shift that grew out of two major changes in the United States. First, the new nation's population grew dramatically in the first forty years after ratification of the Constitution in 1789, and there seemed to be a shortage of land for the white yeoman farmers on whom Americans believed their republic rested. Second, ideas about human difference changed radically. The "civilization" program rested on the belief, rooted in the eighteenth-century Enlightenment, that only education and opportunity kept an Indian from being culturally the same as a white man. The romantic nationalism of the nineteenth century challenged that notion. White Americans increasingly believed that Indians (and Africans) were fundamentally different from them and, therefore, could never be a part of their society.

In 1830 Congress passed the Indian Removal Act, which committed the federal government to the removal of Native people from their homelands in the East to territory west of the Mississippi. By 1850, thousands of Native people from the Southeast and Midwest, in particular, had been forced from their homelands into new territory beyond the line of white settlement. That line of settlement soon blurred, however, as citizens of the United States pushed west into the prairies and journeyed overland to California and Oregon. They placed an enormous strain on Native resources, and their preconceptions of Indians as bloodthirsty savages often led them to respond violently when they encountered Native people. The completion of the transcontinental railway in 1867 and the repeated discovery of gold and silver on Native lands in the nineteenth century only increased the pressure on the United States government to reduce Native landholdings and restrict the movement of Native people.

The United States sought to settle Native people on reservations, land "reserved" from cessions by Native people or carved out of what the federal government considered to be public domain. Never completely abandoning the notion of "civilizing" the Indians, the Bureau of Indian Affairs (BIA), an agency of the federal government, regarded the reservations as training grounds that would prepare Indians ultimately to enter the American mainstream. But many reservations were located in areas that could not sustain the Native population either through traditional subsistence practices or through Anglo-American style agriculture. Consequently, the people on these reservations suffered severe privation that inadequate government rations did little to relieve. Furthermore, agents tried to enforce an Anglo-American construction of gender by issuing rations to men for their nuclear families and employing "matrons" who taught Native women domestic skills. They also outlawed many traditional practices ranging from polygamy and divorce to religious ceremonies. These conditions help explain why Lozen's band of Apaches, along with thousands of other Native people, refused to remain on their reservations. Sustained armed conflict in the West in the period after the Civil War stemmed largely from the attempt of the United States to confine Native people to reservations against their will.[10] Gradually, however, Native people began to carve a life for themselves out of the desolation on the reservations. Preserving as much of their traditional ways of life as they could, they adapted to their situation, and reservations became home.

In the late nineteenth century, a new movement arose to reform Indian affairs and return to the goal of assimilating the Native population.[11] Philanthropists believed that education was an essential component of assimilation, and they established boarding schools for Indian children throughout the United States. On the reservations, agents enticed, cajoled, and threatened parents into sending their children to schools far from home. Some parents, convinced that Indian lifeways had no future, agreed that boarding schools were in their children's best interests, while other parents saw only a cultural cleavage developing between them and their children. At boarding schools, educators first transformed children physically by cutting their long hair and clothing them in corsets and dresses or suits and ties. Then they implemented a rigorous curriculum of academic and vocational training. They also taught the children to be women and men according to Anglo-American standards: girls learned domestic tasks like sewing, cooking, and cleaning, while boys learned economically viable occupations such as carpentry and farming. Forbidden to speak their Native languages, many children began to lose touch with their families and their tribal identities and to forge new relationships with each other and the Anglo-American world into which they were supposed to assimilate.[12]

The essay by Jane Hafen provides a glimpse of how the boarding school experience affected an exceptional Sioux woman, Gertrude Bonnin, who wrote under the name Zitkala Ša. Removed from her family at the age of eight, Bonnin spent the rest of her life mediating between her birth as a Sioux and her education as an "Indian." Estranged from her family and largely ignored by her tribe, she became a "public Indian," that is, an activist for Native rights. As Bonnin discovered, assimilation as envisioned by reformers did not happen, in part because of the persistence of Native culture, but largely because racism in the dominant society precluded the acceptance of Indians.

Philanthropists refused to acknowledge how profoundly the racism and the unbridled greed of the late nineteenth century limited the ability of Native people to assimilate even if they wanted to. Consequently, they failed to anticipate the disastrous effects of the allotment policy enacted into law in 1887 and extended to eastern Oklahoma, where southern Indians had been relocated, in 1893. The premise behind allotment was that reservation land, which Indians held in common, thwarted the individualism essential to assimilation. Only individual landholdings would encourage competitive and acquisitive values. Consequently, the federal government set about allotting millions of acres of tribally held land, usually in 160-acre tracts. Allotments for families went to the head, whom officials normally defined as male, and so divorce, separation, and death frequently left women without any land at all. Although legislation initially placed some restrictions on the sale of land, unscrupulous officials and land jobbers, encouraged by the relaxation of restrictions in 1906, managed to deprive many people of their holdings, and two-thirds of Native land passed out of Indian hands.

Dee Garceau's essay on Mourning Dove, an Okanogan woman, illustrates the poverty that Native people experienced following allotment and the impediments that attitudes about Indians posed for them. Instead of becoming self-sufficient on her land, Mourning Dove had to rent her allotment to whites and take a number of menial jobs that sometimes forced her to move far from home. Mourning Dove's poverty hindered her ambitions as a writer, but the literary world's view of Indians also proved a powerful obstacle. Mourning Dove wanted to write romance novels and screenplays that depicted contemporary Native people, but her literary mentors insisted that she collect and publish Indian folklore, which they believed was vanishing along with the Indians.

Ironically, Native people fascinated an American public that cheated them and refused to accept them as equals. In reaction to the homogenizing influence of industrialization, many Americans found in Native cultural practices, stories, and crafts an authenticity that they believed their own society had lost. Buffalo Bill's Wild West show is only the most famous example of public performances that made a romanticized version of Native life accessible to large audiences in the United States and Europe. As Bunny McBride demonstrates in her essay on Lucy Nicola, a Penobscot woman, many Native people seized the opportunity to perform publicly in order to improve their economic circumstances, experience a wider world, and acquaint non-Indian people with Native culture. The same impulse that brought people into the theater to see "Princess Watahwaso," as Lucy Nicola called herself, initially led them to purchase the pottery of Maria Montoya Martinez, a Tewa woman from the Pueblo of San Ildefonso, and her husband, Julian. As Terry Reynolds reveals in her essay, art critics soon recognized a rare talent, and Maria Martinez's pottery transformed the way that many people looked at Native "craft." At the same time, Martinez refused to succumb to the individualistic ethic of the art world, signing her name to her neighbors' pots so that they would bring higher prices. Just as Lucy Nicola returned home to promote the welfare of her people, Maria Martinez improved the economic situation of her entire community. Although they had experienced many cultural changes, these women, like many others, maintained the value of community.

Anthropologists and other scholars were among the first non-Indians to recognize the value that Native people placed on community and the disastrous effect that allotment had had on them. The Meriam Report of 1928, commissioned by the secretary of the interior, painted a dismal picture of malnutrition, disease, and substandard housing on reservations and overcrowding, sickness, and abuse in boarding schools. By the time Franklin Roosevelt became president in 1933, allotment had been thoroughly discredited. In 1934 Congress passed the Wheeler Howard Act (or Indian Reorganization Act, as it is often called) that formally ended allotment and pledged the federal government to help tribes to recover some of their lost domain, establish tribal governments with constitutions, and incorporate to protect and manage their assets. Indians voted in tribal referenda on whether or not to accept the provisions of the Wheeler Howard Act, but not surprisingly, many Native people wanted little to do with the federal government. Gertrude Bonnin's opposition to the Wheeler Howard Act stemmed largely from her long struggle against the BIA. Alice Lee Jemison, a Seneca woman about whom Laurence M. Hauptman has written, criticized the government's "one size fits all" approach to Indian affairs. The Seneca had not been subject to allotment, and Jemison resented this imposition of federal authority on her people. In the end, 174 Indian tribes voted to accept the provisions of Wheeler Howard in the referenda, 78 opposed, and 13 did not participate. In terms of individuals, 38,000 voted in favor of the act, 24,000 voted against, and 35,000 people who were eligible did not vote at all. Some tribes that voted in favor never complied with its provisions, and the United States Congress failed to appropriate funds to support land acquisition to restore tribal estates. Therefore, the so-called Indian New Deal did not have the far-ranging effects that many had hoped. But it did recognize the desirability of preserving tribal governments and landholdings.[13]

The Wheeler Howard Act and Native opposition to it demonstrates one of the major problems Indians have had in dealing with non-Indians since the arrival of Columbus. People of European descent have insisted on a category called "Indian" or "Native American" for the original inhabitants of the Americas. This categorization belied the enormous diversity of the hemisphere when Columbus imposed it, and its incorporation into U.S. policy has meant that no program is likely to suit the needs of all tribes. Nevertheless, the fiction of "Indian" has persisted, and it has forced Native people to negotiate not only between their own cultures and that of Euro-Americans but also between their own tribal identity and the artificial "Indian." Just as Europeans created "Indians," they also marked off the land into units that they called "private property," "reservations," "allotments," and even "nations." These demarcations did not coincide with how Native people understood the land. In his essay, Phillip Round explores the ways in which Delfina Cuero crossed boundaries of both identity and place, mediating her experiences in order to achieve legal residence in the United States, one of the two nations that divide her homeland.

Even the mixed reaction of Native people to a policy widely believed to be pro-Indian failed to prompt a reexamination of the fundamental premise that the United States had to develop a single policy applicable to all tribes. By the 1950s the pendulum of Indian affairs had once again swung toward assimilation. Congress moved to liquidate tribal assets, terminate tribal governments and their relationship with the BIA, and relocate Native people to urban areas.[14] This policy had devastating effects on the Native people who became subject to its provisions. The Menominee, the first to be terminated, fought back. Led by a university-educated Menominee social worker named Ada Deer, they engaged in many of the tactics of resistance employed by the civil rights movement. Through demonstrations, lawsuits, and lobbying, they challenged both federal policy and their own complicit leaders. As Nancy Lurie recounts in her essay, the struggle catapulted Deer into the national spotlight, and in 1993 she became the first woman to head the BIA. She presided over a policy of self-determination, developed in the 1970s, which permits Native people to chart their own course.

Federal policies often have created deep divisions within Indian tribes. From the earliest years of contact with Europeans, Native people have disagreed about how to deal with the newcomers. Federal officials preferred, quite naturally, to deal with those who agreed with them, a response that privileged Native leaders who sought to conform to U.S. policies. As the federal government through its policies became more central in the lives of Native people, leaders who cooperated amassed more power. Rations, employment, access to education and medical care, and other federal benefits flowed through these individuals. In many tribes leaders acted responsibly, but in some, Native politicians became repressive.

The social unrest of the 1960s and 1970s reached Indian country through the American Indian Movement (AIM). People who grew up in the cities to which their families had been relocated began to return to their reservations, and they were horrified by what they saw. The BIA was not meeting the needs of many Indians, and tribal leaders seemed to be the BIA's tools of impoverishment and oppression. Consequently, AIM challenged both the BIA and Indian leaders who misused their positions. Nowhere was the challenge answered with greater brutality than on Pine Ridge, a Sioux reservation in South Dakota. In her essay on Anna Mae Pictou-Aquash, Devon Mihesuah reveals the tension between Native activism and white feminism. Products of a colonial relationship, Native men in AIM had adopted many of the dominant culture's attitudes about women. Anna Mae Pictou-Aquash took exception to those attitudes and assumed a leadership role. Her tragic example illustrates the complex ways in which Native women must mediate between cultures in both their identities and actions.

Personal mediation—sifting—involves various layers of experience, some of which seem contradictory. While sifting can separate out uniform grains, it can also blend together disparate elements into a cohesive whole that has a richer flavor and texture than any of its original ingredients. All of these women sifted their experiences in order to preserve and refine essential ingredients; then they sifted these ingredients together to create their identities and values. By the same token, we can use each woman's life to understand the uniqueness of her experience and her culture, and we can also blend these lives together to create a richer view of Native America.

NOTES

1. James Mooney, "Sacred Formulas of the Cherokees," *Seventh Annual Report*, Bureau of American Ethnology (Washington: Government Printing Office, 1886), 410.

2. Sarah H. Hill, *Weaving New Worlds: Southeastern Cherokee Women and Their Basketry* (Chapel Hill: University of North Carolina Press, 1997), 52–54.

3. Laura F. Klein and Lillian A. Ackerman, eds., *Women and Power in Native North America* (Norman: University of Oklahoma Press, 1995).

4. For a collection of essays that manage to uncover the experiences of women, see Nancy Shoemaker, ed., *Negotiators of Change: Historical Perspectives on Native American Women* (New York: Routledge, 1995).

5. For images of Native people generally, see Robert F. Berkhofer, Jr., *The White Man's Indian: Images of the American Indian from Columbus to the Present* (New York: Alfred A. Knopf, 1978). For an essay that addresses women specifically, see Rayna Green, "The Pocahontas Perplex: The Image of Indian Women in American Culture," *Massachusetts Review* 16 (1975): 698–714.

6. Gretchen M. Bataille and Kathleen Mullen Sands, *American Indian Women: Telling Their Lives* (Lincoln: University of Nebraska Press, 1984).

7. Mona Etienne and Eleanor Leacock, eds., *Women and Colonization: Anthropological Perspectives* (New York: Praeger, 1980), and Patricia Albers and Beatrice Medicine, eds., *The Hidden Half: Studies of Plains Indian Women* (Lanham, MD: University Press of America, 1983).

8. For other examples, see Beatrice Medicine, "'Warrior Women'—Sex Role Alternatives for Plains Indian Women" in *The Hidden Half*, 267–80; Oscar Lewis, "Manly-Hearted

Women among the South Piegan," *American Anthropologist* 43 (1941): 173–87; Theda Perdue, "Nancy Ward" in *Portraits of American Women from Settlement to the Present*, ed. G. J. Barker-Benfield and Catherine Clinton (New York: Oxford University Press, 1998), 83–100.

9. For a detailed account of United States Indian policy—but one that pays little attention to women—see Francis Paul Prucha, *The Great Father: The United States Government and the American Indian* (2 v., Lincoln: University of Nebraska Press, 1984).

10. See Robert M. Utley, *Frontier Regulars: The United States Army and the Indian, 1866–1891* (New York: MacMillan Company, 1973).

11. See Frederick Hoxie, *A Final Promise: The Campaign to Assimilate the Indians* (Lincoln: University of Nebraska Press, 1984).

12. Among the many books on boarding schools are the following: K. Tsianina Lomawaima, *They Called It Prairie Light: The Story of Chilocco Indian School* (Lincoln: University of Nebraska Press, 1994); David Wallace Adams, *Education for Extinction: American Indians and the Boarding School Experience, 1875–1928* (Lawrence: University Press of Kansas, 1995); Clyde Ellis, *To Change Them Forever: Indian Education at the Rainy Mountain Boarding School, 1893–1920* (Norman: University of Oklahoma Press, 1996); and Brenda J. Child, *Boarding School Seasons: American Indian Families, 1900–1940* (Lincoln: University of Nebraska Press, 1998).

13. See Kenneth R. Philp, *John Collier's Crusade for Indian Reform, 1920–1954* (Tucson: University of Arizona Press, 1977).

14. Donald L. Fixico, *Termination and Relocation: Federal Indian Policy, 1945–1960* (Albuquerque: University of New Mexico Press, 1986).

1

POCAHONTAS

The Hostage Who Became Famous

Helen C. Rountree

The one Native woman most Americans know about is Pocahontas: she was the Indian "princess" who saved the Jamestown Colony by rescuing John Smith and then married John Rolfe to maintain peace. She went to London and died prematurely on the way back home, after which her "warlike" people reverted to type. What a heroine—and what an Anglo-centered legend.

In her own lifetime, Pocahontas was not particularly important. In fact, very few Virginia records dating from her lifetime even mentioned her. No writer left us with more than little snippets about her, suggesting that she did not loom very large in the English scheme of things. Then, in 1624, John Smith wrote a revisionist account of the colony, which compiler Samuel Purchas repeated without editorial comment the following year. Pocahontas appeared as a heroine in that account, with Smith her hero; Smith downplayed Indian diplomacy and emphasized Indian warfare. This was the beginning of the Pocahontas legend. This "history" was written seven years after her death, two years after her husband's death, and after most of the other early eyewitnesses to the Jamestown Colony were deceased. Hardly anybody was left to challenge Smith's new version of events. Additionally, there were no scholarly standards of accuracy to meet at that time; everyone understood that authors wrote with their own interests in mind. So it was acceptable practice for Smith to write a Pocahontas-as-savior account that flattered him, and, being unchallenged, it was natural that this version be repeated by Purchas and later considered authoritative by others. By the twentieth century, when historians tightened their standards and reexamined the earliest Virginia records, Smith's dramatic hindsight about Pocahontas had long since become embedded in American legend. That is a pity. The legendary Pocahontas has far fewer dimensions than the real one must have had. The earlier, more reliable accounts of Virginia history and Powhatan culture indicate that the young Pocahontas made herself the favorite daughter of a powerful father. In adulthood she participated—as a wife, not a heroine—in two rather distinct cultures. Her life was short, but it was not a soap opera: it was an adventure.

Pocahontas was born about 1595–96. Her birthplace and her mother's identity and origin are unknown. As a child, she was given a public name of Amonute and a private, very personal name of Matoaka; neither name can be translated. What little we know about her early life comes from information recorded about her father, the paramount chief of eastern Virginia, whose personal name was Wahunsonacock and throne name was that of his town, Powhatan.

Powhatan was a native of Virginia. He inherited the leadership of several tribes from his mother because his people, like many in North America, traced descent and inheritance matrilineally, or through the mother's line. Powhatan expanded his dominions by both intimidation and outright warfare. His capital town, Powhatan, was originally near modern Richmond; sometime before 1607 he moved to a more central location on the York River that became known as Werowocomoco ("chief's house"). Powhatan's heirs, in the matrilineal succession used by chiefs, were his brothers in order of age, then his sisters in order of age, then his eldest sister's progeny, the sons and then the daughters. This means that Pocahontas was not a "princess" in the English sense of lifelong closeness to the seat of power. Given the age of her father, about 60 in 1607, she could expect fairly soon to be the niece and then the cousin of the reigning chief.

Pocahontas did not spend her early years in her father's capital. She lived instead with her mother, who was only a temporary wife. Powhatan, as the paramount chief, had a dozen or so wives-in-residence when John Smith met him in 1607. After one of the wives delivered a child, she and the baby usually returned to her family while Powhatan took another wife. Either at that point or several years later, when the child was returned to Powhatan's household, the young mother became free to remarry. In his lifetime, Powhatan was said to have had over a hundred wives from many different tribes. Most of these marriages served political purposes, binding various peoples to the paramount chief with kin ties. With tribute paid by his allied towns, Powhatan's household was not only large but prosperous. Furthermore, all members of the house-

hold worked. The women farmed, while Powhatan, on the days when no ceremonies required his participation, performed the same tasks as other men in
the household—hunting, fishing, clearing new fields, and protecting the village.

Pocahontas was a child of separation and later divorce in a society that
expected such behavior of powerful chiefs and made it relatively easy for common folk. She spent her early years wherever her mother lived, either with her
mother's extended family or, if her mother remarried soon, with her stepfather's
extended family. Nonelite Native people of coastal Virginia were patrilocal—
they lived in the households of their fathers—although they may have been
matrilineal, related by blood only to members of their mothers' family. In any
event, Pocahontas lived among a raft of relatives or step-relatives, there being
"6 to 20 in a house," according to John Smith.[1] She was trained in all the wom-
anly arts since she had to contribute to her mother's household and prepare
herself to do the same work under others' scrutiny when she rejoined her father.
That meant another way in which Pocahontas was not a "princess": she grew
up being trained to do the same jobs as all other women in Powhatan Indian
society. She learned to cultivate corn, beans, and squash; gather a wide variety
of wild plants both for eating and utilitarian purposes; paddle a canoe in order
to get to some of those wild plants in the marshes; make cordage, mats, and
pottery; turn plants and animal carcasses into cooked food; collect firewood
daily in order to cook that food; tan hides and make them into clothing; build
sapling-and-mat or sapling-and-bark houses; and participate in the rearing of a
large household's younger children.

Sometime in late childhood, Pocahontas moved to her father's capital. There
she joined a ménage headed by a father she had seen only intermittently. Besides bodyguards and councillors, Pocahontas's new home was peopled by a
host of young wives vying for the paramount chief's attention and numerous
half-siblings, twenty sons and ten daughters in 1610, whose position depended
entirely upon their influence with Powhatan. The careful scrutiny of newcomers and the competition among residents must have been relentless. Pocahontas
apparently exhibited a combination of toughness among peers and vivacity in
dealing with her father, and she became a favorite child. Her method of dealing with Powhatan is indicated in her nickname, "Pocahontas," translated as
"little wanton," which in modern English would be "little mischievous one."[2]

Chief's favorite child or not, Pocahontas remained primarily with the
women and girls. Men's and women's spheres were separate and complementary in the Powhatan Indian world. Both sexes could trade the products of their
labor with strangers, but warfare and diplomacy with foreign nations lay firmly
within the men's world, while domestic affairs, including farming, rested with

women. Like that of other Powhatan girls who had not reached menarche, Pocahontas's hair was still shaved off except for a lock at the back, and she wore only shell jewelry, mulberry-red face paint, and her own skin.

Pocahontas did not set eyes on an Englishman until the end of December 1607, when John Smith was brought to Werowocomoco as a captive. At that point, Powhatan himself had not seen an Englishman either. He had stayed aloof, and the English were only hazily aware of his existence. Powhatan, however, had numerous district chiefs in the James River basin, who were responsible for dealing directly with the English and keeping him informed of their activities. He probably learned about the arrival of the English in late April 1607, and he received reports of their subsequent construction of a fort, their distrust of apparently peaceful local Indian visitors, their expedition up the James, and their pointed questions about enemy territory beyond the falls. Only three weeks after construction of the fort began, several of Powhatan's subject tribes attacked the foreigners, probably at the instigation of local chiefs.

Over the next several months, Powhatan continued to sit quietly in his York River capital as a wary truce ensued. The late summer harvest, however, yielded a poor corn crop. Unable to acquire gifts of corn from their neighbors, a party of Englishmen under the command of John Smith purchased corn from the Chickahominies, who were independent of Powhatan and eager to curry favor with the English. Powhatan wanted to discourage an alliance between the Chickahominies and the English. Consequently, on Smith's third expedition to the Chickahominy, Powhatan's people attacked the Englishmen, took one of them prisoner, and tortured him to death, the standard fate for male enemies. Several miles away an intertribal hunting party led by no less than Powhatan's brother, Opechancanough, captured Smith.

Smith's experience as a captive and his consequent relations with Powhatan and Pocahontas raise questions. He was the only literate witness present, and he wrote three separate accounts of the episode that differ from one another in significant ways. His earliest report, written six months after his capture for his Virginia Company superiors, described his first being "conjured" by priestly diviners and declared harmless.[3] In this account, Opechancanough paraded him through Powhatan's dominions to Werowocomoco, where the Powhatans feted him as a foreign dignitary and negotiated an alliance with him before escorting him back to Jamestown. Smith makes no mention of Pocahontas although she must have been present. Smith's 1612 account, actually written by his friends for publication in England, was much shorter. As a prisoner he charmed the credulous Natives, including Powhatan, and returned to Jamestown with the firm friendship of the Indians in hand.[4] Once again, there was no mention of

Pocahontas. Furthermore, both accounts conformed to what Smith and other writers described elsewhere as Powhatan Indian customs.

Smith's 1624 version, written by Smith for publication after the 1622 Powhatan assault on the colony, was the only one that featured the rescue by Pocahontas. It also included incidents that do not make sense in terms of Powhatan culture.[5] Smith the captive was trundled around a large area of Powhatan's dominions, after which he was "conjured," in a reversal of events that downgrades the influence of the priests, who would not have permitted a potentially harmful person into Powhatan territory. Once in Werowocomoco, Powhatan feasted him as a dignitary. But then, after conferring with his councillors, who included priests, Powhatan became the unpredictable, treacherous savage who ordered that Smith's brains be beaten out, a fate from which Pocahontas saved him.

Two things do not jibe here. First, Virginia Algonquians did not customarily honor a foreigner with a feast and then confer about whether or not to kill him, especially after powerful priests had "vetted" him and declared him benign. For people known to be enemies, a feast might end with sudden ambush, but the sequence of divining, feasting, negotiating, and then killing makes little sense culturally. Second, the death to be meted out to Smith was the wrong kind. The Powhatans brained their own people who committed heinous crimes, but they slowly tortured foreign enemies. The first kind of death was inappropriate because of Smith's ethnicity, the second because of the priests' pronouncement.

The 1624 account claimed that Pocahontas's action caused a complete change of heart in Powhatan, who now wanted Smith as an ally. That desire rings true. Powhatan's wait-and-see policy shows that he had long hoped to make the English colonists allies under his leadership. But no sudden change in attitude was necessary. Powhatan may at some time have ordered a physical test of Smith's bravery, of which he had plenty, and the 1624 account's ritual in the temple makes cultural sense. So does Powhatan's inviting Smith, as his new allied chief, to call him "father" thereafter. But Powhatan probably did not threaten Smith's life directly at any point, as Smith claimed. In other words, Pocahontas probably did not save Smith's life, because, aside from her own tenuous position with her father, Smith most likely did not need any saving.[6]

The Powhatan-English alliance was shaky from the outset since both sides intended to be dominant, but the English needed Powhatan's friendship desperately in the following months. Long overdue supplies arrived from England, only to be destroyed immediately in a fire. Assistance from Powhatan saved the colonists from starvation, but diplomatic relations threatened to falter as the spring of 1608 wore on. Attempting to put the English in his debt, Powhatan gave them a large amount of food and indicated that he expected repayment in English swords; not surprisingly, the colonists never delivered the swords. The spring of 1608, therefore, saw the English plagued with incidents of attempted "theft" and sniping by neighboring Indian men, which ended in late May when the English took some men prisoner. Powhatan sent Pocahontas along with a warrior-messenger to beg for their release.

This was the girl's first appearance in John Smith's 1608 account, which is more reliable because it was written close to the events and for his superiors rather than for publication. His introductory description of her is interesting: she was "a child of tenne yeares old, which not only for feature, countenance, and proportion, much exceedeth any of the rest of his people, but for wit, and spirit, the only Nonpariel of his Country."[7] The messenger who requested the prisoners' release added that Powhatan's esteem for the English led him to trust his daughter to visit them. That pronouncement, coupled with an appeal from Opechancanough, persuaded Smith to release the men to Pocahontas, not to the messenger. If the messenger's words were correctly understood and recorded, then this May visit was Pocahontas's first trip to the fort.

The precarious alliance between the Powhatans and the English continued. Pocahontas seems to have visited the English fort occasionally for a while, though always with an escort. The secretary of the colony, William Strachey, was told upon his arrival in 1610 that she visited at various times. His wording, in the longest passage yet recorded about her, is interesting: "Pochohuntas [sic], a well featured but wanton [mischievous] young girle Powhatans daughter, sometymes resorting to our Fort, of the age then of 11. or 12. yeares, [would] gett the boys forth with her into the markett place and make them wheele [turn cartwheels], falling on their handes turning their heeles vpwardes, whome she would follow, and wheele so her self naked as she was all the Fort over."[8] Some of John Smith's enemies claimed that Smith intended to marry her and become her father's heir. But Smith's friends specifically denied all that in their 1612 account that Smith approved and published under his own name, adding that Smith had no special interest in her, romantic or otherwise. In fact, she and Smith seem to have had only limited contact during the time in which peace officially lasted (January 1608–January 1609), and Smith interacted with her as a nearly middle-aged man to a little girl. In one of their encounters, Smith left us one of the few recorded sentences in the Powhatan language, which translates into English as "Bid Pocahontas bring hither two little baskets, and I will give her white beades to make her a chain."[9]

The fall and winter of 1608 brought Smith and some Englishmen to Powhatan's capital, where Pocahontas helped entertain them, but the focus was naturally on her father. The English tried to "crown" Powhatan as a vassal of King James in a September meeting. Powhatan, understanding the symbolism, was uncooperative, and he backed out of a planned joint attack on the Monacans to the west of Powhatan's territory. The English thereupon went to Monacan country themselves. Their expedition was a failure, and the alliance with Powhatan was essentially at an end. When soon thereafter English emissaries tried to buy corn from several Indian towns, including Werowocomoco, they encountered hostility. Forcing trade with the Native people kept the colony alive but further soured relations with Powhatan. It is unlikely that Pocahontas was allowed to make any more visits to the English fort.

By late December 1608 the English were starving again, and Powhatan knew it. He invited them to trade in his capital with the intention of ambushing them. John Smith accepted the invitation and made plans to loot the paramount chief's storehouses. The actual multiday meeting in January 1609 ended in several skirmishes. In his 1624 account, Smith wrote that after the first skirmish, Powhatan sought to smooth things over again and set him up for another ambush, but Pocahontas warned him of a trap. But no such warning would have been needed by a military man. The English won the skirmishes and got their corn, and then they also raided many of the Indian towns upriver. Powhatan and his household abandoned Werowocomoco and moved westward into the forests at the headwaters of the Chickahominy River, out of reach of English boats. Pocahontas naturally went with them.

John Smith left Virginia in the fall of 1609 after an accident in which he received severe powder burns. He said no good-byes to Pocahontas or any other Indian person. When Pocahontas later inquired about him, most likely through an intermediary, she received word that he had died, probably because his death seemed imminent as he was taken aboard ship. Once the militarily astute Smith was out of the picture, the level of raiding on the part of the Indians escalated. Pocahontas ceased visiting the fort after Smith left, but Jamestown's distance from her father's new capital and the increase in violence, rather than Smith's departure, are more likely explanations of her absence. She was, therefore, out of direct contact with the English when she became a woman.

William Strachey wrote in 1612 that Pocahontas had married a couple of years earlier. Her husband, whose name was Kocoum, was a "pryvate Captayne," which apparently meant a warrior who was neither a chief nor attached to her father's household. We know nothing else about him. Since Kocoum was not a chief, Pocahontas was not being used as a political pawn like her sister, who married a hereditary chief at the age of eleven. Colonists Strachey and Henry Spelman both implied that among common folk men made the first move in courtship and women were free to respond or not, and so Pocahontas probably made a free, personal choice.

From what Strachey, Spelman, and Smith tell us about Powhatan customs, we can reconstruct how Pocahontas would have gotten married. Kocoum would have had to prove that he was a good provider, for Powhatan women set greater store by a man's hunting ability than by any other quality. Then Kocoum would have sought Powhatan's permission for the marriage, after which he and his male relatives would have haggled with Powhatan over the bridewealth, the goods that the groom presented a father to compensate him for the loss of his daughter and her labor. They then would have set to work to accumulate the payment and the household goods needed by the couple. On the day chosen for the wedding itself, Pocahontas's father and mother would have brought her to Kocoum's family's town. The couple would have joined hands, and his father would have broken a long string of shell beads, which would have gone to her father afterward, over their clasped hands. A feast traditionally followed. Eventually the bride's family went home, leaving her to live with her husband— and her in-laws. Pocahontas would never again live with her father.

The Englishmen in Virginia recorded nothing about Pocahontas's young married life. It is impossible to know where she lived, since Kocoum's origins are hazy, if she bore him children, or how she got along with her new extended family. She almost certainly did her share of the women's work alongside her female in-laws. She probably visited her father occasionally, but a sentence in colonist Ralph Hamor's 1615 account indicated that her father had chosen a new favorite daughter. If Pocahontas's mother was still alive, there may also have been visits to her. Keeping up with kin was important in Indian people's lives, a trait shared by the English of that time. However, the English and Pocahontas's people were at war during her married years, and neither side would have been willing to see similarities between their cultures.[10]

War, waged mainly through unrelenting raids, brought Pocahontas back into the English records again. Her value as a hostage probably declined since she had been replaced in her father's affections, but as far as the English were concerned, she was prime hostage material. The problem was catching her. The Indian custom of visiting brought the opportunity. In April 1613 the English captain Samuel Argall was sailing on the Potomac River when he heard that Pocahontas was visiting friends nearby. Argall's report on her capture says nothing about any companions with her, including Kocoum or children of hers or anyone else. The captain merely bribed the local town's chief, Iapazeus (Japazaws), and his wives to help him lure her aboard the English ship to see the sights, and then he refused to let her debark before setting sail for Jamestown.

The English sent word of the capture immediately to Powhatan, who refrained from answering for three months. The English demanded an exchange of Pocahontas for the English weapons his people had taken. The Powhatans returned some items, but not all, and negotiations ended. Pocahontas remained in Jamestown.

Pocahontas, at the still malleable age of seventeen or eighteen, was pulled into a colonial version of English culture for twelve months. During that time she was cut off from her various families, and her hostage status made her a focus of attention for English people. Her captors wanted badly to make her into a voluntary convert to the Church of England as proof that their way of life was better for Native people. The Virginia colony did not have missionizing of Indians as its primary goal, but the colonists considered evangelization important and legitimate. English people openly discussed religious matters at that time, and minor differences in interpreting Church of England dogma led Englishmen to evangelize each other. So when Pocahontas landed amongst people who believed their own culture and religion to be superior to hers, they hastened to tell her so.

The colonists combined their religious instruction with very kind handling. Pocahontas's captors treated her as the daughter of a very important man, a "princess," not as the wife of a commoner. They very likely exempted her from the hard physical work of cooking and keeping house carried out by English women, a respite from the even harder labor of Pocahontas's female relatives. She spent her less physical life, however, in heavier, hotter clothes and with fewer baths. Quartered in a substantial English house with heavy wooden furniture, she ate food served on painted pottery with metal utensils, exotic and high-status items to Indian people. Pocahontas encountered more domestic authority on the part of English males than Indian women experienced, though her elevated social status tempered male demands. Her lenient treatment and the deference shown her may have made a future with the English palatable, even attractive. Furthermore, she probably began to have doubts about Powhatan's relative military strength. The Powhatans and the English were about equally powerful in the James River basin by 1613–14, but Powhatan made a poor showing by delaying his daughter's ransom. A final and very compelling reason for Pocahontas's eventual complaisance as a captive stemmed from her romantic entanglement with one of her English instructors.

John Rolfe was a twenty-eight-year-old widower who had lost his first wife and their newborn child while on the way to Virginia in 1610, after which he concentrated on making his fortune in the colony. He was a gentleman, but not a wealthy one, at least until he helped introduce tobacco into the colony as a cash crop. Rolfe was also a deeply religious man whose interest in convert-ing a "heathen" woman for the salvation of her soul was undoubtedly sincere. Once he and Pocahontas developed a mutual attraction, which all the contem-porary sources that mention them agree that it was, and she asked for baptism, the only honorable course was marriage.

However, neither one of them was truly free to marry. Widower Rolfe's intended was a political prisoner, so he needed the colonial governor's permis-sion to marry her. Pocahontas was still subject to her father's pleasure, in the English colonists' opinion, and she had a living husband in Indian law, which the English ignored. Contemporary records mention only the attempts to get her father's permission. Her capture and prolonged stay among the English probably constituted a divorce by Powhatan standards. Her father's permission may or may not have been needed in Powhatan law for marriage to an English-man, but the English wanted a truce, and the marriage offered an opportunity to seek one.

In March 1614 the colony's governor, Sir Thomas Dale, took Pocahontas, along with John Rolfe and a force of soldiers, and sailed up the Pamunkey River toward Powhatan's new capital, putting down the local people's armed hostil-ity as he went. Finally Dale, Pocahontas, Rolfe, and an escort went ashore, where they opened negotiations for a truce with Powhatan's brother Opechancanough. Dale wrote later that Pocahontas was in such a huff about her father's delay in ransoming her that she threatened to remain with the English "who loved her." Ralph Hamor, another member of the escort, recorded that two of her half-brothers came to see her and report on her condition. She assured them that she was well and told them that she and Rolfe wanted to marry. The marriage promptly became part of the negotiations, but Powhatan continued to procras-tinate. The English party left for Jamestown before Powhatan decided, but a few days later he sent word that he approved of the wedding and would meet the other English demands, a promise he kept.

Pocahontas was baptized in April 1614, and she took the biblical name of Rebecca. At that time she revealed her very personal Indian name, Matoaka, since as a Christian, she no longer feared anyone's learning it and using it to cast evil spells on her. Instead of relinquishing superstition, given the common English belief in witchcraft, she probably switched to other practices (such as wearing garlic) for protection from maleficent people. Immediately after her baptism, she married Rolfe. The couple took up residence somewhere in the English settlements, at Jamestown Island or on Rolfe's property across the river at Smith's Fort, and in 1615 they had a son, Thomas. Since keeping up with kin was important in both the Powhatan and the English worlds, the family might have visited Pocahontas's relatives, but Powhatan did not visit them since he had a policy of remaining in his own dominions.

Pocahontas's marriage marked the beginning of a period of peace. In May 1614 Governor Dale sent Ralph Hamor to arrange a second marriage to reaffirm the peace. Englishmen as well as Indians appreciated the value of marital politics since their own monarchs often cemented alliances with royal marriages to foreigners; their current king, James I, had made just such a match for himself with Anne of Denmark. Dale asked Powhatan for his current favorite daughter as a "bride" for himself although he had an English wife back home in England. The Indians would have expected the governor to be polygynous, and Dale himself probably planned to hand the girl over to a henchman, a gesture Powhatan himself often made with cast-off wives. The matter became moot, however, when Powhatan refused cooperation. His young daughter was married already, and he declined to recall her for Dale's benefit. Having one daughter married and living out of his reach in the English settlements was enough.

The period that followed Pocahontas's marriage to John Rolfe was a "golden age" for the Jamestown colonists. Settlers expanded their territory without encountering Indian snipers and engaged in commerce with Native people. Many colonists believed that the Indians would convert to English culture and religion, as Pocahontas had. And if the Indians took up English-style intensive farming, they would not need nearly as much land. No one realized as yet that the few young Native converts would be the exception, not the rule, for the next century. To the English in the mid-1610s, the future looked bright.

Pocahontas's marriage symbolized the truce that ushered in this hopeful period, but it did not cause it. The real reason for the truce lay in the leaders' negotiations, fueled by the aging Powhatan's waning interest in defending his territories. The marriage, however, created excellent propaganda for the Virginia Company of London, the joint-stock company that owned the Jamestown settlement. The company, which had been paying for supplies and people to colonize Virginia, sought additional investments, mainly from aristocrats, gentlemen, and merchants in London. What better ploy to use in selling such people on a golden Virginia future than introducing them personally to Pocahontas, presumably the first of a flood of Virginia Indian people who would convert and join the English enterprise? Her background in her father's "court" and her aptitude for learning English manners prepared her well for her public appearances. The company, therefore, offered to subsidize a trip to England for Pocahontas, her husband, and their child only two years after her marriage.

The Rolfes took with them Uttamatomakkina, Powhatan's priest/councillor and Pocahontas's brother-in-law, and several young Indian women. They landed at the southwestern port of Plymouth on June 12, 1616, and traveled overland to London, arriving around June 22nd. The Virginia Company fed and lodged them and, since the Rolfe family's purse was not large, purchased for Pocahontas clothing appropriate to English high society. During their trip, Pocahontas learned that John Smith had not died in 1609 and was actually alive and well in London.

Lady Elizabeth Dale, Sir Thomas's wife, introduced Pocahontas into London society. She caused a sensation among the bored glitterati, but none of them bothered to record any details. She had her portrait engraved, which prompted John Chamberlain to remark that she was no beauty by English standards. Her demeanor, however, impressed most people. The bishop of London made a greater effort to entertain her than he ever had done for English visitors. When she met King James, she behaved with such dignity and aplomb that the King invited her to return for his celebration of Twelfth Night. On that occasion, she was well placed among the aristocracy. Meanwhile, English clergymen were evangelizing her Indian entourage. These ministrations deeply offended the priest Uttamatomakkin, but the young women proved more amenable.

As the visit neared its end, bad weather delayed the Rolfes' return to Virginia. They moved into borrowed quarters in the nearby town of Brentford where John Smith finally visited Pocahontas. According to Smith, as soon as she saw him, Pocahontas became very upset, turned her back on him, and withdrew to another room for two or three hours. Perhaps the shock of seeing him after eight years caused her to withdraw, or maybe she was angry because she had been in England for months and he had not called. Whatever emotion she exhibited failed to register with Smith, whose contemporaries often found him insensitive to any negative effects that his self-absorbed behavior had on people. He merely wondered what ailed the woman and waited for her to return. When she did come back, their conversation quickly degenerated into recriminations on her part about his disloyalty to her father. Smith, the only source of information about the encounter, suddenly ended his account at this point.

The ship taking Pocahontas and her family back to Virginia left London in March 1617. Rumored to be reluctant to leave the city where she had been feted, Pocahontas was ill by the time the ship reached the mouth of the Thames. She was taken ashore to the town of Gravesend where she "made a Christian end," that is, professed her faith on her deathbed, and died at the age of twenty-one. On March 21 she was buried in the chancel of the church, but her bones were lost during the reconstruction of that church in the next century. Little Thomas, too ill to make the ocean voyage with his father, remained behind with relatives. Rolfe remarried in 1620 and sired a daughter. He died at age thirty-seven in 1622, but he probably was not a victim of the Powhatan assault on the colony in that year. His widow's father paid for Thomas Rolfe's passage to Virginia in 1635.

Thomas was essentially an Englishman, after being brought up by his father's people, but he knew of his mother's relatives, especially Opechancanough and another half-sister of his mother's whom the English dubbed "Cleopatra." After his arrival in Virginia, he asked the governor's permission to visit them in Indian territory. Eventually Thomas married and, if the traditional genealogy is correct, he became the progenitor of thousands of people alive today who identify themselves ethnically as non-Indians. They take great pride, however, in their descent from the Powhatan "princess," Pocahontas, whom they rediscovered a century ago.[11]

In the late nineteenth century white Virginians became sensitive to the issues of colonization and racial purity, and they found Smith's last account of Pocahontas particularly useful. The Jamestown colony predated the Pilgrim settlement at Plymouth, Massachusetts, by thirteen years, yet the latter got much more attention in American history books. Rectifying that situation involved returning to "original" documents. The Pocahontas legend that John Smith included in his 1624 *Generall Historie* remained the most accessible version of the Jamestown colony's early days because it was published immediately and then reprinted numerous times, while other accounts, like that of William Strachey, did not see print for over two centuries. Historically competitive Virginia elites seized upon Smith's third version of events to passionately defend their state's preeminence, and in the process, they committed themselves to Smith's veracity and to their own racial purity.

In this overtly racist era, white Americans accepted the "one-drop rule," which classified anyone with African or Indian ancestry, however remote, as nonwhite. Only someone with 100 percent European ancestry could be classified as "white," which meant that Pocahontas's many descendants, some of whom were wealthy and powerful Virginians, could not make the grade.[12] The solution was to make Pocahontas a "princess" as well as the "savior" of the colony and to distinguish her from other Virginia Natives. Then her almost-white descendants could hold up their heads, ride in segregated "white-only" railway coaches, and avoid other forms of discrimination. This response provides a tantalizing possibility for why John Smith's rescue by Pocahontas appeared only in the 1624 version of his experiences in America. In 1622 the Powhatans had attacked the colony and killed about one-fifth of Virginia's white population. The English had not anticipated such violent resistance. Smith's new account of the Powhatans, published two years after the attack, suggested that

Smith had long known about the Powhatans' true nature as well as Pocahontas's exceptional qualities. By casting Pocahontas as not a real Indian, her conversion was made to seem a novelty rather than the beginning of a trend. And so when the English brutally retaliated against the Powhatans, they had little reason to fear that they were exterminating people who might become Christian subjects of the English crown. By the same token, nineteenth-century Virginians cleansed Pocahontas's descendants of their Indian ethnicity, while legally oppressing other Native people.

The social and political pressure to preserve the Pocahontas legend remains strong in our more covertly racist modern society. New pressure from the cult of celebrity probably will keep the inaccurate soap opera version of Pocahontas alive for a long time to come. We have few authentic details about Pocahontas's life, but the public's fascination with famous people's personal lives has encouraged fictionalized ones. Disney Studios' 1995 cartoon about her legend, not about her, clouded the issue further with female dependency, teenage angst, and doomed interracial love. The story of a young woman firmly rooted in her own culture, held hostage by bellicose newcomers, forcibly and then willingly assimilated into their culture, killed by a mysterious disease, buried far from her homeland, and ultimately used by the dominant society as a symbol for the oppression of her own people is not only an authentic account of Pocahontas's experiences but is also emblematic of the histories of generations of Native people.

NOTES

1. "A Map of Virginia [and compilation called 'The Proceedings of the English Colony']," in *The Complete Works of Captain John Smith*, ed. Philip Barbour (3 v., Chapel Hill: University of North Carolina Press, 1986), 1: 162.

2. William Strachey, *The Historie of Travell into Virginia Britania,* ed. Louis B. Wright and Virginia Freund (1612; reprint, Cambridge: The Hakluyt Society, 1953), 113.

3. "A True Relation," in *Complete Works,* 1:3–118.

4. "A Map of Virginia."

5. "The Generall Historie of Virginia, New England, and the Summer Isles, 1624," in *Complete Works,* 2: 25–488.

6. Scholars do not agree on whether or not Pocahontas saved John Smith. Philip Barbour, in his works on John Smith, accepted the story as did J. A. Leo Lemay in *Did Pocahontas Save Captain John Smith?* (Athens: University of Georgia Press, 1992).

7. "A True Relation," 93.

8. Strachey, *The Historie of Travell into Virginia Britania,* 72.

9. Smith, "A Map of Virginia," 139.

10. Helen C. Rountree, "Powhatan Priests and English Rectors: Worldviews and Congregations in Conflict," *American Indian Quarterly* 16 (1992): 485–500.

11. Elizabeth Vann Moore and Richard Slatten, "The Descendants of Pocahontas: An Unclosed Case," *Magazine of Virginia Genealogy* 23 (1985): 3–16.

12. Helen C. Rountree, *Pocahontas's People: The Powhatan Indians of Virginia Through Four Centuries* (Norman: University of Oklahoma Press, 1990), 221.

2

MARY MUSGROVE
Creating a New World

Michael D. Green

Coosaponakeesa, the child who would become Mary Musgrove, was born about 1700 in Coweta, Creek Nation.[1] She was the niece of Brims, chief of Coweta and the most prominent and influential town king of the Lower Creeks. Her father, Edward Griffin, was a Charles Town trader. When she was about seven years old, Griffin took Coosaponakeesa and her brother to Pon Pon, a tiny community built around a ferry over the Edisto River in South Carolina not far from Charles Town. Until 1716, Coosaponakeesa lived in Pon Pon with an English family, perhaps related through her father. The family taught her to speak and write English, introduced her to the mysteries of Christianity, and named her Mary. Over the course of her life, Mary married three times. By the first husband, John Musgrove, she bore three children, all of whom died in their youth. Her second husband was Jacob Matthews. In 1744 she married her third, the Reverend Thomas Bosomworth. Thus Coosaponakeesa appears in the written record as Mary Musgrove, Mary Matthews, and Mary Bosomworth. Mary never stopped being Coosaponakeesa, neither in her own mind nor in the minds of her Creek relatives, but increasingly she also became Mary, an English-woman in colonial Georgia. Her story is thus twofold. In part it is the trajectory from Coosaponakeesa to Mary, but in part it is also the relation between Coosaponakeesa and Mary, or more directly, the story of how a Creek woman in colonial Georgia mediated identities in order to create a new world for herself, the English colonists in Georgia, and the Creek people.

Hierarchy and rank were established principles in Creek society, perhaps because the Creeks descended from the Mississippian culture, characterized by social ranking and hierarchical political systems, which flourished in the Southeast from the tenth to the sixteenth centuries. Four Creek towns enjoyed unique status as mother towns, for example, suggesting a recognition of these towns as having special prominence and exercising leadership positions reminiscent of the Mississippian mound centers. Creek towns were not only geographical locations; they were political, social, and economic entities whose sites occasionally changed. Coweta, the town of Coosaponakeesa's birth, was one of these towns.

All early European observers agreed that Coweta enjoyed rank and prestige superior to the other Creek towns. This may have been institutional, like a Mississippian ceremonial center, or it may have resulted from the leadership skills of its chief, Brims. Europeans described Brims as the emperor of the Creeks. Brims "is a man of good appearance and good character," an anonymous Frenchman who knew him wrote. "He has many slaves who are busied night and day preparing food for those coming and going on visits to him. He seldom goes afoot, always having horses well caparisoned. . . . He has a quantity of cattle and kills some of them at times to regale his friends." English, French, and Spanish delegates bearing presents waited on him in the hope of procuring his alliance in their imperial competitions, but Brims chose a different course: "He asserts that he wishes to see everyone, to be neutral, and not to espouse any of the quarrels."[2] In the process, his power and wealth increased (he served visitors dinner on silver dishes), the position of Coweta as a mother town solidified, and Brims's reputation as a wise and aloof emperor widened. As the daughter of Brims's sister, Coosaponakeesa was born into what European observers would have termed the royal household. Mary understood that very well. In her later life, she repeatedly referred to herself as a "princess," and once she asserted the rank of "queen" of the Creek Nation. Mary knew that the Creeks had no emperors, princesses, or queens, but she also knew that within the world of the Creeks, where rank mattered, few could claim rank higher than hers.

Coosaponakeesa's position in Creek society was also determined by her clan, large extended families that traced their lineage to a distant mythical ancestor. Though Coosaponakeesa's clan is not known, she may have belonged to the Wind clan, from which Cowetas probably chose their chiefs. If Coosaponakeesa was a Wind, she was a member of the clan ranked highest by the Creeks. Winds were everywhere in the Creek Nation, in positions of influence and prominence, and according to the rules of kinship Coosaponakeesa was related to all of them.

Coosaponakeesa received her clan affiliation from her mother because the Creeks traced kinship matrilineally, and like other matrilineal societies, the Creeks accorded considerable prestige to women. With each new birth women replenished lineage, clan, town, and nation. Women controlled the land and the crops, and Creek towns were composed of extended families that descended from the eldest women. Husbands lived in the houses of their wives, but because clan kin could not marry, their homes and many of their domestic responsibilities were where their clan kin—their mothers and sisters and their families—lived. When the Creeks called the most prominent towns of the Nation mother towns, they reminded themselves metaphorically of the creative and sustaining power of women and underscored their centrality in society. Creeks reserved special recognition for women of the Wind clan and referred to them respectfully as their grandmothers, regardless of age.

When Coosaponakeesa was born, Coweta was located on the Ocmulgee River in present-day central Georgia. Originally from the Chattahoochee valley in what is now western Georgia, the Cowetas and other Lower Creek towns had moved east in the 1690s to escape Spanish depredations and to be closer to Charles Town, the home base of the English traders who exchanged manufactured goods for their deerskins and war captives. But in 1715, trade abuses led to the Yamassee War. Brims is often credited with masterminding the conflict, which took the lives of virtually all the Carolina traders the Indians could find in their country. Mary recalled that she returned to Coweta when the fighting ended. In 1716 John Musgrove, an experienced trader and member of the Carolina Commission of Indian Trade, journeyed to Coweta to negotiate a treaty of peace. During the talks, Musgrove and Brims agreed to cement the peace with a marriage between Mary and Musgrove's son, also named John. Young John's mother may have been a Creek, and he spoke the language of the Creeks well enough to serve as an interpreter, though he was not as fluent as Mary.

The young couple remained in the Creek Nation until 1725 when they moved to Pon Pon. By the early 1730s they were the parents of three sons, the holders of over 700 acres of land in Colleton County, and well established in the business of trading with the Indians. Because Mary and perhaps John belonged to a Creek clan through their mothers, Creeks considered them to be tribal members, although their lifestyle differed from that of most Creeks. In 1732, at the request of the Yamacraws, a tribe affiliated with the Creeks that lived on Yamacraw Bluff overlooking the Savannah River, the Musgroves relocated to a site on Pipemaker's Creek, near Yamacraw Bluff but about five miles inland from the Savannah River. They erected a house, trading store, and cowpen, and launched a brisk trade selling metal hoes, knives, and hatchets, blankets and cloth, copper kettles, a variety of ornaments including beads and bells, and guns and ammunition to the neighboring Yamacraws and other towns both up the Savannah and west into Creek country. Supplying manufactured goods acquired in Charles Town, the Musgroves took in trade deerskins and other animal pelts, honey and beeswax, bear oil, and other Creek products. Before long the volume of their business equaled one-sixth of the total Indian trade of Charles Town.

In early 1733, Yamacraw Bluff became the site of Savannah, entrepot for the newly established colony of Georgia. Locating an English settlement south of the Savannah River violated the 1716 treaty of peace that John Musgrove had negotiated with Brims at Coweta, however, and demanded quick and careful diplomacy to defuse a potentially explosive reaction from the Yamacraws. Mary later claimed that she was responsible for convincing Tomochichi, the chief of the Yamacraws, that having an English settlement nearby could be to his advantage. Certainly, she was central in the talks between Tomochichi and James Oglethorpe, founder of Georgia. This initial relationship, established moments after the settlers arrived and before they had begun to construct Savannah, began a pattern that reshaped Mary's life. She became Oglethorpe's interpreter, advisor on Indian affairs, diplomatic go-between in the later relations between the colony and the Creeks, troubleshooter, hostess for visiting Creek envoys, recruiter of warriors to support anti-Spanish adventures, and dispenser of the gifts necessary to validate Georgia's friendship with the Indians. At the same time, Mary and John expanded their commercial enterprises to include the fledgling colony. For many years, Georgians ate beef, corn, peas, potatoes, and other crops raised in the Musgroves' fields with the labor of their slaves, largely black and Indian but also sometimes Spanish prisoners of war. Mary later claimed that much of the food she supplied Savannah was never paid for, but she also traded staples at the Savannah commissary for imported goods.

Much of Mary's business career remains a mystery. After the establishment of Savannah, she and John moved to Yamacraw Bluff to facilitate river transport and gain easier access to the colony. There they continued to trade with the Indians as well as the Georgians. In the late 1730s Mary established a trading post on the Altamaha River, Mount Venture, at Oglethorpe's request. Mount Venture, part trading post, part supply depot, part listening post, part recruiting station, and part diplomatic mission, quickly became an important element in Oglethorpe's plans for raiding Florida. Establishing and supplying the posts stretched Mary thin, however, and managing two trading houses demanded a trustworthy staff that was not available. Mount Venture lasted but a few years, it never paid its expenses, and its destruction by enemy Indians cost heavily in lost lives and property. In 1746 Mary opened a second post on the Altamaha, which like Mount Venture had strategic as well as economic purposes. Mary complained bitterly in later years about her losses on the Altamaha, and her claims for compensation included large sums for the goods, livestock, and slaves sacrificed, she argued, in the service of Georgia.

Indeed, Mary's struggle for wealth—and the deference that wealth brought in English society—is central to her story. Many traders made handsome incomes exchanging goods for deerskins, but in the colonial South the path to real wealth lay in the land. And landed wealth conveyed a status recognized in both England and America. According to the terms laid out by the board of trustees responsible for settling and governing Georgia, however, land was available only in small amounts. The grand plan of the trustees was to create in Georgia a middle-class paradise for the hard-working and worthy poor of Europe. Using South Carolina as a negative model, the trustees prohibited the individual accumulation of land for large plantations worked by slaves or for speculation. Rather, they doled out land in limited parcels, fifty acres a head for families up to five hundred acres, refused to permit either its subdivision or sale, and for many years even denied a wife the right of inheritance at the death of her husband. This way, Georgians could not accumulate more land than they could readily use. The trustees also prohibited slavery, believing that proper middle-class folk should do their own honorable work. In place of a plantation economy like that of South Carolina, which produced great wealth for some and limited opportunity for others, Georgians were to have equal hopes for an adequate but modest living. This egalitarian utopia was not for Mary, nor was it for Coosaponakeesa of the Wind clan.

In June 1735, at the time of his death, John Musgrove owned land in South Carolina and a 500-acre grant in Georgia that encompassed the trading post, house, and cowpen on Yamacraw Bluff. The trustees permitted Mary to hold the Georgia grant until her eldest son attained majority, but her sons died. In danger of losing her property, in March 1737 Mary married Jacob Matthews, one of her indentured servants several years her junior. The marriage was, for Mary, the only way she could retain her property. One suspects that for both husband and wife, convenience and opportunity loomed larger than love in their match. Mary was, after all, the wealthiest woman in Georgia. But she was also deeply in debt to her Charles Town suppliers. In recognition of her importance to the colony, the trustees excepted her from the rule against selling land, allowing her to sell some to pay her creditors.

Mary's importance to Georgia related directly to the power of the Creeks and the exposure of the colony. Mary's identity as niece of Brims and member of a large and influential clan was obviously the key to good relations with the Creeks. From the beginning, Oglethorpe appreciated the vulnerability of Georgia and realized that its survival depended primarily on the acquiescence, if not support, of the Creeks. Mary not only facilitated his initial arrangement with Tomochichi, she also arranged a meeting with several Creek leaders that confirmed Tomochichi's permission for the construction of Savannah. They set no boundaries, but extended normal Creek land use practices to the Georgians by agreeing that the settlers could use whatever land the Indians were not using. By the mid 1730s the Creeks and Georgia officials agreed to more definite limits. Georgia would extend west of the Savannah River as far as the high tide line, some thirty to fifty miles, and south to the St. Johns River. This grant included all the sea islands save Ossabaw, Sapelo, and St. Catherines, and excepted as well the tract of several hundred acres on Yamacraw Bluff where Tomochichi's village was located.

Mary's help with these arrangements paled beside her ongoing labors on Oglethorpe's behalf to support his military ambitions. The father of Savannah quickly tired of administrative duties, built Fort Frederica on St. Simon's Island, and prepared for war with Spanish Florida. Garrisoned by Scottish troops, Frederica represented England's most exposed imperial outpost. Oglethorpe spent most of his time there, and he called on Mary repeatedly for advice and help on Creek matters. Although he made one hasty trip to Coweta in the summer of 1739 to reinforce the alliance and confirm the boundary between Georgia and the Creeks, Oglethrope relied largely on Mary in his dealings with the Creeks. Headmen and war leaders wore a path to Savannah to consult with Mary, and she worked incessantly to keep them in the British interest. When trouble loomed, as in the War of Jenkins' Ear from 1739 to 1742, Mary was instrumental in raising Creek warriors to fight with Oglethorpe in his attempts on St. Augustine. The Creeks also rebuffed incursions by Yamassees and other Indians allied to Spain.

Mary was much more, however, than Oglethorpe's Indian agent. The steady stream of Creek guests she entertained at her home outside Savannah included many of the most important chiefs in the nation. Brims never came, but after his death in 1733 his successors and clan kin, Chekilli and Malatchi, visited many times. As a close relative with the inside word on Georgia, Mary was important to Chekilli and Malatchi. They consulted with her on their foreign policy, looked to her for advice and intercession with English officials, asked her to read documents and write responses, depended on her to interpret the motives as well as the words of English diplomats, expected hospitality in her house when they were in town, and loved her as an honored member of their family. Mary gave what she had to them; in a classic example of reciprocity, they gave what they had to her. Her gifts were food, manufactured goods, advice, love, and respect; their gifts were tracts of land, which would enable Mary to live in English society with a status similar to that she enjoyed in the Creek world.

The historians who have noticed Mary have paid little attention to her role as Oglethorpe's Indian agent. They have recorded in deep detail, however, her land deals. This story begins when Tomochichi granted her the Yamacraw Bluff tract containing his village. Actually, he gave Mary the right to claim the land after the Yamacraws no longer used it. Exactly why he did so is not clear, but perhaps he realized that only someone like Mary, knowledgeable of both Creek and English ways, could protect the tiny Yamacraw community from the impositions of the Georgians. Certainly that is what happened. Georgians from Savannah poached game on Yamacraw Bluff, cut trees, and in other ways disregarded the property rights of the Yamacraws. When the Yamacraws complained, the Savannah court announced that it would receive only the testimony of Christians, meaning that the word of Indians was unacceptable. As a Christian with stature in Georgia, Mary could and did defend them in court. On the other hand, Mary may well have asked Tomochichi for the bluff whose speculative value adjacent to Savannah Mary recognized and appreciated.

Tomochichi made the grant in 1737. The next year, during a visit by several dozen Creek chiefs and warriors, Tomochichi again announced his gift. The visiting chiefs confirmed Tomochichi's action in Oglethorpe's presence, and Mary asked that the grant be recorded by the Savannah court. The court refused and referred the matter to the trustees in London. Oglethorpe's presence at the ceremony lent the appearance of legitimacy, but appearance was not enough. Without an English title, Mary could not subdivide and sell the land to English colonists. Whether or not that was Mary's intent in 1738, it became so a decade later and established Mary as a much maligned character in the history of early Georgia.

The problem was that Tomochichi gave the land to Coosaponakeesa, but Mary wanted to hold and profit from it according to English law. The English had nothing to say about Creek land use customs, the details of which they little understood. Creeks allocated the rights to use land according to ancient rules. The rights of the Yamacraws to use the land on Yamacraw Bluff rested on the principle that if no one was using it, they could. As their chief, Tomochichi could share those rights with Coosaponakeesa or any other Creek or group of Creeks as he pleased. When the Yamacraws gave up those rights, according to Tomochichi's grant, they became Mary's. When Mary asked the Savannah court to recognize the grant, she ran afoul of English law.

As a matter of English law, all land titles derived from the Crown. The whole imperial enterprise rested on that legal principle. The fundamental issue was sovereignty. English claims to sovereignty in America arose from the doctrine of discovery, which took precedence over the Indians' right to use the land. While Indians could grant or exchange land freely among themselves, they could not sell or grant land to individual Englishmen. They had to convey their limited rights only to the Crown, which, in turn, granted land to its subjects. In Georgia, the agents of the Crown were the trustees. So while Coosaponakeesa as a Creek could receive land from Tomochichi, Mary as an Englishwoman could not legally gain English title to it and sell it to Georgia colonists since she had received it from an Indian and not from the trustees. For Mary, English jurisprudence must have seemed inappropriate and irrelevant in a world where her ancestors had lived for thousands of years. Nevertheless, it was a reality with which Mary had to contend if she wanted to sell her land to English colonists.

During the late 1730s and early 1740s, Mary's life was complicated by her service to Oglethorpe and her trading activities, and her efforts to acquire title and sell lots on Yamacraw Bluff were sporadic. In 1742, Jacob Matthews died, leaving Mary a widow for the second time. That same year, Oglethorpe's war with Spanish Florida ended, and he left Georgia in 1743 never to return. He gave Mary the diamond ring from his finger, two hundred pounds sterling as partial payment for her services, and the promise of more. He also told his successors in command at Frederica that Mary was indispensable to their success. They must, he warned, listen to her, depend on her, take good care of her, and above all else respect her.

In 1744, the Yamacraws abandoned their bluff and moved to St. Catherines Island, one of the three sea islands retained by the Creek chiefs when they granted land to Oglethorpe for the colony of Georgia. No longer occupied by the Yamacraws, the bluff was now vacant land that Mary could offer for sale in clear conscience, if only she held an English title to it.

Also in 1744, Mary married her third husband, Reverend Thomas Bosomworth. Bosomworth arrived in Savannah in December 1741, appointed by the trustees to serve as secretary to William Stephens, president of the Savannah court and for all practical purposes governor of Savannah. Bosomworth was a young man, educated for the clergy but not ordained, ambitious, and easily bored. Stephens, who could not keep him busy with secretarial duties, gave him additional jobs to fill his time, including the task of administering the regulations governing trade with the Indians. This is probably how Thomas and Mary first met. Still bored, in the fall of 1742 Bosomworth went to Frederica to work for Oglethorpe, only to leave a few months later to return to England to receive ordination as an Anglican priest. Once ordained, the now Reverend Bosomworth returned to Georgia, appointed by the trustees rector of the Savannah church. Bosomworth found Frederica more to his liking, however, and much to the disgust of both Stephens and the trustees, he went there rather than Savannah. In July 1744, within six months of his return to the colony, he and Mary married while Mary was in Frederica on military business. Bosomworth abandoned his ministerial duties shortly thereafter, concentrating instead on helping Mary manage her various enterprises. Mary needed the help. She also needed an ambitious, aggressive, well-educated, and well-placed partner to support her own ambitions. From this point until her death some twenty years later, Mary and Thomas Bosomworth set out to become, and became, landed gentry. The key to their effort was Mary's access, as Coosaponakeesa, to Creek land; their challenge was to gain English title to it as loyal subjects of the Crown.

Bosomworth entered the marriage deeply in debt. To satisfy his creditors, in 1747 Mary petitioned the British government for back pay, compensation for lost property and profits, and title to the Yamacraw Bluff tract granted her by Tomochichi in 1737. This was the first of many petitions. Like the others, this petition began with a brief autobiography in which Mary identified herself as princess of the Creek Nation. She then recounted her contributions to the establishment, survival, and security of Georgia, and closed with a listing of the financial sacrifices her services had cost her and a plea for recompense. The sum, in 1747, was about 5,700 pounds sterling. Her petition wound its way slowly through various bureaucracies, only to be shelved. No one wanted to alienate the Creek princess who seemed to hold the power to damage, if not destroy, Georgia, but neither did anyone wish to grant her request and thus make her and her English husband enormous exceptions to British claims to sovereignty in America. Her financial claims were rejected for lack of supporting evidence.

While awaiting a reply from London, Mary turned her attention to St. Catherines Island. The Yamacraws had already relocated there, and in 1747 Thomas moved in a herd of Mary's cattle. Fenced by water, the island was perfect grazing land and what little tending the cattle needed could be taken care of by Yamacraw cowboys. Thomas also took six black slaves imported from South Carolina to the island, in violation of the trustees' prohibition of slavery, to construct buildings and prepare fields.

Because Creek land law rested on the principle of common ownership and use, Mary needed no permission to develop any of the tribal domain that was unused by others. She could have occupied and used the island however she pleased for as long as she pleased, mindful only of the rights of the handful of

Yamacraws living there. After the buildings were completed, the island ranch became her main residence. But Mary's plans for St. Catherines went beyond a desire to develop the largest cattle ranch in America. As her many petitions sent to London in the next several years demonstrate, she wanted an English title for the island, which could only mean that she intended to subdivide it and sell off lots, just as she hoped to do with Yamacraw Bluff. The timing must have seemed propitious.

England and France went to war in 1744. Operating out of Louisiana, the French were an active presence in the Southeast, and since 1717 they had occupied Fort Toulouse on the Alabama River in the heart of Upper Creek country. With diplomatic maneuvering, generous distribution of presents, and dire warnings about the dangers posed by the expansionist English, French officers won allies among the Creeks. The English colony of Georgia, always isolated, vulnerable, and dependent on Creek friendship, could have been obliterated by a concerted French-Creek effort. Everyone knew it, apparently, except the Savannah court and its president, William Stephens. Stephens liked neither Indians in general nor Mary in particular. Oglethorpe's attentions to Mary appalled him, Mary's regal bearing and haughty manner offended him, the behavior of the Creeks who visited Mary at Savannah disgusted him, and when Oglethorpe was not around he took no pains to hide his contempt. It was Stephens who refused to accept Indian testimony against Georgians in court, and in his reports to the trustees, he repeatedly described Mary as dangerous, overbearing, unstable, disloyal, and unruly. Mary expected the respect and deference due both her rank and her contribution to the well being of the colony. From Stephens and his Savannah court, she received neither.

Mary reacted to Stephens and the court with "an equal Mixture of a Real Grief of Heart, and Indignation [over] being Insulted, Abused, contenmed and Dispised by those ungratefull People who are indebted to [me] for the Blessings they Injoy." She also understood that she held the fate of Georgia in the palm of her hand. Her "Interest" with the Creeks had enabled the settlement and survival of Georgia, and she could at any moment "command a Thousand fighting men" to defend it from the French. But without "Suitable Encouragements" from London she could do nothing and the "Jealousies and uneasiness which his Majestys Enimies have so Industriously fomented and Spirited up Amongst" the Creeks would be confirmed.[3] Lieutenant Colonel Alexander Heron, Oglethorpe's successor at Frederica, agreed. "It is Impossible for me to establish a Strict Friendship with the Creek Indians without the Friendship of Mrs. Mary Bosomworth," he wrote in September 1747. "She is a most usefull person, and if properly Applyied to, May be of Infinite Service to the Crown."

Three months later he informed London that Mary "is looked upon by the whole Creek Nation, as their Natural Princess, and any Injury done to her will be equally resented as if done to the whole Nation. . . . If she is drove to the Necessity of flying to her Indian friends for bread It will be morally Impossible for me to maintain his Majesty's Peace and Authority Amongst them." On the other hand, with her goodwill, to be secured by a favorable response to her petition, Heron promised that he could defend Georgia from any enemy attack.[4]

While her petition worked its way through various government offices in London, Mary arranged with Malatchi, Brim's successor, for an additional grant of land. Creek leaders already had confirmed Tomochichi's gift of Yamacraw Bluff, and they were also aware that Mary had stocked St. Catherines. That island, along with the adjacent islands of Sapelo and Ossabaw, remained in Creek hands, off limits to English settlement according to the original treaty with Oglethorpe. Mary arranged with Malatchi for all three. They struck the deal in December 1747 when he and about one hundred Creek leaders traveled to Frederica to discuss business with Colonel Heron. The deed for the lands is written in English legalese, probably by Thomas, and it stipulates that in return for various goods and in recognition of the "Signal Services done to my Nations by my Sister Mary Bosomworth," Malatchi, "Emperor" of the Creeks, "granted and sold and by these presents give Grant Bargain sell enfeoff and confirm" the three islands to Thomas and Mary Bosomworth and their "Heirs and Assigns forever."[5] Mary's campaign for English title to her vast landed wealth thus expanded to include the islands.

When England and France made peace in October 1748, Georgia was demilitarized, Fort Frederica closed, and the southern coast of Georgia virtually depopulated. Savannah and the Savannah River replaced Frederica and the Altamaha as the center of political and economic gravity in relations between Indians and Georgians, and, with the army gone, Georgia was more vulnerable than ever before. Part of the solution to this problem was to institutionalize the distribution of presents to the Creeks. Presents were essential to Indian diplomacy. Gifts made words true. They were symbolic representations of the ideas and agreements discussed, and in their exchange, they signified the peaceful and honorable intent of the parties. An exchange of gifts marked and validated all peaceful relations between tribes. More often than not, Europeans misunderstood the Native meanings and interpreted the gifts as bribes, with which they were very familiar. But in a sense it made little difference. Europeans learned very quickly that whatever arrangements they made with Indians amounted to nothing if gifts were not included. Mary had played a central role in this aspect of relations with the Creeks, dispensing gifts from her trading posts and billing Oglethorpe and his successors for the costs. Much of her claim for losses covered the expense of these gifts, most of which were never paid for. Peace meant that Creek military alliances became less important than general goodwill. Peace did not mean that Georgia could now ignore the Creeks. The problem was that in wartime, giving gifts to warriors could be understood as payments for services rendered; in times of peace, it was hard for the English to agree that gifts to allied Indians were worth the cost.

Moving the seat of Georgia's relations with the Creeks from Frederica to Savannah meant that William Stephens and his court were now responsible for preserving the alliance. Oglethorpe and his successors had respected the Creeks as important allies, whereas the civilians at Savannah saw them as troublesome problems. Nevertheless, in cooperation with South Carolina, the Savannah authorities agreed to an annual distribution of presents to be paid for by the Crown. Mary claimed a portion of the goods in compensation for past generosity. She also needed stock in order to reopen her store, which she had closed when she had neither credit nor cash to stock her shelves.

Planning to use Malatchi's support for her demands, during the summer of 1749 she invited over one hundred Creek headmen to travel to Savannah to collect their gifts and pressure the colonial government to act on the land grants. Her scheme backfired. The Savannah officials shared Stephens's contempt for her and were badly frightened by the unexpectedly large number of chiefs and warriors who came to town. In hopes of shutting her out of the talks and thus removing her influence, they refused to appoint her interpreter for the conference. When she demanded to be included, they asked her who she was, an Indian or an Englishwoman. Challenged like never before, a furious Mary announced that she was the sovereign queen of the Creeks, an ally but not a subject of the king, to whom she owed no allegiance, and that no business could proceed without her participation. Rejecting this argument as treasonous, the magistrates then tried to evict her from the chamber. When she resisted, they threw her in jail. Only an abject apology from Thomas effected her release. The chiefs then announced that Mary should not be compensated with gifts designated for them. Malatchi could not convince them otherwise, and Mary was effectively silenced. Furthermore, the magistrates leveled such a scathing attack on her, denying her "royal" birth and claiming that she was the daughter of a strumpet without standing who commanded no respect, several headmen began to doubt her influence and ability to act for them.

Publicly humiliated, denied a share of the presents, and thwarted in her ongoing attempt to gain a title for her lands, Mary had never been in a weaker or more difficult position. The Savannah magistrates took advantage of the situation and attempted to undercut Malatchi, replace him with a puppet, and gain a cession of the controversial lands for the king. Their efforts failed, perhaps in part because Mary sent a string of "bad talks" into the Creek Nation charging that the English intended to steal the lands of the Creeks and denouncing the bad faith of the Georgians, including Oglethorpe. These talks underscored the French propaganda and rang true in Creek council houses. Malatchi, following the policy of his deceased uncle, Brims, opened talks with French officials.

Mary spent much of 1750 in the Creek Nation. She did not travel there often, but this trip was clearly necessary to recover the status lost at the debacle in Savannah the year before. Malatchi threatened to go over to the French, he visited Mobile to talk to French officers and collect a present, and when he returned home he flew a French flag over his house. Mary talked him into replacing it with an English flag, perhaps hoping to curry favor in Savannah. Mary also got more signatures on another document giving her the islands and the bluff. Her plan seems to have been to arm herself with paper in anticipation of a trip to London where she would apply personally to the Board of Trade for compensation and title.

In May 1752 Mary and Thomas arrived in Charles Town with passage booked on a ship to London. They arrived in the midst of a crisis, however, that threatened to embroil South Carolina in a war already underway between the Creeks and the Cherokees. James Glen, governor of South Carolina, had been trying to end the war, believing that conflict in Indian country disrupted trade and threatened to spill over into English settlements. He hosted a delegation of Cherokee leaders to confer about peace, and as they left Charles Town, a party of twenty-six Lower Creek warriors killed four of them and took another prisoner. Not only did this exacerbate the war, it also demonstrated that Glen could not assure the safety of the chiefs who visited him in his capital. The only way to defuse the tension was to convince the Creeks to give satisfaction by killing some of the warriors involved. Glen could find no one in Charles Town willing to go to the Creeks with such a demand. Mary agreed to try. If she succeeded, she would earn badly needed cash and win an enormously valuable ally in Governor Glen.

With Thomas and a small entourage of servants, Mary set out for the Creek Nation. They first went to Coweta, home of Malatchi and Chekilli, the leading figures among the Lower Creeks. There they learned that Acorn Whistler, an Upper Creek war leader of great repute, had encountered the warriors in the woods on their way to the Cherokee Nation and talked them into going to Charles Town with him instead. There they met with Glen, professed peaceful intent, smoked with the Cherokee delegates, and then left, having convinced the Cherokees that they could travel home safely. But Acorn Whistler, a "hott head" with a reputation as one of the "most dangerous men" in the Nation, talked the young warriors into lying in wait for the Cherokees. Because Acorn Whistler outranked them, they did as he suggested. Clearly, then, Acorn Whistler was responsible for the treachery. But it was "hard," Malatchi argued, to ask the Creeks to execute their own warrior for having killed the enemies of the Nation. Chekilli agreed, as did the other headmen consulted.

Mary changed their minds. Governor Glen did not ask for satisfaction for killing Cherokee enemies, she argued. He demanded satisfaction for defiling Charles Town, the "beloved white town" of the English. This made sense to the Creeks. Beloved white towns were towns of peace, safety, and security. And they understood that if Charles Town was such a town, they wished to be safe there when they visited. Killing enemy Indians close to Charles Town was thus an affront to Glen and the king. Mary also reminded them of the consequences if they refused to do as Glen asked. At the least, he would recall the traders and impose an embargo, which would hurt everyone. But he might also invade, in which case innocents would be killed.

As she swayed the opinion of the headmen, she also raised an extremely touchy problem. If the Creeks ordered some of the young warriors killed, the clan kin of the victims would be outraged and trouble would ensue. If only Acorn Whistler were killed, however, the leaders had only one clan to worry about. Malatchi, Chekilli, and the others agreed to the latter plan, but killing Acorn Whistler posed its own problems. According to clan law, the kinsmen of the victim had to avenge his death on the clan of the perpetrators. If Malatchi ordered Acorn Whistler's death, as he was not of the same clan, he or one of his clan kin could expect to be killed for it. The only solution to this problem was to find a clan relative of Acorn Whistler to do it. Murders within the clan were clan business alone, obligating no one outside the clan. Among the nearby chiefs, Cusseta King was of Acorn Whistler's clan. Malatchi brought him into the discussion, and with Mary's help convinced him that "the Blood of Acorn Whistler should be spilt for Satisfaction to the English and for the Good of our own Nation." How it should be done they left to Cusseta King to decide, but it had to be done quickly and secretly before Acorn Whistler or his followers learned of the scheme.

Cusseta King pitched on a young nephew of Acorn Whistler as the executioner. The two had had an earlier disagreement over a woman, and in the heat of it, Acorn Whistler had threatened to kill the young man. If he did it, the nephew could announce afterwards that he had settled that old grudge, and no one would know that Malatchi and the others had sacrificed Acorn Whis-

tler to please the English. But Cusseta King ordered the nephew followed. After
he had killed his uncle and explained why, Cusseta King's spy, fearing the boy
would tell the truth too soon, silenced him forever. When news reached Coweta
that "the Business was done," Mary and Thomas, the Cusseta King, and others
set off for the Upper Towns where they successfully convinced Acorn Whistler's
relatives of the "Justice and Necessity of his Death."

Mary and Thomas had two other missions to perform in the Creek Nation.
One was to recover property, primarily horses, stolen from Carolina traders in
the Cherokee Nation by Creek warriors; the other was to arrange a peace with
the Cherokees. By mid December 1752, both missions were accomplished.
Thomas prepared to return to South Carolina, but Cusseta King asked that Mary
remain in the Nation until the headmen made a formal parade to Charles Town
to settle the peace with the Cherokees. "She had been instrumental in promoting [our] Happiness," he explained, and he wished "that she might see it completed, when every Thing was confirmed before the Governor." Mary remained
among the Creeks for several months, leaving Thomas to return alone to Charles
Town and make his reports. The commission was in Thomas's name, but as he
pointed out to the governor, "Nothing but Mrs. Bosomworth's Interest, and
Authority could have induced them to comply with" his demands. "The Merit
of the Whole is chiefly due to her."[6]

In May 1753, Malatchi, an entourage of Creek headmen, and Mary went
to Charles Town to settle the Cherokee peace with Governor Glen. At the same
time, the Creeks raised a number of other issues important to their relations
with the English. Malatchi said he wanted everything settled that threatened
their friendship, but one thing "lay heavey on our Minds." It was the question
of Mary's land claims. "My Sister, Mrs. Bosomworth," he announced, "I do not
look upon as a white Person. She is an Indian, intitled to all the Rights and
Privaledges of an Indian, and was entitled to the Lands she possessed, but of
late the People of Georgia pretend to take these Lands from her by Force, therefore I am willing that the Matter be now settled." Glen explained that he had
no authority in Georgia, a separate colony, but promised that he would inform
that colony of Malatchi's wishes. Later in the conference, Malatchi returned to
the problem of Georgia and Mary's lands. After repeating his interpretation of
Mary's right to the land, he launched into a denunciation of Georgia and reaffirmed his conviction that "the People of Georgia have taken Mrs. Bosomworth's
Land from her, which was given her by the Indians, and it belonged to us, when
it was given her, and as I should be very sorry to have any Difference with the
English, I thought it best to lay this Matter before your Excellency hoping that
it might by you be properly represented."[7]

Mary and Thomas did not sail for England until the summer of 1754, largely because the South Carolina legislature refused to pay them the promised salary and expenses for their embassy to the Creeks in 1752. While they pestered the colony's politicians for payment, they won two grants of land in Colleton County adjacent to the land Mary and John Musgrove had accumulated in the 1720s. This was apparently all Governor Glen was willing or able to do on their behalf. When they sailed out of Charles Town harbor, they did so on borrowed money. Shortly after they arrived in London, Thomas and Mary sold half interest in her claims to a London merchant and speculator, Isaac Levy. Desperate for cash, they accepted three hundred pounds plus Levy's agreement to return his half interest to them for one thousand pounds, if they chose to redeem it.

Between October 1754 and June 1755 Mary and Thomas sent two petitions to the Board of Trade, one to the Treasury, and one to the King's Privy Council. All claimed the same things—compensation for back salary and losses in the royal service and title to the sea islands and Yamacraw Bluff. The Board of Trade, armed with a vast array of countervailing evidence, including documents and memos from the trustees and reports from Stephens and the Savannah court, rejected everything. Indeed, the commissioners concluded that Mary was a swindler, that Thomas was worthless, and that Malatchi had been bribed. Remarkably, however, the board kept its conclusions secret and ordered John Reynolds, newly appointed royal governor of Georgia, to settle the controversy. In consultation with Mary and Thomas, who returned to Savannah in the fall of 1755, Reynolds turned everything over to his attorney general, who recommended that the affair be settled by a jury in court.

During the winter, about three hundred Creek chiefs and headmen met in Augusta to receive their presents from the royal government. Mary met them there, they discussed her ongoing problems about the land, and they confirmed the original grants made by Tomochichi and Malatchi. Mary got all this on paper, witnessed by a dozen traders, and notarized. Mary and Thomas then settled into their ranch on St. Catherines Island. Unoccupied for several years, the property was beset by large numbers of squatters who could not be evicted because the Bosomworths lacked a title that would command respect in court. By this time Mary was well into her fifties, obese, and sickly.

During the winter of 1756–57, with Mary's land claims still unresolved, the British government removed Reynolds from office and appointed Henry Ellis governor of Georgia. Ellis's arrival early in 1757 coincided with a period of crisis in Georgia. The French and Indian War, formally underway since 1756, renewed the threat to the security of Georgia. Still exposed as the southernmost colony

with a hinterland that was claimed and occupied by French and Spanish enemies, Georgia remained as dependent as ever on the goodwill of allied Indians. Affairs among the Creeks were in a turmoil. After Malatchi's death in 1756,
leadership was unsettled, the hard work of French and Spanish diplomats to
win Creek friendship seemed to be succeeding, and, frustrated and angry, Mary
and Thomas were entertaining large numbers of Creeks at their home and telling them who knew what. With no army and only about seven hundred citizens capable of bearing arms, Georgia was in a very threatened position. On
arrival in Savannah, Ellis also learned that no court in the colony would hear
the Bosomworths' case out of fear that if things went badly, Mary and Thomas
would order the Creeks to attack them. Ellis concluded that the security of
Georgia thus depended on two interconnected things: settling Mary's claims
and increasing the English population of the colony. The sea islands contained
some forty thousand fertile acres that could not be occupied legally by immigrants until Mary's claim was settled, nor could Mary's goodwill be secured until
her claim was settled.

In the fall of 1757, after discussions with Ellis, Thomas proposed a compromise. For title to St. Catherines and three thousand pounds plus one thousand more to pay off Levy, Mary would surrender her claims to Yamacraw Bluff
and the islands of Sapello and Osabaw, as well as her claims for back salary and
lost property that she had estimated in 1747 at some 5,700 pounds. At the same
time, Ellis convinced the new Creek leadership, less loyal to Mary than Malatchi
had been, to rescind Malatchi's grants, leaving Mary without a claim. With this
added pressure on Mary, Ellis urged the Board of Trade to accept the compromise as the quickest and easiest resolution to a problem that had soured Georgia's
relations with the Creeks for nearly twenty years and had inhibited the growth
and prosperity of the colony. In November 1758 the Board of Trade authorized
Ellis to work out the details and settle the controversy. The plan became to give
Mary and Thomas title to St. Catherines, put Sapello, Ossabaw and Yamacraw
Bluff on the market, and pay Mary from the proceeds. In July 1759 Mary settled
for 2,100 pounds. Shortly thereafter, she went to the Creek Nation as Ellis's
representative to invite the Creek chiefs to Savannah for talks. Importantly, she
convinced Togulki, Malatchi's successor and an enthusiastic ally of the French,
to lead the delegation from Coweta. Mary also served Ellis as official interpreter
as he worked to patch up the frayed alliance. Later that summer she traveled to
Savannah to interpret and mediate another conference with Creek leaders. These
were Mary's last public actions. Afterward, she and Thomas settled into an
apparently quiet and uneventful life on St. Catherines, where she died in the
summer of 1765.

Mary died on land conveyed to her by the Creeks and confirmed by the English, but the title was her own. Similarly, she was a Creek woman and an Englishwoman, but she did not regard herself as having a dual identity. She understood the cultural differences of the two worlds in which she lived, but did not construct a life that vacillated between worlds. Instead, she created an identity that mediated and merged the two. Although she almost always appears in the documentary record as Mary, this remarkable woman was also Coosaponakeesa. Born into one of the most rank-conscious societies in Native North America, she refused to relinquish her Creek identity or the perquisites that went with it. When she moved into the English colonies, she worked to acquire those symbols of power—property and wealth—that the English recognized, and she demanded that the Crown honor not just her diplomatic service to the colonies but her elevated status as a Creek woman of the Wind clan. Extraordinarily comfortable in English circles, she refused to bow to English law. Her efforts to force Georgia to acknowledge her land titles were not merely arrogant acts of self-aggrandizement. Instead, she insisted that Georgia—and by extension, the Crown—work out a corporate identity that mediated between Indian and English. Indeed, her public service to Georgia embodied this process. Just as no internal boundaries separated Coosaponakeesa and Mary, no rigid frontier needed to demarcate the Creek Nation and Georgia. Her life represented a distinct vision for the future of the English in America, a future that was never realized.

NOTES

1. The most complete book-length account of Coosaponakeesa is Doris Fisher, "Mary Musgrove: Creek Englishwoman" (Ph.D. diss., Emory University, 1990). Supplementing that are Helen Todd, *Mary Musgrove: Georgia Indian Princess* (Chicago: Adams Press, 1981); E. Merton Coulter, "Mary Musgrove, 'Queen of the Creeks': A Chapter of Early Georgia Troubles," *Georgia Historical Quarterly* 11 (1927): 1–30; John Pitts Corry, "Some New Light on the Bosomworth Claims," *Georgia Historical Quarterly* 25 (1941): 195–224; Rodney Baine, "Notes and Documents: Myths of Mary Musgrove," *Georgia Historical Quarterly* 76 (1992): 428–35; Michele Gillespie, "The Sexual Politics of Race and Gender: Mary Musgrove and the Georgia Trustees," in *The Devil's Lane: Sex and Race in the Early South*, ed. Catherine Clinton and Michele Gillespie (New York: Oxford University Press, 1997), 187–201. The chief printed primary sources are *Colonial Records of Georgia*, v. 1–19, 21–26, ed. Allen D. Candler (Atlanta: Charles Byrd, State Printer, 1904–16), v. 20, 27–31, ed. Kenneth Coleman and Milton Ready (Athens: University of Georgia Press, 1976–); *Colonial Records of South Carolina: Documents Relating to Indian Affairs, 1750–1765*, ed. William L. McDowell (2 vols.,

Columbia: South Carolina Archives Department, 1958, 1970); *Early American Indian Documents: Treaties and Laws, 1607–1789*, v. 11: *Georgia Treaties, 1733–1763*, ed. John T. Juricek (Frederick, MD: University Publications of America, 1989).

2. John R. Swanton, "Social Organization and Social Usages of the Indians of the Creek Confederacy," *Forty-Second Annual Report of the Bureau of American Ethnology* (Washington: Government Printing Office, 1928), 308.

3. Mary Bosomworth's Memorial to Heron, 10 August 1747, *Georgia Treaties*, 144–45.

4. Heron to Deputy Secretary of State Andrew Stone, 8 September 1747, *ibid*, 146; Heron to Stone, 8 December 1747, ibid., 154.

5. Deed from Malatchi to the Bosomworths for three Coastal Islands (Revised Version), 4 January 1748, ibid., 159–60.

6. The most comprehensive account of this affair is Journal of Thomas Bosomworth, 12 January 1753, and Appendix to the Journal and Proceedings of Thomas Bosomworth, 24 January 1753, *South Carolina Indian Affairs Documents, 1750–54*, 268–337.

7. Proceedings of the Council Concerning Indian Affairs, 31 May 1753, ibid., 396–97, 405–6.

3

MOLLY BRANT

From Clan Mother to Loyalist Chief

James Taylor Carson

In the fall of 1777, on the heels of English General John Burgoyne's disastrous defeat at Saratoga, the pro-English chiefs of the Iroquois confederacy began to question their alliance with the Crown. The Mohawk, Oneida, Onondaga, Cayuga, Seneca, and Tuscarora nations of New York and southern Canada made up the Iroquois confederacy, and several of their leaders met to consider the situation. A Cayuga chief, Cayengwaraghton, denounced the English and urged the others to reconsider their loyalty as well. Molly Brant, a Mohawk woman, spoke and reminded the chief of his long-standing ties to the English. Tears rolled from her eyes as she recounted the close friendship between the Iroquois and King George, and she urged the assembled men to fulfill their obligations to the Crown as military allies. In the end the council affirmed its support for the English war effort, but the outcome of the meeting meant more than the reaffirmation of a long-standing alliance. When Molly Brant challenged the Cayuga leader, she moved beyond the traditional rights and privileges the Iroquois associated with women and claimed for herself powers traditionally exercised by male chiefs.[1]

Both men and women had power in Iroquois society, but they derived their powers from different sources and displayed them in different arenas. Women's power rested on their importance as farmers and as mothers. Mothers and daughters had custody of the land, and they contributed the corn, beans, and squash that they grew to the subsistence of their households and villages. Men moved in the forests that lay beyond the fields and villages, and they supplemented the bounty of the women's gardens with meat procured by the hunt. The complementary economic relationships between women and men, however, extended far beyond their different contributions to their people's diet. Male chiefs governed the villages and the larger confederacy, but in order to build a powerful consensus behind their leadership, they redistributed foodstuffs and trade goods. Such a system made the men beholden to the women for one of the most important currencies of chiefly leadership—food—which enabled them to hold feasts, help those in need, and promote community spirit. Once chiefs established broad networks of support through distribution and other evidence of leadership, they were free to negotiate matters of diplomacy and to convene and preside over council talks. Even at these levels of government, however, female councillors held a powerful voice that the men could not discount. In politics as in economics, Iroquois men and women enjoyed particular rights and prerogatives, but for the whole to function, the two halves had to be in agreement.

Beyond the community granary and the council house, women like Molly Brant controlled other expressions of power and authority. In kinship, for example, the Iroquois traced descent exclusively through the female line, so children belonged to their mother's clan and had no blood relationship to their father's clan. Clans formed the basis of Iroquois society. Clans bound children to many people, rather than merely their birth parents and siblings. Iroquois women, for example, did not distinguish between their own sons and daughters and those of their sisters. Children of the same clan and generation regarded their biological mother, her sisters, and all clan women of their mother's generation to be their mothers. Extended families connected by women lived together in longhouses where they shared communal living spaces. The heads of these households were the clan mothers, usually older women so honored for their wisdom and industry, who sought to foster the family's influence and power. These matrilineal clans performed many of the functions Europeans associated with government. When an individual was killed, for example, the clan exacted revenge in order to redress the imbalance created by the death. If a clan member perished in war, clan mothers harangued male warriors to avenge the loss. By the same token, women might block a declaration of war for fear of the danger war posed for their kinfolk. Mothers also increased their clan's influence and prestige by arranging marriages for their children with desirable partners and by using their political clout to invest relatives with political and ceremonial titles that were inherited through the clan line. Clan mothers chose chiefs, and, if those chiefs failed to meet expectations, these same powerful women deposed them. Only men, however, actually served as chiefs. Men controlled redistribution, went to war, and negotiated with foreigners. They could do none of these things, however, without women and the essential kin ties women provided.

Few European officials understood the dynamics of Iroquois society like Molly Brant's future husband, William Johnson, an expatriate Irishman who served the Crown as superintendent of northern Indian affairs. He cultivated his closest ties with Canajoharie, the most important Mohawk town located in what is today upstate New York, and its most powerful chiefs, the brothers Abraham and Hendrick. An astute student of Native politics, Johnson realized that the Mohawks associated status and legitimacy with kinship. In 1752, after his first wife, Catherine Weissenberg, died, Johnson engaged Caroline Hendrick, Abraham's daughter and Molly Brant's aunt, as his "housekeeper," a relationship that the Iroquois considered marriage.[2] The kin relationship that bound Abraham and Hendrick to Johnson after the marriage symbolically brought the English nation under the roof of the longhouse since men lived with their wives. Although Caroline moved into the house Johnson had built in western New York, she and her relatives almost certainly regarded it as her house, not his. According to the matrilineal kinship pattern, Abraham, Caroline's father, was not a blood relative of his daughter although they enjoyed a special relationship. His status as Johnson's father-in-law, therefore, meant little to the Mohawks' reckoning of family ties, but it placed Johnson in the same relationship to Caroline's clan as Abraham himself stood. It also presumably brought special consideration from the English, who regarded in-laws as family members. Regardless of the incompatibility of matrilineal and patrilineal patterns of kinship, the Mohawks ultimately adopted Johnson into their society and gave him the name Warraghiyageh, which meant "in the midst of affairs."[3]

The bonds that linked Johnson to the Mohawks took on added significance when in 1756 the Seven Years' War, a conflict known in United States history as the French and Indian War, erupted between England and France across the globe. Johnson entreated the Mohawks to enter the war on the side of the English, and one sachem responded favorably to his adoptive kin. "We look upon [you]," he told Johnson, "as our own flesh and Blood."[4] Mohawk women, however, were reluctant to see their sons die in another people's war. At a meeting held in Canajoharie, female councillors spoke out against the war and feared that if Hendrick and the other chiefs had their way, "perhaps they would have no body left to take Care of [them.]"[5] The men won the argument, but to placate the women, Abraham pledged that a sufficient guard would be left in the villages to protect them from marauding French forces. The Mohawk alliance worked well for the English, but the deaths of Hendrick in 1755 and Caroline in 1759 imperiled the superintendent's diplomatic efforts. The war was not going favorably for the English, and they could not risk losing the Mohawk alliance. To retain his status among the Mohawks, Johnson cultivated the friendship of another prominent Canajoharie chief, Nickus Brant, who was Molly Brant's stepbrother.

The Brants were not only a prominent Mohawk family but they also had begun adopting some European practices. Molly's parents, Peter and Margaret, practiced Iroquois Christianity, a Catholicism that retained many vestiges of Iroquois practices and beliefs. Several years after Molly's birth in Canajoharie in 1736, they moved to the Ohio River Valley, where their son Joseph was born. Peter died, and when the family returned to Canajoharie, Margaret married Brant Canagaraduncka. Molly and Joseph, who had no surname at this point, took their new stepfather's first name as their family name. The Brants were a prominent and prosperous family. A traveler who visited their homestead in 1750 remarked that they inhabited a two-story, European-style house filled with "middle class" furnishings.[6] Since Molly remained her mother's daughter and clan kin, she enjoyed no specific kinship connection to Brant Canagaraduncka and his son Nickus Brant. Nevertheless, she took their name, and her position in the Brant household gave her entry into the upper echelons of both Mohawk and English society.

Johnson's frequent visits to Canajoharie helped him form a close relationship to the Brants that replicated his ties to Abraham's family. Nevertheless, the Mohawks refused to let Warraghiyageh forget his subordinate position within the tribe. On one occasion, the superintendent planned to conduct a diplomatic mission to the other Iroquois nations, but Nickus Brant insisted that Johnson speak only with him or, at the very least, that Johnson obtain the chief's permission. Prominent women seconded Nickus's demand. "Brother, by this belt of wampum," they implored Warraghiyageh, "we, the women . . . earnestly beg you will give ear to our request, and desist upon your journey." Johnson complied.[7]

Only through another marriage could Johnson hope to achieve some sort of reciprocal partnership with the Brants. During his stay with the family in April 1759 Johnson probably caught his first glimpse of Molly. That same year she took up residence in his home. While vicious rumors about Johnson and his propensity for Mohawk wives circulated in London, the marriage pleased the Brants and Johnson. The couple ultimately had nine children, an unusually large number of children for an Iroquois woman. These children made Molly the head of her own substantial Mohawk lineage as well as consort to the most powerful representative of the Crown in Iroquois country.

The new relationship between the Brants and Johnson benefited both parties. The Crown won invaluable military and political support in its struggles with France and other Indian nations while the Brants received access to goods and favors that augmented their status accordingly. The superintendent often used Nickus as an emissary, and when Johnson visited Canajoharie, he stayed in the Brant home. In 1759, for example, he paid the Brants for horses, firewood, food, and lodging. He also provided money when family members were sick and once gave Nickus a gun as a gift. Likewise, Molly Brant used her position to advance the interests of her family. She was particularly solicitous of her younger brother Joseph. Through his family connection to Johnson, Joseph gained admission to Eleazor Wheelock's school for Indians, which later became known as Dartmouth College. Johnson was so impressed with the young man that he permitted Joseph to speak for him from time to time and to encourage other Native boys to enroll in Wheelock's school. Kinship obligations, however, extended beyond the Brants' immediate family, and Molly's marriage to William positioned her to help other Mohawks. When the nephew of a Mohawk woman died, for example, the mother and her sister requested from Brant black mourning shrouds. The two women saluted "Miss Molly" because through her marriage to Johnson they now could assert traditional claims to important ceremonial goods that were formerly obtained from traders.[8]

Although William Johnson recognized the importance of having a Mohawk wife, he refused to countenance women's considerable political influence in councils. On one occasion Johnson's brother Warren visited the Mohawks and noted that because women could overrule declarations of war, they might hinder the Crown's war effort. During a visit to Canajoharie in 1763, Johnson met with a council of thirty-six men and thirty-three "principal women." The issue at stake was land, and the Mohawks refused to cede any. Johnson tried to limit the talks to the assembled men, but the Mohawk men demurred. One sachem asserted that the women were "the Truest Owners being the persons who labour on the Lands, and therefore are esteemed in that light." Granted the authority to make the final decision on the proposed cession, the women refused to agree to it.[9] Johnson was frustrated, and he attempted to have them excluded from further council discussions by citing the increased expenses they incurred on his Indian accounts. Iroquois chiefs, however, refused to participate in the superintendent's scheme to silence the women. "It was always the custom," one Oneida chief remarked, "for [women] to be present [at councils] being of much estimation among Us, in that we proceed from them, & they provide our Warriors with provisions when they go abroad."[10] That is, men obtained their physical and social existence as well as their sustenance from women, and so they valued women's views. Molly Brant's role in her husband's diplomatic efforts is unclear. Nowhere does her voice appear in the minutes of the various councils Johnson held, but in a chance encounter with a traveler in the 1780s, she recounted that "she often persuaded the obstinate chiefs into compliance with proposals" during her years with Sir William.[11] There is no evidence, however, that she joined his attempts to subvert the power of women.

Johnson's attitude toward the Iroquois women who sat in council was widespread in Anglo-America. English women had little political authority compared to Native women, and Englishmen regarded the power exercised by women as proof of Native "savagery." They believed that women's submission to men's will characterized "civilization," and they denied that women's productive and reproductive roles entitled them to a public voice. Englishmen normally refused to negotiate with Native women, and they preferred to conduct trade as well as diplomacy with men. For many Native women, the result was a decline in their status, particularly as the relative power of the English and other Europeans increased to the point that they could demand compliance with their gender conventions. A few unusual Native women like Molly Brant, however, managed to exploit the few opportunities Europeans afforded women without surrendering power rooted in their own culture. As a result, they forged new roles for Native women.

In 1774 William Johnson died, and Molly Brant moved back to Canajoharie with their eight surviving children. She used the money her husband left her in his will and perhaps the funds and goods he bequeathed to their children to set up a household from which she distributed trade goods among her people. Extending hospitality was an important custom of Iroquois women, but Molly Brant expanded the practice until it began to resemble redistribution, a prerogative of male chiefs. Opening her home to the Mohawks enabled her to achieve the prestige and influence that came with the control of goods, but she had lost for the time being the potential diplomatic and political power that came from being married to a high-ranking English official.

The Revolutionary War, however, gave Molly Brant the opportunity to exploit her association with William Johnson and, consequently, to increase her family's power and influence among the Iroquois and within the British Empire. At the same time, she enhanced her own power. While her younger brother, Joseph Brant, used his connection to Johnson to win accolades on the battlefield, her diplomatic efforts behind the frontlines made her an even more important asset to England's war effort. At the outbreak of hostilities, she began gathering vital intelligence for the English army from her home in Canajoharie. In one case, she relayed to the high command information that rebel forces were moving on nearby Fort Stanwix. Her warning enabled the English to marshal a small force that ambushed the American column at Oriskany on 6 October 1777. After the victory, Loyalist Indians ransacked the homes of pro-American Oneidas, burning houses, destroying crops, and killing livestock. The Oneidas recognized Brant's role in the attack and singled her out for revenge.

After the Patriot Oneidas looted and burned her house, Molly Brant fled to the Cayugas where her kinfolk gave her shelter. Far from cowed by the destruction of her home, she became an even more outspoken Loyalist. An opportunity to make public her support for the Crown came in 1777 at the meeting where she confronted Cayengwaraghton. She wept before the council at the mention of Johnson's name, and was, one observer wrote, "considered . . . by them as his relict."[12] By casting herself as her husband's "relict," Molly Brant established a claim to political authority that lay outside of the normal sphere of Iroquois women's power. Iroquois women derived status from their own accomplishments and from their clans, not from their husbands, but Molly Brant used the English conception of spousal relationships to assert greater authority among the Iroquois. She was, however, far from a Loyalist pawn. Although she used her status as Johnson's widow to legitimate her own exercise of power, she nevertheless sought to restore Mohawk land and sovereignty. "I hope," she wrote to a friend in 1778, "the time is very near when we shall all return to our habitations on the Mohawk River."[13]

From Cayuga, Molly Brant moved to the English outpost at Niagara where she continued to broker military information. She was most interested in the actions of her brother, who had assumed command of a party of Loyalist Mohawks and colonists. On one occasion, fearful of Joseph's safety, she tried to block his ambitious plan to take his men and link up with the English army of New York. In exchange for monetary payments, Molly Brant also dispatched reports of American troop movements and descriptions of Native attitudes. Because of her close association with the military high command, she had easy access to English money, friendship, and favors. The money she received for her information sustained her family, but it was not enough to insure their future, so she pressed the governor of Canada, General Frederick Haldimand, to allow some of her children to attend boarding school in Montreal. Just as she had used her marriage to Johnson to secure Joseph's education, so too did she draw on her friends in the colonial government to grant her children the same opportunities.[14]

Molly Brant constantly insisted that the manner in which she needed to live at Niagara was "pretty expensive," which irritated colonial officials who believed their payments to her were more than fair.[15] The cost of her lifestyle, however, did not reflect any extravagance on her part but instead revealed the very real costs of building a network of support based on the redistribution of goods. During her stay at Niagara, she was, one English officer observed, "obliged to keep, in a manner, open house for all those Indians that have any weight in the 6 Nations Confederacy." Perfectly willing to facilitate this redistribution in order to reap political rewards, her imperial benefactors told her that they would "not see her in want," and they supplied her with goods.[16] Such official support enabled Molly Brant to achieve both political and diplomatic authority through redistribution, which enabled her to exercise chiefly power in wartime Iroquoia. Whereas Joseph's battlefield exploits incited "Envy & Jealousy" among the Crown's Native levies and diminished his prestige, military men considered Molly to represent an important pan-Indian consensus that respected her leadership and supported the Crown.[17]

Molly Brant, however, worried that her residence at Niagara was undermining her influence among the Mohawks because it put her out of touch with affairs among her own people. She wanted to return to her homeland where formerly she had sat at the head of a "society of Six Nations matrons," the council of clan mothers. Aware that the Iroquois might attribute her absence from her home to fear, she made preparations to depart for Canajoharie.[18] She had good reason to regret her distance from her homeland since chiefs across the region were again reconsidering their alliance with the Crown. One chief from the Mohawks' St. Regis reserve in Lower Canada denounced the English for failing to protect his people from American rebels.[19] Deiaguanda, an Onondaga chief, shared his counterpart's concern. He charged the Crown with surrendering the Six Nations' homeland in western New York without so much as a fight. The Indians were, he argued in council, "left to be Sacrificed after having drawn on themselves the resentment of the Rebels by their Signal Service to Gouvernment."[20]

The two hundred or so Iroquois and Missassaugas who had resettled with Deiaguanda at Fort Haldimand on Carleton Island, near present-day Kingston, Ontario, shared the chief's frustration. After the loss at Saratoga, the English hinged their defense of Canada on Fort Haldimand, and the growing dissatisfaction of their Native allies alarmed the high command. The inability of the English to meet the various chiefs' demands for trade goods lay at the heart of the matter.[21] Unable to patch over differences between the English and the Indians, General Haldimand ordered Molly Brant from Niagara to Carleton Island where he hoped she might impose order and discipline on his disenchanted allies. The new mission precluded her return to Canajoharie, but she looked forward to rendering to the Crown what she considered to be her "little services."[22] The Indian inhabitants of Niagara "greatly regretted" her departure.[23]

Molly Brant identified jealousy between the chiefs and resentment against the English as the most important problems among Carleton Island's Native community. The chiefs who favored a continued alliance with the English felt that the chiefs who threatened to abandon the Crown received more presents for their disloyalty than they did for their constancy. Moreover, under Haldimand's orders the officers refused to permit the Indians to enter either the fort or its harbor facilities for fear of treachery. The fact that the military and Native communities of Carleton Island lived in uneasy isolation from one another only exacerbated the tension. No one in the garrison was willing to conciliate the Indians. One officer went so far as to inform General Haldimand that he "most heartily despise[d] gaining popularity among the Indians & abominate[d] them as the most treacherous worthless and ungrateful race of Men on the face of the Earth."[24] The task of repairing the damage done by mutual mistrust fell to Molly Brant. After a few months' residence on the island she was able not only to patch up factional divisions among the Indians but also to restore a measure of faith between her community and the garrison. The same officer who deplored the Indians as "worthless" later informed his superior that "the Chiefs were careful to keep their people sober and satisfied, but their uncommon good behavior is in a great Measure to be ascribed to Miss Molly."[25]

Aside from her work in the Native community on Carleton Island, Molly Brant continued to play a significant role in the war as an informant and diplomat. In one case, the sister of a Mohawk chief informed her that a St. Regis headman had visited a French commander in Rhode Island and brought back with him letters imploring the "Indian Canadians" to forsake the English. She also relayed information on the movements of Generals Horatio Gates and Benedict Arnold and on a planned American invasion of Canada.[26] Setbacks to her efforts occurred from time to time, which challenged her ability to maintain the Loyalist Native constituency. For example, during an overnight stay at Niagara Joseph had his life threatened by some English and Native troops. Molly Brant feared that such conflicts would undermine all that she and her late husband had worked for. While she regretted that Joseph had been put in such a dangerous situation, "what I am most concerned about," she wrote to a friend, "is that it may affect the Kings Indian Interest."[27] Informed observers told Haldimand that Brant was not overstating her family's importance to the northern war effort.[28] One officer went so far as to say that she had an influence "far superior to that of all their Chiefs put together."[29]

Molly Brant's successful contribution to the English war effort further enhanced her authority among the Carleton Island Native community. Employing the chiefly strategies, particularly the distribution of goods, she first had implemented at Niagara allowed her to unite Loyalist Indians of several nations. From time to time she visited the island's stores and took whatever she wanted to "give to her particulars," earning her the reputation for avarice among the English that reached up the chain of command. An officer at Fort Haldimand wrote to his superior that "she is insatiable."[30] Still, he believed it was a small price to pay for her friendship and for her vital service to the king. She even began to bring the military and Native communities together under her own roof. During the winter of 1780 Molly Brant held a ball for the soldiers and Indians in her home, which afforded her the opportunity to distribute gifts and supplies to the entire island community.[31]

In spite of her success on Carleton Island, in the summer of 1780 Molly Brant asked General Haldimand to transfer her back to Niagara. The reasons for the request and for the subsequent denial issued by the high command are unknown. Maybe Molly Brant wanted to shore up friendships she had culti- vated while she was posted at Niagara. Perhaps the English feared her depar- ture from Carleton Island would unleash the old forces of factionalism and mistrust. Or they might have worried that the warriors who had threatened Joseph's life would endanger hers as well. Whatever the reasons, the request unnerved Haldimand. An officer at Fort Haldimand warned him that if Molly Brant did not get her way, "she may by the violence of her temper be led to create Mischief."[32]

In spite of her request and her threats, Molly Brant remained on Carleton Island and passed the last two years of the war uneventfully. Just as the war gave her an opportunity for enhanced status and political power, the peace took it away because the end of the war marked the end of her tenure as a Loyalist chief. General Haldimand acknowledged her contribution to the war effort, and, more importantly, he recognized her efforts as a clan mother. In reward for her and her family's services, the Crown granted Molly Brant a pension of one hundred pounds annually for life.[33] While her brother Joseph led a reconsti- tuted Mohawk Nation on the Grand River reserve in western Upper Canada, Molly retired to a fine home overlooking the Cataraqui River in Kingston and, still mindful of her maternal duties, married five of her daughters to promi- nent Canadian gentlemen. Her sole surviving son, George, found employment in the British Indian department. Having fulfilled her family obligations, she became involved in the local Anglican church and passed away quietly in 1796.

Molly Brant's life provides an exception to the assumption that Native women's power and authority declined as a consequence of contact with Euro- peans. As an important daughter, wife, and clan mother she enjoyed the tradi- tional privileges and prerogatives that the Iroquois associated with women. Had she accepted the possibilities and limitations of her gender and of her culture, her life would have differed little from the lives of other prominent Iroquois women of the eighteenth century. But Molly Brant used the traditions of her own culture as a base from which she could expand her power in a time of crisis. She seized opportunities presented by the Revolution to construct a new kind of power, and she transformed herself from Mohawk clan mother to Loyalist chief. Molly Brant appropriated the strategies of male leaders as well as those of clan mothers to build patronage networks that underwrote her political and diplomatic authority. In mastering the intricacies of chiefly leadership and Native factionalism, Brant also earned the grudging respect of the English high command. Finding and holding a middle ground between the two sides was impressive enough; translating it into real authority where none had existed before was nothing short of remarkable.

NOTES

1. Recent studies of Molly Brant have commented on her role as a mediator who managed to bring together the Iroquois and the English, but they have neglected her significance as a Native leader. See Clara Sue Kidwell, "Indian Women as Cultural Mediators," *Ethnohistory* 39 (Spring 1992): 97; Earle Thomas, *The Three Faces of Molly Brant* (Kingston, Ont.: Quarry Press, 1996); Gretchen Green, "Molly Brant, Catherine Brant, and Their Daughters: A Study in Acculturation," *Ontario History* 81 (September 1989): 242; and Henry Pearson Gundy, "Molly Brant—Loyalist," *Ontario History* 44 (1953): 98.

2. Gundy, "Molly Brant," 98.

3. Journal of Warren Johnson, 29 June 1760–3 July 1761, *The Papers of Sir William Johnson* (14 v. Albany: University of the State of New York, 1921–65), 13: 192, and William N. Fenton, *The Great Law and the Longhouse: A Political History of the Iroquois Confederacy* (Norman: University of Oklahoma Press, 1998), 449, 510.

4. "Conference between Major-General Johnson and the Indians, June 1755," *Documents Relative to the Colonial History of the State of New York*, ed. E. B. O'Callaghan (15 v. Albany: Weed, Parsons, and Company, 1854–1887), 6: 967.

5. Goldsbrow Banyar to William Johnson, 23 September 1755, *Papers of Sir William Johnson*, 2: 80.

6. Daniel Claus and Conrad Weiser, "A Journey to Onondaga [1750]," trans. and ed. Helga Doblin and William A. Starna, in *In Mohawk Country: Early Narratives about a Native People*, ed. Dean R. Snow, Charles T. Gehring, and William A. Starna (Syracuse: Syracuse University Press, 1996), 239.

7. Journal of Indian Affairs, 4 April–18 November 1758, *Papers of Sir William Johnson*, 13: 111–12.

8. Peter Ogwitontongwas to William Johnson, 9 February 1770, ibid., 7: 379.

9. "A Meeting with Canajohares [10 March 1763]," ibid., 4: 50–58.

10. Indian Proceedings, 21–28 April 1762, ibid., 3: 707–8, 711–12.

11. George Starr, *Old St. George's* (Kingston, Ont.: R. Uglow and Company, 1912), 30.

12. Daniel Claus to Frederick Haldimand, 30 August 1779, Claus Papers, MG 19-F1, reel 2: 132, Public Archives of Canada, Ottawa, Ontario, Canada.

13. Mary Brant to Daniel Claus, 23 June 1778, ibid., 2: 29.

14. Earle, *Three Faces*, 110–11.

15. Taylor Duffin to Daniel Claus, 26 October 1778, Sir Frederick Haldimand, *Unpublished Papers and Correspondence, 1758–84* (London: World Microfilm Publications, 1978), 51: 21774, Queen's Archives, Queen's University, Kingston, Ontario, Canada.

16. Taylor Duffin to Daniel Claus, 26 October 1778, ibid., 51: 21774.

17. Daniel Claus to Frederick Haldimand, 30 August 1779, Claus Papers, 2: 133.

18. Daniel Claus to Frederick Haldimand, 6 September 1779, ibid., 25: 119.

19. Alexander Fraser to Frederick Haldimand, 29 September 1779, *Unpublished Papers*, 58: 21787.

20. Guy Johnson to Frederick Haldimand, 30 September 1779, ibid., 47: 21766.

21. George McDougall to Frederick Haldimand, 26 May 1779, ibid., 58: 21787. For a fuller account of Molly Brant's residence at Carleton Island and Kingston, see Sarah Katherine Gibson, "Carleton Island 1778–1783: Imperial Outpost during the American Revolutionary War" (Master's thesis, Queen's University, 1999).

22. Molly Brant to Daniel Claus, 5 October 1779, Claus Papers, 2: 135.

23. Daniel Claus to Frederick Haldimand, 30 August 1779, ibid., 2: 132–33.

24. Alexander Fraser to Frederick Haldimand, 29 October 1779, *Unpublished Papers*, 58: 21787.

25. Alexander Fraser to Frederick Haldimand, 21 March 1780, ibid., 58: 21787.

26. Alexander Fraser to Frederick Haldimand, 5 November 1780, ibid., 58: 21787.

27. "Extract translated from Mary Brant's Letter to Col. Claus dated Carleton Island, 12 April 1781," ibid., 51: 21774.

28. Daniel Claus to John Johnson, 26 July 1780, Claus Papers, 20: 17.

29. Alexander Fraser to Frederick Haldimand, 21 March 1780, *Unpublished Papers*, 58: 21787.

30. Alexander Fraser to Frederick Haldimand, 21 March 1780, ibid., 58: 21787.

31. Gilbert Tice to Daniel Claus, 18 February 1780, Claus Papers, 2: 175.

32. Alexander Fraser to Frederick Haldimand, 21 June 1780, *Unpublished Papers*, 58: 21787.

33. Frederick Haldimand to Joseph Brant, 27 May 1783, Joseph Brant and Family Papers, MG 19-F6, Public Archives of Canada, Ottawa, Ontario, Canada.

4

SACAGAWEA

The Making of a Myth

Donna Barbie

A Shoshone woman—child-captive of the Hidatsas, subsequent wife of a French fur trader, and purported guide to the Lewis and Clark expedition—stands as a legendary figure in America. Sacagawea, whose name is variously spelled "Sacajawea," "Sacagawea," and "Sakakawea," is that celebrated woman. Since 1805, when she made her first appearance in print, hundreds of histories, paintings, and novels have told her story. An abundance of statues and landmarks have been named in her honor, and a United States one dollar coin bears her image. As is true of any legend, Sacagawea's proponents fashioned an idealized woman, according to their own definition. In doing so, they formulated a satisfying narrative of her life, while also using it to address compelling contemporary issues in America. At the end of the twentieth century, this Native woman's story continues to endure in the society that first endowed it with significance.

Historically, we know little with any certainty about Sacagawea. The only written materials documenting any significant aspects of her life are the journals of the Lewis and Clark expedition (1804–6). Even within their logs, members of the Corps of Discovery merely mentioned her, generally suggesting that she played a relatively insignificant role in the mission. Not a single notation described her physically, and entries usually referred to her as "the squar" (squaw) or "the Indian woman." In nearly two years, only rarely did any of the journalists attempt to use her name. The journals do offer some details of Sacagawea's life. Captured as a child during an intertribal raid, she was taken to the Mandan's country where she became Toussaint Charbonneau's wife and gave birth to a son, Baptist. Shortly following the birth, she and Charbonneau embarked on the westward trek with the Lewis and Clark expedition in the spring of 1805. Sacagawea served, along with her French husband and other Natives whom they met along the way, in the chain of translators who conveyed the captains' words to various tribes.

Although we know little about Sacagawea, scholars have often ventured beyond notations in the journals to find meaning in her life and actions. Some suggest that her presence signaled the Corps of Discovery's peaceful intentions. Most controversial have been claims that Sacagawea "guided" the captains in the vicinity of the Shoshone camps of her youth and during William Clark's crossing of the Rockies on the return trip. Much later, in the entry written during the return trip that later fueled much mythologizing, Clark acknowledged Sacagawea's usefulness. He wrote that she had pointed out a passage through the mountains. A week later, he described her as "[T]he indian woman who has been of great service to me as a pilot through this country."[1] But we actually know little about her as a person.

During the long journey, the members of the expedition regarded Sacagawea as a "savage," a baser person with simple needs, few emotions, and little intellect. When she fell ill and seemed unlikely to recover, Meriwether Lewis wrote, "This gave me some concern as well for the poor object herself, then with a young child in her arms, as from the consideration of her being our only dependence for a friendly negociation [sic] with the Snake Indians on whom we depend for horses."[2] Lewis seemed concerned for the "poor object." But the entry also reflected his view of her as a mere tool of the expedition, and his chief concern was losing someone who might prove useful. Ironically enough, his notations inadvertently acknowledged Sacagawea's unique value and spared her for a moment from undifferentiated savagism. He acknowledged her ambiguous position: she was savage but also serviceable.

Shortly after Sacagawea's recovery, the men camped on the site of her childhood capture, and she related the circumstances under which the Hidatsas took her. No one recorded her account. Lewis merely observed, "I cannot discover that she shews any immotion of sorrow in recollecting this event, or of joy in being again restored to her native country; if she has enough to eat and a few trinkets to wear I believe she would be perfectly content anywhere."[3] As Sacagawea recounted this horrendous event, Lewis remained emotionally detached. He essentially denied that she possessed the capacity to feel. Instead, he described an impassive creature, content as long as her basic needs were met. Living in the present and responding solely to immediate sensory input, Sacagawea could not reflect. In his view, she experienced no pain in recollecting her past, nor could she anticipate the future with hope or desire. She epitomized ignoble savagery.

Despite the men's perceptions of Sacagawea as savage, other entries offer more complex glimpses of her. When the captains did not initially include Sacagawea in a trip to see a whale, for example, Lewis wrote, "the Indian woman was very impo[r]tunate to be permited to go . . . she observed that she had travelled a long way with us to see the great waters, and that now that monstrous fish was also to be seen, she thought it very hard she could not be permitted to see either."[4] The captains ultimately relented and permitted her to go. Although Sacagawea's protest did not change Lewis's assessment of her as "squaw," it forced him to confront her capacity to feel, her desires beyond food or trinkets, and her ability to use logic to bolster her demands.

The men of the Lewis and Clark expedition left the only written materials documenting Sacagawea's existence, and when the expedition ended, she returned to historical anonymity. These non-Indians perceived and portrayed her as a squaw although a few entries also provided glimpses of a unique woman, distinguishable from other savages. Their scant references and their omissions have served as fountainheads from which others have erected a legend.

Two factors account for the genesis of the Sacagawea legend and for its lasting importance. Inextricably linked to national myths, the legend personified the United States' sacred history and justified continental expansion. The Lewis and Clark expedition, the "epic" American journey, embodied a host of frontier myths. As the sole Native member of the Corps of Discovery, Sacagawea came to signify Indian compliance with the mission that symbolically incorporated the Louisiana Purchase (1803) into the United States and consecrated the wilderness to national purpose. Depicted as the Indian princess of the expedition and often proclaimed the key to its success in the years following the expedition, Sacagawea became synonymous with frontier traditions.

Another factor accounts for the enduring nature of the legend. Flexible within its mythic framework, the narrative has enabled those who retell it to confront diverse social and political issues in several historical periods. Propagators of the legend have used it to address women's suffrage, miscegenation, and modern feminism. Both timely and timeless, Sacagawea's story has represented and reinforced abiding national myths, while simultaneously fueling debates on critical issues within a dynamic and diverse society. Combining these purposes, Sacagawea's admirers have created a legend.

The most compelling Euro-American myths sum up the colonists' sacred duty on the continent and define the Natives who occupied the "empty" land.

The American nation dawned, according to these accounts, when Europeans first settled the New World with the help of a beneficent God. Labeling these ideas "manifest destiny" in the 1830s, United States citizens conceptualized the continent as empty and asserted their right to convert the wilderness into civilization. Intrepid pioneers rescued the land from profane neglect and abuse. They protected it, through constant vigilance, from savage violation, infringement, and encroachments.

As reflected in traditional narratives, one unique circumstance profoundly influenced Euro-American culture—the movement westward. Each successive American "wilderness," located just west of pioneer communities, required transformation into consecrated territory. Trailblazers repeatedly enacted the sacred drama of original settlement for more than two centuries. As a result, America's primal moment recurred until the end of the "frontier period" in the late 1880s. Cultural texts depicting these moments continuously revitalized America's frontier myths and reinvigorated the sense of sacred duty. One means of constructing these myths was by stereotyping Native groups who occupied the land. In a profusion of texts, writers collapsed tribal and individual distinctions into a stereotype of undifferentiated beings possessed of innate savagery. In print, on canvas, and in marble and bronze, non-Indians conflated complex Native existences into simplified patterns in order to explain the rectitude of "civilizing" the continent.

Two general patterns have delineated "Indians." Portrayed as either noble or ignoble savages, both stereotypes relentlessly outline an inferior species. Cruelty, barbarity, and treachery have characterized the ignoble or howling savage. These depictions first arose from sensational accounts of Euro-American captivities by tribal groups. Narratives of confrontations between Natives and Europeans, such as those produced during the wars of King Philip and the Pequots, supplemented and amplified earlier portraits. Other texts have illustrated very good Indians, virtuous, albeit primitive, noble savages who exuded qualities of self-sacrifice and trustworthiness. Although their docile behavior did not mandate extermination, these very good Indians also obstructed the progress of civilization. They were expected to assimilate or vanish.

Native American women have, by no means, remained exempt from Indian stereotyping. "Squaws" behaved as savagely as their ignoble male counterparts. Slavish and servile, they also committed gruesome acts, wielding tomahawks and knives, torturing hapless captives. The squaw's eradication, like that of the male savage, was necessary to create a safe haven for civilization. While Euro-Americans condemned squaws, they canonized Indian "princesses." Although traditional Native groups had no concept of royalty and never ordained any Native woman a "princess," this "heroic" figure, emanating primitive virtues of innocence, respect, and trustworthiness, has captivated Euro-Americans.

Stories of the noble female savage are particularly insidious. The princess does not fit into the context of her own culture. Instead, she occupies an ambiguous position between savagery and civilization. Her skin is lighter than most Natives, but darker than whites. More important, she exists only as a reflection of her relationship with Euro-American men. As Rayna Green, a folklorist of Cherokee descent has phrased it, the princess is noble only when, in order to aid a white man or men, she defies "her own people, exiles herself from them, becomes white, and perhaps suffers death."[5] The Indian princess is receptive to and fosters invasion by a superior "civilization," even though her tragic demise may result.

Although the journals of the Lewis and Clark expedition depicted the Shoshone woman as a squaw, the Sacagawea of myth became a "princess." She was deemed the most astute primitive of the trans-Mississippi West, she alone realized that Euro-Americans endowed aboriginals with the blessings of a more advanced civilization. Tapping into culturally satisfying images of western conquest and Native inferiority, Sacagawea's interpreters created a Euro-American legend. But Sacagawea did not become a heroine immediately. Rather, the legend arose nearly a century after the Corps of Discovery first "captured" her in print. Beginning in the 1890s, novelists, sculptors, historians, painters, and playwrights of the Progressive period jettisoned her ignoble savagery and pronounced her a "princess." Focusing on the progress of civilization through democratization and reform, they recast Sacagawea as an overt reflection of manifest destiny. Her life and actions signified the rectitude of America's conquest of the continent.

Several writers of this period employed Sacagawea's story for an additional purpose. Suffragists latched onto her as the prototype for an emancipated woman. Sacagawea demonstrated how women, without voting power, still helped to create an American empire. She also exemplified what women could achieve. Rather than literally blazing trails like Sacagawea, American women were exhorted to venture into social and political arenas and to take their rightful places in society. Guided by enduring frontier myths and embracing timely issues, these writers expanded on the expedition journals.

Perhaps Sacagawea's most important legend builder was Eva Emery Dye. Encouraged by her publishers to write the Lewis and Clark expedition story just before the mission's centennial year, Dye produced her fictionalized account, *The Conquest: The True Story of Lewis and Clark* in 1902.[6] Active in the woman suffrage movement, Dye was not satisfied with retelling a narrative of male heroes. Dye highlighted Sacagawea. As she wrote in her journal, "Out of a few dry bones I found in the old tales of the trip, I created Sacajawea and made her a living entity. For months I dug and scraped for accurate information about this wonderful Indian Maid."[7] Dye did not accept Sacagawea's status as an ignoble "squaw." Since the men of the Corps recorded that her brother was a Shoshone chief, the novelist claimed that she was a "Princess, come home now to her Mountain Kingdom" (228). The Indian princess's innate superiority was not fully realized, however, until Dye enumerated Sacagawea's activities throughout the expedition. These attested to her true nobility.

Dye presented a heroine whose actions served as a template for American women. Highlighting the whale incident, Dye wrote that "This was a staggering blow to Sacajawea, but her woman's determination had been aroused and she took the rostrum, so to speak" (250). Unswayed by the captains' decision, Sacagawea thrust the baby at her husband and argued her own case. Humbled by this "brave little woman" (250), Clark acquiesced. In this passage, Dye abandoned the historical evidence. Neither Lewis nor Clark wrote in their journals that the force of her arguments or the authority of her person had the least effect on them. Instead, Clark apparently simply indulged Sacagawea's whim. Rather than being acted upon or passive, Dye's Sacagawea initiated action and demanded a response.

Thousands of readers embraced the first fictional Sacagawea. Commenting on the popular response in her journal, Dye remarked, "The beauty of that faithful Indian woman with her baby on her back . . . appealed to the world."[8] But the Indian heroine was not the sole aspect of the novel that attracted an audience. Dye also glorified the exploration and subsequent settlement of the West and intertwined an account of righteous national expansion with Sacagawea's story.

The novelist extolled Sacagawea's contributions throughout *The Conquest*, but in her version, the princess actually determined the fate of the mission during the return trip. With Clark's party near the Continental Divide, Sacagawea "led the way into the labrynthine Rockies," crying "'Onward!' . . . 'the gap there leads to your canoes!'" (283–84). Later, when a network of peaks bewildered the men, Sacagawea again indicated the route, and Clark merely followed (285). Unlike the "squar" of Lewis's accounts, this woman did not simply accompany the explorers. She ventured into the wilderness with men, and at times she superseded them. She also gave a female imprimatur to wilderness. Not merely the domain of men, the West—and by implication, the whole nation—belonged to women as well. The explorers' departure from Fort Mandan on the return journey provided Dye with the opportunity to sum up the legend: "Sacajawea, modest princess of the Shoshones, heroine of the expedition, stood with her babe in her arms and smiled upon them [the expedition men] from the shore. So had she stood in the Rocky Mountains pointing out the gates" (290). No savage squaw, Sacagawea was an Indian princess and an American heroine who led the way for Euro-Americans to expand across the continent.

During the Progressive Era, Sacagawea became an icon for expansionism as well as suffrage. In 1905, the Federated Women's Clubs of North Dakota initiated a campaign to erect a monument to honor Sacagawea. A promotional brochure, *Sakakawea (Bird Woman) Statue Notes*, listed reasons a statue should be dedicated to Sacagawea.[9] Not only did she provide a variety of essential services to the Lewis and Clark expedition, but she was also "a princess of uncommon grace of mind and of person" (2). Therefore, she "welcomed with intelligent appreciation the civilization of the white race" (n.p.). Devoted to manifest destiny, Sacagawea was heroic because she had the sagacity to understand and support the wilderness mission. The fund drive, conducted entirely by non-Indians, was enormously successful.

Five thousand gathered in Bismarck on October 13, 1910, to dedicate Leonard Crunelle's larger-than-life bronze statue of Sacagawea. Entitled *Bird Woman*, the statue linked women and frontier traditions. During the ceremony, the chair of the "Sakakawea Committee," Mrs. C. F. Amidon, announced that "The True pioneer spirit has passed along from the first pioneer . . . to the western women of today."[10] Judge B. F. Spalding, accepting the statue on behalf of the state, commended Sacagawea for the selfless services she performed in "the land of promise and of plenty, which she helped save to this great nation." In every speech, presenters espoused frontier myths and incorporated Sacagawea into that tradition.

The dedication ceremony also suggested that Sacagawea's actions had benefited America's Native peoples. The secretary of the state historical society, Dr. O. G. Libby, proclaimed that she had assured that "our good friends," the Indians, were now able to receive educations in government schools. Gros Ventre James Holding Eagle, for example, graduated from Santee Nebraska government school and influenced his parents to "farm and make a home for themselves." Shoshone Mattie Johnson, a graduate of Haskell in Kansas, taught in the laundry department in the Bismarck Indian school. Arikara James Beauchamp, also a graduate of a government school, was "one of the successful Indian farmers and stock raisers on the Berthold reservation and one who is doing much for the betterment of his brother in the way of getting better acquainted with better methods both in farming and living." Never having heard of Sacagawea before the monument drive began, according to the *Tribune* article, such Native peoples did not recognize traditional ties between themselves and this woman. Their achievements, however, illustrated the benefits that all Indians had realized by the U.S. conquest of the continent.

Both the unveiling and the monument itself tied Sacagawea to manifest destiny. According to the *Tribune*, the 14th U.S. Infantry Band played "The Star Spangled Banner" as the ribbon was cut to "release the folds of the National Flag that veiled the bronze features." Heralded by the national anthem and wrapped in the American flag, the twelve-foot statue appeared to emerge from a block of rough granite. The imposing bronze woman, dressed in traditional garb of fringed buckskin and blankets, raised her right hand to her shoulder, assuring the security of the sleeping baby on her back. At first glance, the statue might seem to represent any Native woman. The inscription, however, read, "Sakakawea—the Shoshone Indian 'Bird Woman,' who in 1805, guided the Lewis and Clark expedition from the Missouri River to the Yellowstone." The statue honored Sacagawea not because of her Native origins but because of her actions during the expedition. Facing directly west, *Bird Woman*'s intense gaze confirmed her devotion to the wilderness mission.

Following Dye's *The Conquest* and Crunelle's *Bird Woman*, the Sacagawea legend proliferated. Fewer than eleven works about the Lewis and Clark journals were published before 1905. Over two hundred titles, however, came to press in the next seven decades.[11] Each touted the narrative of America's "epic journey," and each embraced the Sacagawea legend. Although World Wars I and II temporarily diverted attention from stories of Indian princesses, by the mid 1940s, Sacagawea once again became the focal point of numerous works. She resumed her place as a vaunted American heroine, but her message underwent subtle changes.

Between 1940 and 1970, Sacagawea became the essential helper in the wilderness. Creators of this period, like their predecessors, used Sacagawea to explore and question aspects of a dynamic American culture. Several historical novels, for example, engaged in the debate over Native acculturation; others examined American strictures against interracial relationships. In doing so, they elaborated on the legend. No longer was a nebulous commitment to manifest destiny the sole reason for Sacagawea's behavior. Novelists of this period asserted that a romantic attachment spurred her cooperation. Although previous works scrupulously avoided references to Sacagawea's sexuality, these writers framed the story around the potential for interracial romance. In the 1940s, Sacagawea fell hopelessly in love with a gallant and heroic captain.

Although texts of the era shared this interpretation, men and women related the narrative differently. Writers of both sexes praised Sacagawea for her helpfulness and cooperation, but most male novelists suggested that she possessed no real understanding of the mission and was motivated by love alone. This woman lived and thought on a basic level, comprehending the world through the lens of her narrow life and limited emotions. Male authors minimized her most important legendary achievements, such as her guidance of Clark in the mountains. More often acted upon than acting, Sacagawea depended upon a man for direction and motivation.

Typical of Sacagawea works penned by men during this period, Donald Culross Peattie's *Forward the Nation*[12] championed manifest destiny. The momentous trip symbolized the continuous, inexorable process of "civilizing" the continent, Peattie reminded readers. America moved, not only westward but also "forward" as the nation absorbed wildernesses. In the midst of a novel retelling America's glorious conquest of the continent and documenting civilization's triumph over savagery, Peattie related the story of Sacagawea. Like previous writers, Peattie established that Sacagawea was not a common squaw. Physically distinct from other Native women, the petite Sacagawea had a lovely face and obsidian, almond-shaped eyes. She was "beautiful," even by "white standards" (6, 72, 83). She was also bright and energetic, not a woman cowed by harsh treatment and the burdens of savage existence (70). Appearance, however, was not the sole indicator of Sacagawea's nobility. Extolling her cooperation during the expedition and reiterating the traditional legend, Peattie proclaimed that Sacagawea "will be remembered as long as Americans love their country, for in its history no other woman ever served it better" (109).

Peattie rejected the implication that Sacagawea's devotion to manifest destiny caused her to act. Instead he asserted that a woman "seldom has any genuine attachment to a cause. It is a man she follows, and she espouses whatever cause he upholds. . . . In serving, she serves him; this is her single purpose; this is her strength" (56–57). Sacagawea was helpful, Peattie concluded, because she met a man worthy of her love and devotion, namely, Meriwether Lewis. Although Peattie celebrated that because of Sacagawea's efforts "the continent, like a flag, was fully unfurled" (248), he claimed that she did not really understand the significance of her actions. Reacting conservatively, perhaps due to the demands that World War II was placing on women in his own society, Peattie may have tried to impart traditional, comfortable meanings to new roles. The women who replaced men in the workforce during the war took these unfeminine jobs, like Sacagawea, out of love for their men rather than the nobler love of country, which only men truly understood.

Although female writers of the period concurred with some interpretations advanced by their male contemporaries, they did not deprecate Sacagawea's accomplishments. Reiterating her heroic deeds, they praised her strength and intelligence. These women agreed that Sacagawea devoted herself to one of the men, but they did not conclude that love alone inspired her. Sacagawea's esteem for a "civilized" man stimulated her understanding of the superiority of Euro-American culture. Rather than being the cause of her behavior, emotions merely deepened Sacagawea's understanding of more important cultural realities.

In *Sacajawea of the Shoshones*, representative of texts written by women during this period, Della Gould Emmons portrayed an exceptional heroine.[13] Like other writers, Emmons excluded Sacagawea from ignoble savagery by indicating her royal heritage and enumerating her contributions during the expedition. In accord with precepts of Indian princesses, Sacagawea was vivacious and pretty with a luminous face. Reflecting the racist views of the period, Emmons described her skin as lighter than that of most Natives, no darker than the hand of a tanned trader. In this version, Sacagawea saved the mission on several occasions, including the time she guided Clark through the mountains. In another incident, Sacagawea saw items drifting in the river during a squall. She acted quickly: "Those prized possessions! What matter if there was danger. She must save all that she could. Like lightning she worked. Quickly she grasped one here, two there . . . she tucked them into her lap and reached for more, oblivious to personal danger" (166). At the end Lewis proclaimed, "we must not forget that our success was due largely to Sacajawea . . . I pray God that we will always remember it" (245).

Emmons also embraced the love story. Sacagawea's heart and soul belonged to William Clark. Constantly watching him "with a worshiping look" (132), Sacagawea saw him as "her God" (183). She adored Clark, but her love did not define the totality of her existence. Clark and the expedition served as Emmons's vehicle for exploring savagery and civilization. She embarked on the journey, not simply for the love of a single man, but with the belief that he and his kind would change the continent. As Emmons wrote, Sacagawea's "heart was singing, her face alight with worship for these white men going to her people, . . . going to free them from hunger and fear" (106). Despite the romance, Emmons did not downplay Sacagawea's heroism. She emphasized that women could excel in male roles without sacrificing their femininity. While Emmons's popular novel disseminated the legend to a broad readership, her efforts reached even more people with a screenplay. *The Far Horizon*, a major Hollywood film produced in 1955, drew thousands of viewers.

Despite significant differences in Peattie's and Emmons's works, both novelists explored the possibility of Native acculturation and assimilation, goals widely discussed in America during this period. Despite the New Deal's emphasis on preserving Native cultures and communities, Indian policy by the late 1940s began to turn toward terminating the special status of Native people and incorporating them into the American mainstream. At the same time, the nascent civil rights movement was raising crucial questions about the role of racial minorities in the United States. Few issues provoked a more emotional response than interracial sex. Nevertheless, interracial marriage appeared to be a logical extension of assimilation, and Indian princesses long vivified that prospect. Taboos of miscegenation nonetheless functioned as a cultural "reality" in Euro-American society. Consequently, the interracial romances of Indian "princesses" invariably ended tragically. "Princesses" recognized the superiority of Euro-American men and culture, but prohibitions against miscegenation prevented consummation of their love.

Peattie and Emmons upheld cultural proscriptions against miscegenation. Peattie emphasized Lewis's emotional indifference to Sacagawea, despite her feelings for him, but he also pointed out the potent sexuality of this young Native woman. Lewis was all too aware of her allure. He noticed that she revealed the "round bronze apple" when she nursed her baby (121). In another scene, the captain observed that Sacagawea's breasts had "a brave young lift to them" (148). She was not simply a maternal nurturer; she was also a sexual being. Although Peattie hinted at a potential romance, he ultimately concluded that an interracial relationship was unacceptable. Writing of Sacagawea, he declared that "In her own blood ran an unalterable devotion to them . . . the marriage of the American soul with the soul of aboriginal America" (236). Offering the only acceptable alternative to the obscenity of interracial mixing, Peattie condoned a "marriage" of disparate souls, but not of bodies.

Emmons also examined miscegenation in *Sacagawea of the Shoshones*. Less circumspect than Peattie, Emmons openly admitted that Sacagawea affected Clark. He became emotionally involved with Sacagawea, and in several scenes, he seemed prepared to put aside racial difference. Disconcerted by his feelings for Sacagawea, Clark wondered if race was really so important. He asked, "was she so different temperamentally from a white girl?" (135). In a dream, he visualized "a bewitching composite" of a civilized woman and the "savage" Sacagawea (137). Despite his musing, Clark answered his own question. The difference not only existed; it was too important to challenge. Savagery, which he linked to race, separated Sacagawea from himself and civilization, and he could not cross the barrier. Emmons assured her audience that Sacagawea aroused only "chivalry" in Clark (136). Other emotions were unacceptable.

The heroine of Emmons's tale embraced manifest destiny and accepted the superiority of "civilization," but her most important discovery was the evil of miscegenation. From the time the corps arrived, Sacagawea possessed a vague awareness of this impediment to romance, and she "sighed at the impassable canyon that yawned between" herself and Clark (157). Nevertheless, Sacagawea hoped to win him. Thrilled by Clark's protective embrace after a flash flood, she asked him why he rescued her. When he replied that any "self-respecting civilized man" would have done the same thing, her "glow died slowly out and left her cold and weary. Gently, but firmly, she drew away from him" (189). Sacagawea understood that the canyon must never be breached.

During the 1970s and 1980s, in the midst of contentious dialogues about imperialism and race relations, the Sacagawea legend remained vital as it changed with the times. Popular works offered the traditional narrative of a Native woman who earned her title as an American heroine by helping civilized men in the savage wilderness. Most works of this period justified western conquests and upheld the bifurcation of savagery and civilization. Many referred to her as an Indian princess and incorporated variations of the legend, especially the romance between her and Clark. At least one representation, however, broke with typical mediums and used the story to question the "truths" of frontier traditions.

Under an advertising banner, "Sacajawea: A Brave and Noble American Heroine," the 1989 Hamilton Collection plate "Sacajawea" revealed the continued attraction of Indian princesses and frontier myths. The script read, "Gentle, serene and knowledgeable, Sacajawea helped lead her party over plains and rivers and through Montana mountain passes." Designed and executed by David Wright, the plate displayed a woman with all the physical attributes of the Indian princess. Young and beautiful with lightly tanned skin, the Indian princess sits serenely in the foreground and dominates the scene. Her clothing of fringed buckskin may not indicate a "royal" station, but the accoutrements adorning her dress, such as fur trim, extensive beading and quillwork, and jewelry, attest to Sacagawea's nobility. Colors of red, white, and blue dominate the image and visually associate Sacagawea with the nation. Red beads or quills against a white background, a design remarkably similar to the stripes of an American flag, decorate the baby's cradle board, which she holds in her lap. As the portrait suggests and the advertisement copy confirms, she simultaneously fulfilled her obligations as a protective mother and as the American heroine of the Lewis and Clark expedition. A "bold and brave Indian woman," this Indian princess assured the nation of the rectitude of manifest destiny.

The Hamilton Collection's approach to Sacagawea is not an aberration, even in an era of dissension over issues of conquest, race, and gender. Others offered the same formula, including Anna Lee Waldo in her 1,407-page romance novel,

Sacajawea.[14] Although the book received unanimously negative reviews, American audiences loved it. Demonstrating how easily Sacagawea's story can be molded to the form of a modern romance novel, Waldo offered a heart-wrenching tale of the Indian princess who loved Clark and saved the mission but who could never participate in civilization because of her Native heritage.

True to the legend, Waldo's story embraced frontier traditions. The back cover of the novel proclaimed that Sacagawea "stood straight and proud before the onrushing forces of America's destiny." Through this "great woman," Waldo told the story of the "great nation." In addition to employing the rhetoric of conquest, Waldo interminably illustrated Native savagery, especially as it affected women. She declared that Sacagawea was an Indian princess, far above the common squaw, and enumerated her many accomplishments during the expedition. Despite those qualities, Waldo, like so many others before her, proclaimed that Sacagawea could not become a part of civilized society, a tragedy illustrated all too vividly in hundreds of pages of frustrated love. Taboos against interracial relationships prevented Sacagawea and Clark from fulfilling their desires: "[T]his feeling had roots between them, but the roots could never be nourished and kept alive" (664).

Despite the tawdriness of Waldo's romance, she too used Sacagawea as a model for American women of their own times. Like Dye and Emmons, she portrayed her as a heroine who rose above many of the constraints of her day. In a romance novel about one of America's most renowned Indian princesses, Sacagawea became a prototype for modern feminists. Waldo used the story to discuss the repression of women and the control of female sexuality and reproduction. Furthermore, Waldo's Sacagawea was not a weakling to be manipulated by men. Rather, she was strong and independent, a woman who resonated with modern feminists.

In the same year that the Hamilton Collection first advertised the "Sacajawea" plate, two Euro-American men produced another iteration of the Sacagawea legend, the musical drama *Sakakawea: The Woman with Many Names*. Librettist William Borden and composer Thomas Peterson, however, used the story of the expedition and Sacagawea's role in that mission to challenge frontier traditions and the dichotomy of savagery and civilization. As this play demonstrated, manifest destiny no longer retained uncontested authority in America. Instead, contrary narratives competed for "reality" status on the continent.

Produced in celebration of North Dakota's centennial year, the musical was performed before sellout crowds in 1989. In some ways, Peterson and Borden did not depart from previous versions of the legend. The heroic Sacagawea was a cooperative helper in the wilderness. She translated for the captains and conveyed the expedition's peaceful intentions to suspicious Indians. When the men were starving because they could not find meat, she arrived with vegetables and roots that she had dug, and the entire chorus sang, "What would we do without you?" (1.19).

Again, in keeping with five decades of legend, *Sakakawea* included a love story. Returning Sacagawea's affection, Clark sang to her when she was ill, "I don't need you to buy horses. I don't need you to find food. I need your bright laugh, I need your warm hand in mine. I need you close to me" (1.25). Nevertheless, their love is doomed. Arguing with Sacagawea over the hopelessness of their situation, Clark explained that he has plans when he returns to civilization: "It's different in the city. It's different in the white man's world. I love you, Janey, but it's not a city love. A General can't have a People [Indian] wife" (2.17). Marrying a Native woman would destroy Clark's political ambitions.

Despite these hackneyed approaches to the narrative, *Sakakawea* disputed some common Euro-American assumptions about Native peoples. Borden and Peterson, for example, confronted a passage in Lewis's journal that implied Sacagawea's savage impassivity. Overlapping each other's disparate conversations, Sacagawea and Lewis sang,

Lewis: Here she was captured by enemies only a few years ago . . .

Young Sakakawea: Only a few years ago, horses thundered over that hill. An arm scooped me up . . .

Lewis: I cannot discover . . .

Young Sakakawea: I rode behind him . . .

Lewis: . . . that she shows any emotion . . .

Young Sakakawea: . . . all day, the horse's spine . . .

Lewis: . . . of sorrow in recollecting this event . . .

Young Sakakawea: . . . hard against my buttocks . . .

Lewis: . . . or of joy in being restored . . .

Young Sakakawea: . . . the man's back sweating, his smell heavy in my nostrils.

Lewis: . . . to her native country.

Young Sakakawea: It was like dying—. (2.1–2)

Sacagawea related to the members of the expedition the pain and anguish of her capture. Frontier myths, however, had shaped Lewis's sensibilities, and he uncritically believed that savage women were unemotional creatures. Although he heard her tale, he also understood that she was unquestionably savage. Nothing, not even her own testimony, swayed his opinion. As the audience witnessed two intersecting, yet conflicting narratives, Sacagawea's story remained believable and poignant. Lewis's judgments became pointedly ironic.

Although other writers have cast doubts on Lewis's interpretation of Sacagawea's impassivity, most have not countered broader notions of Native savagism, as did Borden and Peterson. When Clark first met Sacagawea, they talked about the mission. She asked, "You'll see many Peoples? We call ourselves People. You call us Indians" (1.8). First, she pointed out the error of conflation. Natives are "peoples," many groups embracing different traditions and customs. She emphasized that Native people are not lesser beings, but human. *Sakakawea* also questioned the intent of the journey and documented the destruction of Native cultures. A moment after the young Sacagawea pleaded with her brother to provide horses for the corps, the setting shifted. The elderly Sacagawea mused:

> They were very strange, and they meant well. But they did not understand the consequence of their journey. None of us understood. We did not know that traders would follow. We did not know that railroads would follow. We did not know that treaties would follow, that reservations would follow, that Wounded Knee, boarding school, BIA would follow. (2.7)

Although Sacagawea claimed that neither she nor other members of the corps could have foreseen the results of the expedition, she highlighted issues that other texts did not raise. Citing the consequences of confinement and paternalism, Sacagawea delivered a message about the horrors of conquest. Borden and Peterson retold a story of one of the nation's most celebrated women, but they also offered a new variation of the legend, one that had important implications for their own time.

The texts examined here are but a few representative works, produced over nearly a century, that have embraced the Sacagawea story. As they illustrate, Sacagawea has long struck a responsive chord in American creators and in the nation's audiences. She is still in the forefront of American cultural heroines. From casual references on popular television programs like "thirtysomething" to perennial "answers" on the game show "Jeopardy!" hundreds of texts proliferate Sacagawea's name and her fame. They also demonstrate the power and endurance of cultural ideas and imagery.

The latest installment in the legend is the use of Sacagawea's "image" on a gold-colored dollar coin slated to come into circulation in 2000. Six versions of the "portrait" appeared widely in daily newspapers in December 1998. Although a U.S. Mint spokesman admitted that no one knew what Sacagawea looked like, he also claimed that the images were realistic portrayals of Native women. The mint invited the public to comment on the likenesses to narrow the field to three, with the U.S. Fine Arts Commission making the final selection. Some might applaud this action. They might suggest that the time has come for America to celebrate a Native woman and that a coin is an appropriate vehicle for such recognition. As this study reveals, however, Sacagawea's animation does not speak of her as a person nor does it illuminate Native cultures. Instead, the legend reflects the needs and aspirations of Euro-America. With no means of uncovering or knowing anything about the historical woman, Euro-Americans have transformed Sacagawea, "inventing" the story of an enduring, yet flexible, Indian princess who serves the needs of white men without requiring them to make fundamental changes in their own values. Indeed, she usually has validated those values. Despite narrative variations and diverse goals, fundamental descriptions and meanings behind the legend remain relatively constant.

Therein lies the dilemma. Few dissenting portraits of Native American women have ever been produced, in part because Euro-America has been unwilling to give up satisfying legends. Perhaps America will soon be ready to retire Indian princesses. Perhaps the culture will champion other visions of Native cultures and of Native women. Scholars agree that this can be accomplished, at least in part, as Natives increasingly produce works portraying aboriginal life of the past and present. Works written by Leslie Silko, N. Scott Momaday, Louise Erdrich, James Welch, Michael Dorris, Mary Crow Dog, Wilma Mankiller, and others echo and reinforce evidence that tribal peoples have been important to the nation, although not in the ways the Sacagawea legend embodies. Through reading about and interacting with Native peoples, Euro-Americans can break free of persistent visions that cripple their ability to see, to understand, or even to concede the existence of the polyphonous voices that comprise American culture. Someday, we may be ready to erect statues in celebration of different Native women. In the meantime, *Bird Woman* still faces West.

NOTES

1. Reuben Gold Thwaites, ed., *Original Journals of the Lewis and Clark Expedition, 1804–1806* (8 v., New York: Dodd Mead, 1904–1906) 5: 250, 260.

2. Ibid., 2: 162–63.

3. Ibid., 2: 283.

4. Ibid., 3: 315.

5. Rayna Green,"The Pocahontas Perplex: The Image of Indian Women in American Culture," *Massachusetts Review* 16 (1975): 703–4.

6. (Chicago: A. C. McClurg, 102). Page numbers of quotations appear in text.

7. Quoted in Alfred Powers, *History of Oregon Literature* (Portland: Metropolitan Press, 1935), 93.

8. Quoted in Ella Clark and Margot Edmonds, *Sacagawea of the Lewis and Clark Expedition* (Berkeley: University of California Press, 1979), 94.

9. (Fargo, ND: Porte Company, 1906). Page numbers of quotations appear in text.

10. "Statue Unveiling at State Capitol Is Unique Event," *Bismarck Tribune*, 14 Oct. 1910.

11. Paul Russell Cutright, *A History of the Lewis and Clark Journals* (Norman: University of Oklahoma Press, 1976), 202.

12. (New York: G. P. Putnam's Sons, 1942). Page numbers of quotations appear in text.

13. (Binfords and Mort, 1943). Page numbers of quotations appear in text.

14. (New York: Avon Books, 1979). Page numbers of quotations appear in text.

5

CATHARINE BROWN

Cherokee Convert to Christianity

Theda Perdue

In July 1817 Catharine Brown, a seventeen- or eighteen-year-old Cherokee woman, enrolled in the Brainerd Mission School. The daughter of a relatively prosperous but uneducated Cherokee couple, she had no previous formal education, and the missionaries harbored strong doubts about her ability
to adjust to the regimen of the mission school. In the six years before her un-
timely death in 1823, however, she achieved everything missionaries sought
in converts: she was pious and chaste, industrious and humble, absolutely committed to the conversion of her people to Christianity. Catharine Brown's brief
life illustrates the goals of Protestant missions among Native peoples—and the
limitations imposed on their efforts.

Protestant missions in North America lagged far behind those of the Roman
Catholic Church. Catholic priests accompanied early French and Spanish explorers, and well before the United States won its independence, their successors had
built mission communities across Canada, throughout what is now the southwestern United States, and in Florida. Protestant efforts in the English colonies
seem paltry by comparison—scattered individual ministries and a few "praying
towns," communities of Native converts, in the northeast. The Great Awakening in the 1740s kindled interest in missions, but the real impetus to intensive
evangelical effort was the waves of revivalism that swept the United States in the
early nineteenth century. Having had an intensely emotional religious experience, converts brought unbounded zeal to the task of saving all the world's people.

The American Board of Commissioners for Foreign Missions, which founded Brainerd at the present site of Chattanooga, Tennessee, provides an example of this religious enthusiasm. Begun in Boston in 1810, the American Board intended to blanket the globe with missionaries and accomplish universal salvation in just a few years. Drawing members primarily from Congregational and Presbyterian churches, the American Board organized local chapters throughout New England and collected funds to support its missionary activities. The board did not limit its activities solely to preaching, singing, and praying. Like most other missionary societies in this period, the American Board committed itself to the complete transformation of Native people.

Members believed that "civilization" and Christianity were intrinsically linked. For an Indian to become a true Christian, he or she would have to learn to live like Anglo-American citizens of the United States. Men would have to abandon hunting and take up the plow while their wives tended to hearth and home. Their children would have to enroll in schools where they learned to read and write English. Native style of dress would have to give way to the modest apparel of Anglo-Americans. Families would have to conform to the patriarchal model of Anglo-America, and government would have to embody republican principles like those of the United States. At missions Indians were taught by rote and by example. Native children attended schools and learned the appropriate chores for "civilized" households along with their ABCs. Model farms demonstrated the cultivation of "civilized" crops like wheat—instead of corn, a "savage" Native American crop—and mills provided local Native households with a place to process their grain and lumber. Missionaries provided an example as well as a sermon.[1]

In the summer of 1817 when she arrived at Brainerd, Catharine Brown seemed to epitomize the "savagery" of Cherokee society. In a memoir of Catharine, the assistant secretary of the American Board, Rufus Anderson, described the Cherokee Nation as "susceptible of the highest cultivation. But most imperfect was their agriculture." The Cherokee language, which no missionary had yet learned, was reputed to be "precise and powerful," but the Cherokees had failed to develop a system for writing their language. Anderson lamented: "Not a book existed in the language. The fountains of knowledge were unopened. The mind made no progress." The Cherokees recognized that the missionaries promised them a better way of life, according to Anderson. Therefore, the National Council gave permission to the American Board in 1816 to establish schools with the hope that "they will be of great advantage to the nation." The Cherokees needed not only the technology of "civilization," missionaries believed, but also the values of hard work, discipline, and humility that Christianity inculcated.[2]

Like the Cherokees, Catharine was full of potential. Anderson described her as "an interesting girl: her complexion blooming; her features comely; her person erect, and of middle stature; her manners easy; her demeanor modest and prepossessing." She had done little, however, to cultivate that potential. She was a young woman, not a child, but she barely knew how to read and write. Furthermore, according to missionary Cyrus Kingsbury, "she had a high opinion of herself, and was fond of displaying the clothing and ornaments in which she was arrayed." Kingsbury worried that "her feelings would not easily yield to the discipline of our schools, especially to that part of it, which requires manual labor of the scholars." Catharine accepted the school rules, however, and she quickly learned to "read the Bible intelligibly."[3]

Although she was of marriageable age, Catharine came to the missionaries with her virtue intact. Anderson assured his readers that "her moral character was ever irreproachable," a circumstance that he found "remarkable, considering the looseness of manners then prevalent among the females of her nation, and the temptations to which she was exposed." United States soldiers stationed near her home during the Creek War of 1814 provided the "temptations," although Anderson's remark that "once she even forsook her home, and fled into the wild forest, to preserve her character unsullied" suggests that rape was more likely than seduction. None other than General Andrew Jackson, who commanded the soldiers in Alabama in 1814 and became president of the United States in 1829, reportedly described Catharine as "a woman of Roman virtue, and above suspicion."[4]

As for the "looseness" of her contemporaries, Cherokee women enjoyed considerable sexual freedom before marriage as well as easy divorce and remarriage.[5] These practices, needless to say, deeply offended the missionaries. Furthermore, some Cherokees lived in polygamous households in which a man had more than one wife. Missionaries regarded such arrangements not only as sinful but also as degrading to women. In any event, Catharine grew up in a household in which Protestant notions of morality had little place. Her father was married three times. Catharine's mother, his second wife, and his third wife lived with him at the same time. Furthermore, Catharine's mother had previously been married to another man by whom she also had children.

Cherokee families clearly lacked the familial order that missionaries associated with "civilization," and matrilineality only compounded the situation. In Cherokee culture, children belonged to the clan of their mother, not their father, and their mother had control over them. In the event of divorce, children remained with their mother in her house. Missionaries constantly confronted the problem of fathers bringing their children to school and mothers removing them. They soon learned to ascertain the wishes of mothers before enrolling their children, but they did not approve of the practice. In the missionaries' worldview, fathers headed households and mothers as well as children were subordinate to them. When Catharine Brown decided to go to school, Anderson wrote, "she besought her parents to send her, and they granted her request."[6] In this compromise version, missionaries accorded father and mother equality. In reality, Catharine's mother almost certainly held sway.

One of the ways that missionaries sought to reorder Cherokee families was to change gender roles, that is, the appropriate behavior for men and women. Women farmed in Cherokee society while men hunted, but missionaries sought to turn the men into farmers. Therefore, in the mission schools, young men plowed and hoed, fenced fields, planted orchards, harvested corn and ground it into meal, tended livestock, and performed other tasks, such as chopping and carrying wood, traditionally done by Cherokee women. Young women worked in the kitchen and laundry, sewed clothing, swept and mopped floors, and attended to other domestic chores. Presumably, manual labor, to which missionaries at first thought Catharine would object, taught discipline and the value of work as well as new tasks. Without such student labor, however, the mission schools could not have survived.

Missionaries recognized that their primary objective was converting Native people to Christianity, an essential step in the "civilizing" process. In this respect, Catharine did not disappoint them. Many concepts of Christianity were alien to Cherokees. In particular, they did not regard human beings as innately sinful, and death did not hold the promise of reward or punishment for actions in this life. Catharine did not know that she was a sinner, and the heaven of which she vaguely conceived had "fewer points of attraction than the earth."[7] Consequently, when Catharine began to express interest in Christianity, "she did not seem to be greatly influenced by a fear of the punishment threatened against sin." Instead, she merely wanted to "know the will of God, and do it." The anguish she felt was for her people: "For them she wept and prayed, in secret places, and in the company of her female friends at their weekly prayer-meeting."[8] The missionaries interpreted her behavior as evangelical, the ardent desire of believers to spread the gospel, but Catharine's concern may have stemmed from the Cherokee concern for community. Unlike Christianity, which concentrated on the salvation of individual souls, Cherokee religion focused on community well-being. Convinced of the correctness of Christianity, Catharine agonized not over her own soul, but over the collective soul of her people. In January 1818, Catharine became the first Cherokee baptized by the American Board. Her baptism seems to have opened the door for other Cherokees. Soon over a hundred adults joined her in Christian fellowship, no doubt a gratifying development for the missionaries.

Catharine revealed her intense desire for a Christian community in a number of ways. She frequently expressed her concern for her people. In a letter to missionary Moody Hall and his wife, she agonized: "My heart bleeds for my people who are on the brink of destruction."[9] The salvation that she envisioned, however, incorporated the Cherokees into a broader community: "O, how great, how rich is the mercy of our dear Redeemer, who has made us the subjects of his kingdom."[10] Her vision of heaven also focused on community: "And when time with us shall be no more, may we be permitted to meet in that world, where Christians will be collected to sing through eternity the song of Moses and the Lamb."[11] At the same time that she sought and found community in her new faith, conversion drove a wedge between her and the vast majority of Cherokees. When she visited her parents, "all around her were engaged for the riches and pleasures of the world; and because she could not unite with them as formerly, they were telling her, they supposed she thought herself very good now; that she expected to go to heaven alone, &c."[12] Instead of uniting her people through Christianity, Catharine found herself estranged from many of them because of her faith.

The mission provided a concrete example of Catharine's abstract notions of Christian community, and she loathed separation from her mission family, as residents of Brainerd called themselves. While at home with her parents, she wrote the missionaries: "O beloved friends, you know not the love I bear to that blessed spot, where I have spent so many happy hours with you."[13] To other missionaries, she revealed her belief in the eternal nature of their relationship: "I think of you every day, and long to see you once more in this world. . . . I hope, if we may not meet in this world, we may meet in heaven, where we will never be separated."[14] Within the mission family, she had special feelings for the women whom she joined in separate prayer meetings. According to Jeremiah Evarts, secretary of the American Board, soon after her baptism Catharine had begun collective prayers with other students in their quarters just before bedtime. One of the missionaries overheard her "pouring forth her desires in very affecting and appropriate language." When questioned about the unauthorized and unsupervised prayer sessions, Catharine responded that "she had prayed with the girls, because she thought it was her duty." She also joined in the prayer meetings of all the women at the mission two nights each week. She took her turn at prayer: "Her prayers are distinguished by great simplicity as to thought and language, and seem to be the filial aspirations of the devout child." She developed strong relationships with the women of the mission family, who had "the most intimate knowledge of her conduct, and receive[d] a most frank disclosure of her feelings."[15] She felt the departure of women from the community keenly, writing to one: "We were lonesome when you left us, especially at out prayer-meeting; but I hope our hearts were united in love."[16] Upon learning of Isabella Hall's illness, she wrote: "It is with pleasure I take time this morning to assure you, that my love for you is as great as ever. You cannot tell how painful it was to me to hear that you had been sick. . . . O could we see each other, how would we talk, and weep, and sing, and pray together."[17]

The women at Brainerd embodied the roles of middle-class white women in the Northeast. Expected to be pious, chaste, and submissive, women sought each other's company to reinforce those values. Missionary women distanced themselves socially from their Cherokee neighbors, who did not necessarily share their views on feminine propriety, and developed very close personal ties. With the help of the female students, they performed all the domestic labor of the mission together. In addition, they attended the births of each other's children and shared child-care responsibilities. They nursed each other and cared for the families of invalids. Lack of privacy, fatigue from overwork, and a variety of illnesses produced serious tensions that occasionally demanded intervention by the board's headquarters, but this community of women replicated in some ways the world in which Catharine grew up.

Women in Cherokee society traditionally lived very separate lives from men. They hoed their corn together and conducted appropriate rituals without men present. They delivered their children alone or with other women, and they sequestered themselves from men during their menstrual periods. Households were their domain, and men spent relatively little time in the vicinity of dwellings. This Christian society of women, working and praying together, must have seemed comfortably familiar, and, when her Christian duty led her far from Brainerd, Catharine mourned the loss of sisterhood.

The years that Catharine spent at Brainerd Mission were turbulent ones in the Cherokee Nation. Cherokee leaders recognized the land hunger in the United States and took measures to secure their people's homeland. The Cherokees had long held annual national council meetings, but most governmental functions rested with clans and town councils. Each town, which was a social and political unit as well as a place, sent representatives, but no system of apportionment existed, and national councils tended to be enormous gatherings. With so many people involved in government, unscrupulous treaty commissioners usually could find a few individuals willing to sell land, particularly if they offered bribes. In order to prevent unauthorized land cessions, the Cherokees reorganized their government to provide for the election of male representatives from electoral districts and to empower specific officials to negotiate treaties. Gradually the new government took over many of the responsibilities of clans and local councils, and in the process, it eliminated women, who had been included in clan and local decisions, from political participation.

This new government mirrored the republican political institutions in the United States, and Cherokee leaders sought to broaden that reflection. They permitted the American Board and other missionary societies to enter the nation so that their children could learn to live like white people. The purpose of this cultural transformation was to make Cherokees less threatening and more acceptable to their non-Indian neighbors so that they could remain in their homeland. Many Cherokees clung to the old ways, but others, including Catharine Brown's family, began to take steps toward "civilization." For Catharine, the mission represented hope for the future. It also provided a sense of community at the very time that Cherokee communities, centered on town councils, seemed to be disintegrating. The mission incorporated women, although in a subordinate position, while the new Cherokee national government excluded them altogether. The rituals of the mission replaced the religious rituals that traditionally had taken place in council houses. And Christianity offered certainty when little else seemed certain.

In February 1820, Catharine's father called on the missionaries at Brainerd with a message from the headmen of his town, Creek Path. Noting "the good effects arising from education," they requested a school and promised the enrollment of twenty to twenty-five students from the neighborhood. Daniel Butrick, the only American Board missionary with any facility in the Cherokee language, and John Arch, a young Cherokee man, promptly opened a school for boys at Creek Path, but residents soon requested a girls' school as well. The missionaries decided to send Catharine, who had grown up in Creek Path, located in what is today northeastern Alabama. She accepted her charge with mixed emotions. She recorded in her diary that "it is truly painful to part with my dear Christian friends" and with "the place, where I first became acquainted with the dear Savior." But she recognized the importance of the work before her: "He now calls me to work in his vineyard, and shall I, for the sake of my Christian friends and of my own pleasures, refuse to go, while many of my poor red brothers and sisters are perishing for lack of knowledge? O no. I will not refuse to go. I will go wherever the Savior calls me."[18]

Catharine's arrival at the Creek Path Mission presented a new challenge for Butrick. Of all the American Board missionaries, Butrick was the only one who exhibited any real interest in Cherokee culture. He had learned the Cherokee language ostensibly to enable him to preach sermons without a translator and to instruct individual Cherokees who exhibited an interest in Christianity but did not speak English. Butrick, however, also used the language to conduct research on Cherokee history and culture. He sought out elderly, knowledge-able Cherokees and interviewed them about their religious beliefs and ways of life.[19] He certainly learned about the prominent position of women in Chero-kee society and about their sexual autonomy. The disdain that most mission-aries felt for traditionalists appalled Butrick, but his fascination with "savagery," as the missionaries considered traditional culture, probably frightened him a bit. The sympathy that he developed for Cherokees, ultimately expressed by his journey west with them in 1838–39 on the Trail of Tears, must have seemed at times like seduction. Then Catharine Brown arrived at Creek Path. Young and, by all accounts, physically attractive, she represented for Butrick the people whom he had come to love. He agonized over his attraction to her and wrestled with his conscience: "My wicked passions rage, the storm beats on my foun-dering bank, and gaping waves and towering surges threaten my immediate ruin."[20] At this remote station, far from the prying eyes of other missionaries, a sexual liaison would have been quite easy, but Butrick resisted temptation. As for his infatuation with her, Catharine remained oblivious.

Catharine's students at Creek Path included more than twenty girls as well as several of their mothers. She conducted a weekly prayer meeting for the women, and she helped organize and recruit members for a "female charitable society."[21] She was so affected by the work that she decided to become a mis-sionary herself. Catharine taught at Creek Path for about nine months until a missionary couple, the Potters, came to relieve her of the responsibility of the school, permitting her to continue her own education.

While she was at Creek Path, Catharine also taught a number of slaves in the community. Having accepted many aspects of Anglo-American culture, these Cherokees no longer thought that it was appropriate for women to labor in the fields. Nevertheless, few Cherokee men were willing to compromise their masculinity by farming. Therefore, in the late eighteenth century, some Chero-kees began acquiring African-American slaves to cultivate their crops for them. Slave labor also enabled these Cherokees to expand production, and they began to sell surplus corn and wheat. The Creek Path community was home to many of these Cherokees because the broad, fertile valleys made large-scale agricul-ture possible. According to Mrs. Potter, Catharine, "at her own expense, put a spelling-book into the hands of each of the younger ones, [and] she began with zeal to teach them to read."[22] By the time of her death, at least two slaves read quite well.

Catharine's greatest pleasure at Creek Path came from the conversion of her family. Her brother David, who was a student at the Foreign Mission School in Cornwall, Connecticut, had become a Christian while he was a student at Brainerd, but as she wrote David in 1820, "even our dear parents are yet living without any hope in God."[23] Not long after her arrival at Creek Path to teach school, however, her mother, father, brother John, and sisters converted to Christianity. Their conversion ended long-standing tension between her natal family and her mission family.

Since her arrival at Brainerd in 1817, Catharine had struggled with a serious conflict between her obligation to her parents and her duty to God. She had been at Brainerd only six months when her father arrived to remove her from school so that she could join the family in emigrating to Arkansas. In response to white pressure for their land, the Cherokees had ceded large tracts of their homeland in the Southeast and received land west of the Mississippi. The United States hoped that ultimately all Cherokees would decide to relocate to this new territory. Although Catharine's father's family remained in the east, the children of Catharine's mother by her first husband had already departed for the West, and apparently their mother wanted to reunite her family. As a dutiful daughter, she accompanied her father to their Creek Path home to make preparations for the journey. After a month, the family decided to delay departure and Catharine returned to Brainerd, but a heavy cloud hung over her:

> I do not know whether I shall go to the Arkansas [country], or not. I feel grieved when I think of leaving my Christian friends, and of going far from all religious people, into a wild howling wilderness, where no star shines to guide my wandering feet to the babe of Bethlehem; where no warning voice is heard to keep me in the straight path that leads to heaven. When I look to that dark region, I start back; but when I think of my two brothers there, and my dear parents, who are to go soon, I feel reluctant to stay behind, and leave them to perish alone.[24]

Her internal struggle is evident in a letter she wrote six weeks later to missionaries from her home: "It is not my wish to go to the Arkansas; but God only knows what is best for me. . . . It may be possible, that I may see you once more; it would be a great happiness to me if I don't go to the Arkansas; perhaps I may; but if I should go, it is not likely that we shall meet in this world again."[25] She expected her family to leave in a month, just after Christmas, but once again they delayed departure. In May 1819, Catharine rejoined the mission at Brainerd. She believed that her family's departure was imminent, but they permitted her to remain in the East. She attributed this change of heart to divine intervention, according to Anderson's memoir: "After one of her seasons of private devotion, she returned to her family, with a delightfully confident hope, that God had listened to her requests; and as she entered the room where her parents were sitting, she found they had been consulting on the expediency of sending her back to Brainerd; and had actually resolved upon her return."[26] Although she had permission to remain with the missionaries, Catharine dreaded her family's departure, which they postponed repeatedly. Ultimately, the Browns moved west four years after Catharine's death.

The victory of the mission family over her parents presumably confirmed that Catharine's conversion was complete. Her appearance served as a metaphor for the transformation from "savage heathen" to "civilized" Christian. Before her arrival at Brainerd, "she was vain, and excessively fond of dress, wearing a profusion of ornaments in her ears." After her conversion, "her trinkets . . . gradually disappeared, till only a single drop remains in each ear."[27] However, even in her biography, written primarily to convince potential contributors of the efficacy of Indian missions, evidence emerges that calls into question the missionaries' success in the complete eradication of Native culture. The only source of information that we have about Catharine is from the missionaries, and there are no clear examples of apostasy. Instead, we have ambiguous practices that probably represent a blending of Cherokee and Christian beliefs.[28]

In the Cherokee worldview, spiritual beings inhabited this world and interacted with humans. Most landforms, rivers, forests, and fields had an association with particular spirits. People sought guidance and assistance from those spirits, often alone. Unlike non-Indian members of the mission congregation who usually prayed indoors in groups, Catharine frequently meditated out-of-doors: "In the warm season of the year, the adjacent woods was the place of her retirement."[29] She often spent entire days praying by herself. She also fasted in solitary. Although Christians demonstrated their commitment through occasional fasts, Cherokees fasted to acquire spiritual purity and access to spiritual power. The most powerful spirits lived in deep pools and high mountains, and when Catharine went to those places to fast and pray, the missionaries worried about her physical safety.

The religious conversion of Catharine and members of her family should not be doubted, but Christianity did not meet all their needs, so they also turned to their traditional practices and beliefs. Perhaps most significantly, Christianity offered little help in healing illness. Certainly Christians prayed for the sick, but nineteenth-century evangelical Protestants did not expect their prayers to cure patients. Instead, they sought acceptance of God's will and left treatment of physical illness to physicians. Cherokees, on the other hand, regarded physical illness as a manifestation of spiritual malaise, and they combated illness with sacred rituals. They found appalling the failure of Christians to perform religious ceremonies to counteract disease. Consequently, even Christian Cherokees resorted to traditional medicine, which was a significant part of Native religion, to treat illness. American Board missionaries disapproved, but they offered no acceptable alternative. Even Catharine Brown, that most Christian of Cherokees, was not immune to the lure of Cherokee religious practice.

In September 1821 Catharine's brother John began exhibiting symptoms of consumption, or tuberculosis. Catharine, who had just returned from an exhausting visit to her sister, rejoiced "to get back to be with Christians," but Cherokee duty compelled her to help heal her brother.[30] She and John's wife decided to take him to a sulfur spring in Alabama. Unable to travel that far, they stopped instead at a spring with similar properties and made camp. He drank the water and bathed in it, but his condition deteriorated, and six months later he died. Although Europeans believed in the therapeutic benefits of mineral springs, this journey to take the waters had distinctly Cherokee overtones. Cherokees invested water with significant spiritual properties. They bathed in running streams daily before sunrise in order to purify themselves spiritually, and rituals normally involved "going to water," as they phrased it. In Cherokee terms, seeking healing waters made perfect sense. Furthermore, the responsibility for treating illness lay with a person's clan. Clans were matrilineal, and Cherokees did not marry members of their own clan. Therefore, John needed a clan member to accompany him and his wife to the medicinal spring. As his sister and clan kin, Catharine fulfilled that role.

After her brother's death, Catharine returned home to care for her elderly parents, who had been living with him. She still visited the missions at Creek Path and Brainerd, but she accepted her responsibility to her parents. When her siblings from Arkansas arrived for a visit, they sparked renewed enthusiasm for emigration to the West. Catharine wrote her brother David: "You know mother is always very anxious to remove to that country; but father is not. For my own part, I feel willing to do whatever is duty, and the will of our parents. I feel willing to go, or stay. The Lord will direct all things right, and in him may we put all our trust." She still regarded Arkansas and the Osage country, where her brother Walter Webber had just acquired a salt spring (today Webber's Falls, Oklahoma), as a "wilderness . . . far from Christian society," but she saw signs of hope. Walter had "given up trading, and has commenced farming," a significant step toward what Catharine and the missionaries considered "civilization." Furthermore, he had enrolled his younger half-brother Edmund in Dwight, an American Board mission school west of the Mississippi.[31]

Catharine, however, was already showing symptoms of the same illness that had claimed John's life. She sought treatment from Dr. Alexander Campbell, a white physician who lived in Limestone, Alabama, but as her condition worsened, her parents grew desperate. To the horror of missionaries at Brainerd and Creek Path, these Christian converts entrusted their daughter's care to traditional healers. Their prescriptions reportedly did little good, and after a severe hemorrhage of the lungs, they sent for the missionaries. A week later, Dr. Campbell arrived, but by then, Catharine was so weak that he recommended she be transported to his home so he could provide constant care. Her mother and sister accompanied her on the arduous journey by litter, canoe, and carriage. On the morning of July 18, 1823, at Dr. Campbell's home, Catharine Brown died. "Thus fell asleep this lovely saint, in the arms of her Savior."[32]

The missionaries had lost their most treasured convert, and they were unwilling to let her memory fade. Therefore, the American Board commissioned Rufus Anderson to compile a biographical article for their magazine, the *Missionary Herald*. Anderson uncovered so much material, however, that the organization's governing body decided to publish a book-length work, *Memoir of Catharine Brown, A Christian Indian of the Cherokee Nation*. The author clearly stated the purpose of this endeavor: "The hope is cherished, that this little volume will augment the courage, animate the zeal, and invigorate the efforts, of the friends of missions, in their benevolent attempts to send the Gospel of Jesus Christ to all nations."[33] As Anderson and other missionaries extolled the virtues of this Christian Indian, however, they suggested that Christianity had virtually wiped out all evidence of Catharine's Cherokee identity.

When the author first introduced Catharine's family, he carefully noted the ancestry of her parents: "Mr. John Brown was the son of a man named Brown, who has long been dead. It is not known whether he was a white man, or partly Indian. The mother of Mr. Brown was a 'full-blooded' Cherokee. So also, was the mother of Mrs. Brown; but her father was white."[34] Jeremiah Evarts's description of them was more blunt: "Her parents are half-breeds."[35] Although the move to Christianize and "civilize" Native people stemmed from the eighteenth-century belief that Indians could change culturally through education and opportunity, this characterization of Catharine's ancestry suggests that newer ideas about human difference were infiltrating mission work. Race was beginning to matter; ancestry instead of opportunity determined aptitude. Yet Evarts, ambivalent about this shift in racial ideology, admitted the limits of ancestry: despite their white fathers, Catherine's parents could not speak English.

Nevertheless, Catharine's appearance reflected her education and her Christian faith. Evarts described her: "If you were to see her a[t] a boarding-school in New England, as she ordinarily appears here, you would not distinguish her from well-educated females of the same age, either by her complexion, features, dress, pronunciation or manners."[36] Dr. Campbell wrote Reverend Potter that during Catharine's visit to his family in Alabama, "Some of my acquantance [sic] were unwilling to believe she was an Indian."[37] Differences between Catharine Brown and other Native people went further than appearance: "Catharine possessed nothing of that stoical insensibility to pleasure, or pain, for which the Indian character has been considered remarkable. There was never anything in her deportment like unfeeling hardihood. The very reverse of this was true. She had a heart for friendship, for sympathy, for tender emotion."[38] The implication is that physical appearance and innate character traits made her more susceptible to the Christian message and more educable in academic subjects. If that was the case, what hope did missions and the "civilization" program hold out for Cherokees who looked and thought like Indians?

The missionaries' own attitudes, therefore, as well as the Cherokees' reluctance to abandon totally satisfying cultural practices, hampered mission work. Only a small minority of Cherokees joined Christian churches before the Cherokee Nation's removal west of the Mississippi in 1838–39, and mission records reveal that half of them became backsliders. Cherokees who did not belong to churches practiced their traditional religion, which stood at odds with Christianity on fundamental issues. Cherokee religion promoted cosmic balance, not sacred hierarchy, and community welfare, not individual salvation. It promised to heal the sick and make the corn grow, and it connected Cherokees to a particular place in this world rather than a nebulous existence in the next. Male and female spirits inhabited the Cherokee world, and religion gave both men and women access to them. The role of women as presenters of the new crop in the Green Corn ceremony, the Cherokees' most important annual religious rite, recognized and confirmed their centrality in Cherokee society as farmers and mothers. Even a convert as pious and as subservient as Catharine Brown could not easily abandon her culture. Catharine's omnipresent spirituality, her women's prayer and philanthropic societies, and her fasting and prayer in the forests and mountains helped her link her Cherokee world to that of Christian missionaries. Only with her death could missionaries separate those worlds and claim Catharine for their own.

NOTES

1. For an overview of missionary activities in this period, see Robert F. Berkhofer, Jr., *Salvation and the Savage: An Analysis of Protestant Missions and American Indian Response, 1787–1862* (Lexington: University of Kentucky Press, 1965).

2. Rufus Anderson, *Memoir of Catharine Brown, A Christian Indian of the Cherokee Nation* (2d ed., Boston: Crocker and Brewster, New York: John P. Haven, 1825; reprint, Signal Mountain, TN: Mountain Press, n.d.), 11.

3. Ibid., 14–15.

4. Ibid., 12, 126 n. 3.

5. For the changing lives of Cherokee women, see Theda Perdue, *Cherokee Women: Gender and Culture Change, 1700–1830* (Lincoln: University of Nebraska Press, 1998).

6. Anderson, 13.

7. Ibid., 108, 110.

8. Ibid., 17, 18.

9. Brown to Mr. [Moody] and Mrs. [Isabella] Hall, 30 May 1819, ibid., 37.

10. Brown to a Lady in Connecticut, 12 Jan. 1820, ibid., 48.

11. Brown to Isabella Hall, 8 March 1820, ibid., 50.

12. Ibid., 28.

13. Brown to Mr. and Mrs. [William] Chamberlain, 12 Dec. 1818, ibid., 32.

14. Brown to Mr. and Mrs. Hall, 19 Nov. 1820, ibid., 74.

15. Ibid., 24.

16. Brown to Mrs. [Loring] Williams, 1 Nov. 1818, ibid., 30.

17. Brown to Isabella Hall, 8 March 1820, ibid., 49.

18. Entry for 30 May 1820, ibid., 53.

19. Butrick's surviving ethnographic papers are in the John Howard Payne Papers, Newberry Library, Chicago.

20. Butrick's Journal, 27 Jan. 1820, Papers of the American Board of Commissioners for Newberry Library, Chicago. Foreign Missions, Houghton Library, Harvard University, Cambridge, MA. See also Carol[yn] Johnston, "Burning Beds, Spinning Wheels, and Calico Dresses," *Journal of Cherokee Studies* 19 (1998): 3–17.

21. Anderson, 58.

22. Ibid., 57.

23. Brown to David Brown, 16 May 1820, ibid., 51.

24. Brown to Mrs. Williams, 1 Nov. 1818, ibid., 31.

25. Brown to Mr. and Mrs. Chamberlain, 12 Dec. 1818, ibid., 33.

26. Ibid., 35.

27. Ibid., 24–25.

28. William G. McLoughlin, "Native Reactions to Christian Missions," *The Cherokees and Christianity, 1794–1870*, ed. Walter H. Conser, Jr. (Athens: University of Georgia Press, 1994), 9–33.

29. Anderson, 115–16.

30. Entry 9 July 1821, ibid., 63.
31. Brown to David Brown, 18 Jan. 1823, ibid., 82–83.
32. Ibid., 102.
33. Ibid., preface, ix.
34. Ibid., 124 n. 1.
35. Ibid., 23.
36. Ibid., 23.
37. Ibid., 69.
38. Ibid., 113.

6

LOZEN

An Apache Woman Warrior

Laura Jane Moore

During the waning days of the nineteenth-century Indian wars, five thousand American soldiers pursued a band of thirty-six Apache men, women, and children. Led by the chief Naiche and the shaman Geronimo, the group had holed up in the Sierra Madre mountains in northern Mexico. These Apaches never suffered a decisive defeat, but by the summer of 1886 they were tired of running and wanted to be reunited with their families back on the reservation. Two women assumed the dangerous mission of approaching United States troops in order to begin negotiations. While the American soldiers proudly recorded the names of the Apache men whom they met during these military campaigns, only Apache oral traditions identify Lozen and Dahteste as the "squaws" who played such an important role. Well suited to their task, the women were fighting members of the band, able to defend themselves and speak for their people. Each no doubt carried a knife, rifle, and cartridge belt, but since they were women, the soldiers did not assume that they posed much threat.

Both Lozen and Dahteste stepped outside the position usually occupied by Apache women, and both of them fought bravely in battles against U.S. and Mexican troops. Dahteste had found her way to warfare, as Apache women often did, by extending her role as a wife and accompanying her husband, Anandia, on raids and war expeditions. Lozen was more unusual. Probably in her forties in the 1880s, she had never married and had no children. Lozen's choice to opt out of the roles typically adopted by Apache women, however, did not lead to her marginalization or degradation within her Apache community. Rather, she became one of the most revered Apache warriors of the late nineteenth century. As a woman warrior, she possessed qualities that Apaches associated with both men and women that, in their eyes, made her especially powerful. Convinced that she was responsible for much of their success against their enemies, her comrades and kin celebrated her spiritual power and physical prowess. Geronimo and the rest of the group knew they could trust her to represent them to the American soldiers.

Lozen's life exemplifies the permeability of gender roles in a complex Native American culture even when those roles seem to be rigidly defined. Anthropologists describe Apaches as having strict divisions between men and women who performed different work and even occupied separate space in dwellings. "The feeling is," explained one Apache, "that a man should go his way with his friends and a woman her way with her friends."[1] This separation of the sexes was extreme enough that it made men and women quite shy in the presence of each other.[2] Unmarried women, in particular, refrained from spending time with men. Moreover, kin relations imposed further expectations of avoidance. Once grown, brothers and sisters dodged each other's company. Since Apaches considered people whom Euro-Americans call cousins to be siblings, avoidance often extended to many people. "If we even spoke" to the adolescent girls, recalled one Apache man of his own youth, "we could do so only with a bush between us, and back to back."[3]

In contrast to these rules, Lozen was an unmarried woman who rode with male warriors by the side of her brother, the chief Victorio. She was an important enough member of the fighting force that Victorio called her "my right hand. . . . Strong as a man, braver than most, and cunning in strategy." By adopting the unusual but respected role of a woman warrior, Lozen stood in a powerful cross-gender position from which she could act as "a shield to her people."[4]

Lozen and Victorio were Chiricahua Apaches, one of seven different Apachean tribes that lived in the southwestern United States. In the mid-nineteenth century the Chiricahuas occupied an area west of the Rio Grande, including what is now southwestern New Mexico, southeastern Arizona, and part of the Mexican borderlands. The Chiricahuas were highly decentralized and did not necessarily recognize each other as related, even if anthropologists have identified them as the same cultural group. Four major bands of Chiricahuas occupied this area: the Chihene, the Bedonkohe, the Chokonen, and the Nednai. These bands were composed of local groups that in turn each consisted of ten to thirty extended families. Most activities, including marriages, were carried out within the local group. Raiding and war parties, for example, usually were composed of members of a family or local group. Within a local group, a leader or "chief" gained prominence and influence through personal traits of generosity, bravery, integrity, eloquence, and ceremonial knowledge. By 1870, Victorio had assumed a leadership role in one of these local groups, the Warm Springs Apaches.

Apaches organized their society around a sexual division of labor embodied in the matrilocal extended family. That is, when a man married a woman, they lived near her mother. Generally property also followed a matrilineal line. The women of an extended family worked together gathering and processing the wild plants that were an essential food source. Meanwhile, men of the same family hunted in pairs or small groups, providing the game that supplemented their diet. Despite the disruptions of reservations and warfare in the late nineteenth century, Apaches living on reservations maintained this social organization. For example, Charlie Smith remembered that sometime in the 1880s his family received permission from the Indian agent to travel to an area where there was a good piñon crop. In the morning "usually by twos, the men left to hunt. . . . The women also divided into small groups." They brought the young children along and followed trails of pack rats to their dens, where they could sometimes gather as many as two gallons of nuts from one nest. They also placed skins under piñon trees and beat the lower branches to gather more nuts. "When the men returned in the evening, the women dressed the game" and began the process of tanning the hides.[5]

The sexual division of labor did not put women in a subordinate position to men, but instead led to complementary roles for women and men. Women controlled a family's economic activities and managed its wealth; men, more mobile in their responsibilities for hunting and raiding, took command of relations with those outside the group. With marriage, a man assumed obligations not only to his wife but to her extended family as well, obligations that divorce or a wife's death did not automatically terminate. Though marriage for Euro-American women meant economic and legal dependence in this period, in many ways it was the opposite for Apache women. Marriage did, however, lead Apache women to be assigned certain roles within the community, roles that an unmarried woman such as Lozen could eschew, especially the domestic tasks of food preparation, child care, and house building.

Lozen's orientation toward more typically male activities probably emerged during her childhood. When they were small, girls and boys played together and competed in foot races. When they were about six, however, the community began to separate them. During puberty, girls were initiated into womanhood and boys into manhood, and they then avoided each other's company except within strict limits. Lozen apparently did not make this transition, but instead continued to participate in the boys' activities. She was not castigated for her seemingly masculine skills. After all, girls were "urged to be strong and fast. It is simply accepted," the anthropologist Morris Opler explained, that some individuals "have carried the requirement further than is strictly necessary. The attitude of those discussing them is never one of ridicule or condemnation but rather one of admiration."[6] Eventually even girls who excelled at masculine pursuits usually married and entered into typically female roles. Lozen, instead, remained unmarried and became a warrior. That this was the right choice for her may well have been confirmed during puberty.

When a girl began to menstruate, it was a cause for celebration. A crowd of relatives, friends, and members of neighboring communities attended an elaborate four-day ceremony in her honor. During the ceremony the girl became "White Painted Woman," the central Chiricahua deity, and emerged at the end as a woman. No moment so definite as a girl's first period signaled when a boy was ready to make the transition to adulthood. Instead, once he was strong enough, perhaps when he was about fifteen, he volunteered to become an apprentice warrior. He then had to participate in four raids during which he followed special rules, used a special apprentice's language, and was called "Child of the Water" after the son of White Painted Woman. Once he had successfully joined four raids, he was considered a full-fledged warrior.

We can only speculate, based on what we know of Chiricahua culture, about Lozen's youth and how she chose the route of the woman warrior. Perhaps not long after her puberty ceremony Lozen volunteered to become an apprentice warrior, and the men in her family, recognizing her unusual talents with horses and hunting, agreed. It is also likely that she acquired the spiritual power that contributed to her skill as a warrior during adolescence, another sign, perhaps, that she was well suited for the alternative life of a woman warrior.

Both men and women had access to the supernatural world that infused nature. Apaches tapped into this power through visions that sometimes occurred in dreams but often were brought on by fasting in isolation during a "vision quest." In such a vision a supernatural force visited, usually in the guise of an animal, and taught the person a ceremony by which he or she could call on the force for aid. This ceremonial knowledge or "power" was an individual's own, and it normally could not be passed on or shared. Still, Apaches understood that their power was to be used for the good of their community. Those who did not were witches. Apaches might go on vision quests in order to make contact with the supernatural world, but they could not choose which "power" would visit them. Most of these powers involved healing. Some Apaches also could call on the supernatural world to help them diagnose illness, find lost objects, even withstand bullets.

Ceremonial knowledge was an essential complement to a warrior's physical skills and intelligence. Geronimo based his leadership role, for example, on his abilities as a shaman. He had the power to foretell the result of a battle and to "handle men." Another chief, Chihuahua, had "the Power over horses" so that he "could gentle and ride the wildest" and "heal them of sickness or wounds." The chief Nana's "Power was over ammunition trains and rattlesnakes." Even when he was over eighty and crippled, he could make a successful raid for ammunition when younger men failed.[7]

Lozen had the ability, through ceremony, to ask for supernatural aid in locating the enemy. The power that she received related to warfare, and so it may have helped confirm her special standing as a woman warrior. She summoned this power through a ritual in which she stood with arms outstretched and palms up. As she turned slowly in a circle, she sang a prayer such as:

> Upon this earth
> On which we live
> Ussen has Power
> This Power is mine
> For locating the enemy
> Which only Ussen the great
> Can show to me.

During this ceremony a tingling in her palms indicated the direction and distance to the enemy. If the enemy were very near, her palms would turn purple.[8]

Lozen's ceremony illustrates central aspects of the Apache worldview. Her power stemmed from her relationship with the supernatural, called in this case Ussen, the life-giver. Through her individual vision quest she had obtained the ability to manipulate this power, which she used to help her community. In another of her prayers she sang, "Ussen has Power. Sometimes He shares it. . . . This Power he has given me [f]or the benefit of my people. . . . This Power I may use [f]or the good of my people."[9]

Shamans whose ceremonial knowledge related to warfare, such as Lozen's, always accompanied war expeditions, which departed only after certain ritualistic dances and singing were held. While both women and men had equal access to the supernatural world, traditionally warfare was strictly in the male domain, an extension of men's roles in hunting and raiding from which women were normally excluded. This exclusion stemmed from women's reproductive abilities, which made them especially powerful but also potentially dangerous to men, particularly men at war. Because menstruation was so powerful and so uniquely female, it could also cause harm. Boys learned early that contact with menstrual blood would make their joints swollen and painful and that sex with a menstruating woman could lead to deformity. The bodily discharge that accompanied childbirth was equated with menstrual blood, so men were well advised to avoid it. In other words, at the moments when a woman was most a woman, at menstruation and childbirth, she was also most dangerous to men. The rheumatism or deformed joints that resulted from such contact would, in turn, hinder a man's ability to perform his duties as a warrior and hunter. The necessary separation of the sexes, however, could be bridged by a woman warrior such as Lozen. Her skills as a warrior would not be compromised by contact with women, for she shared their unique powers as well. Her powerful cross-gender position combined the most respected aspects of Apache femininity and masculinity.

As a warrior, Lozen displayed impressive talent at the masculine pursuits of hunting, raiding, and warfare. While raiding was a means to obtain supplies and, like hunting, an economic activity, a war party exacted revenge when a member of the group was killed. Apaches explained that "it is the duty of a man to avenge injury to his relatives." Moreover, "when the enemy does something, there have got to be consequences. If there aren't, things get out of balance. Pretty soon everything is upset."[10] Apaches went to war, therefore, to preserve a necessary balance. War parties also reflected Apaches' kin-based social organization: "The relatives of the father of the dead person or of his wife get it started and try to enlist as many as possible."[11]

Although women did not typically participate in war parties, they were as concerned as men were with the importance of exacting revenge. Sometimes women called for the organization of war parties. Sometimes married women followed the expedition in order to provide domestic services such as cooking or dressing wounds. And occasionally women who had accompanied their husbands found themselves participating in the fighting. If her husband were killed, for example, a wife might take his place and personally assume the task of avenging his death. Indeed, it was far easier for women to cross into the men's domain than for men to assume typically female tasks. Whether warriors or not, women needed to be prepared to participate in skirmishes, to handle weapons, and to defend themselves and their families. But even if respected for fighting bravely beside her husband, a woman observed the strict rules that governed relations between the sexes while raiding or warring. Warriors practiced strict sexual abstinence before and during war expeditions because a woman's strength could impede a man's. "Women could go with their husbands, but they could not live together," one Apache later explained.[12]

Women's ability to participate in raids and war parties may have increased in the late nineteenth century. After the United States won the Southwest from Mexico at midcentury and increasing numbers of Anglos began passing through and settling there, the U.S. military waged a campaign to move the various Native American residents onto reservations. The land set aside for reservations was often far from traditional homelands, overcrowded with a conglomeration of traditionally hostile Indian groups, and incapable of supporting the numbers expected to live there. During the last few decades of the century, various bands alternatively fought and negotiated with U.S. troops, agreeing to live on reservation lands for a time and then leaving when their situation became untenable.

Apache groups that resisted reservation life had to be increasingly mobile to elude capture. Warfare severely circumscribed life for Apaches on the run. If families were to stay together, women and children often had little choice but to accompany warriors. Constant movement and the possibility of attack and capture made it difficult for women to perform their normal productive roles as gatherers and processors of food. Raiding instead became the main means of obtaining food and other supplies, especially the all-important horses and ammunition that were necessary to keep up the fight. Not only did women participate in raids and skirmishes themselves but they dug trenches and acted as lookouts and scouts. It was not easy to keep warriors' activities within war parties separate from the activities of women and children. Charlie Smith remembered that frequently "Geronimo had the women and children along. . . . If pursued he, as did all Apaches, tried to protect them by sending them ahead; but ordinarily, when fighting occurred, it was because he laid an ambush, and every one of the band was there." He added that "some of the women were very good shots," Lozen most of all.[13]

In 1870 the Warm Springs Apaches had agreed to live on a reservation called Ojo Caliente (Warm Springs) within their traditional lands in southwestern New Mexico. Because of bureaucratic complications between Washington, D.C., and the presiding military officers, along with the hostility of the local American and Mexican population, the site of the reservation kept changing. But the elder Warm Springs leader, Loco, and the younger and more hotheaded Victorio kept their bands settled and at peace with the American troops. Then in 1875 the American authorities began a new policy of trying to concentrate all Apaches on one reservation, called San Carlos, along the Gila River in eastern Arizona, far from where the Chiricahuas had agreed to live. Ace Daklugie, whose parents were Geronimo's sister, Ishton, and the Nednai chief, Juh, later claimed that it "was the worst place in all the great territory stolen from the Apaches." No one had lived there permanently before because there was no grass and no game, and the only vegetation was cacti. "The heat was terrible. The insects were terrible. The water was terrible. What there was in the sluggish river was brackish and warm. . . . Insects and rattlesnakes seemed to thrive there."[14] James Kaywaykla, who was a few years younger than Daklugie, recalled the malaria, summer temperatures reaching well over a hundred degrees, and insects that "almost devoured the babies."[15] At San Carlos, disease-ridden, inadequately supplied, and overcrowded with different Indian groups who were unfamiliar, suspicious, or even overtly hostile toward each other, Chiricahuas found themselves hungry, sick, and tense. The Warm Springs Apaches tried to live there for a time, but many found it intolerable. Loco and his followers, determined to pursue peace with the Americans, decided to remain, but at least three hundred others, including Victorio's band, left in 1877. Many of them were caught or killed; others made it across the border into Mexico.

Victorio's band eventually returned to their old reservation, Ojo Caliente, which the military had shut down, and indicated their willingness to surrender but not to live at San Carlos. Some of the Warm Springs group, following another chief, Nana, registered at the Mescalero reservation in New Mexico, while Victorio continued to pressure American officials to honor their promise of the Ojo Caliente land. Meanwhile, other Chiricahua leaders, including Juh and Geronimo, were arrested and imprisoned at San Carlos. In July 1879 the Warm Springs band heard a rumor that Victorio was to be arrested too, and the group again left the reservation and fled into the mountains. While family members hid in caves, Victorio and about sixty warriors attacked a contingent of cavalrymen near their old reservation. This battle opened a bloody war in which the Warm Springs Apaches fought to avenge the deaths of their kin and to live where they chose.

When the Apaches fled from the reservations, they left quietly at night in small scattered groups in order to evade pursuit. Their means of escape reflected their gender organization. Women took charge of helping young boys and girls and moved separately from the warriors. Kaywaykla's grandmother woke him one night and told him they were leaving. He had his emergency rations handy. At first she carried the sleepy boy on her back as they ran, and then they crawled slowly. Shielded from sight by mesquite and cactus, they froze when they heard a jingle of metal indicating that soldiers were nearby. They traveled carefully for a few days before they rendezvoused with the rest of their band on the banks of a swollen river.

While deeply ingrained ideas about the proper roles of women and men influenced this dangerous flight, the story also suggests the permeability of those roles. Kaywaykla's grandmother took charge of his safety because his mother accompanied her husband and the other warriors. When they reached the river, Kaywaykla's parents were there, as were the leaders Nana and Victorio. Kaywaykla spoke only briefly with his mother. When he later asked for her, his grandmother explained that "she rides with your father and Nana on another raid."

Meanwhile, the women and children needed to cross the river before the cavalry discovered them. Kaywaykla's grandmother tried to lead her horse into the water, but it balked. They seemed to be stuck in this dangerous position, between the rising water and the American soldiers who could find them there at any time. But then arrived "a magnificent woman on a beautiful black horse— Lozen, sister of Victorio. Lozen, the woman warrior!" She held her rifle over her head as she turned her horse into the torrent, and it began to swim against the current. The others followed across safely, with Lozen having to rescue just one horse and rider who began to wash downstream. On the other side of the river, Lozen gave Kaywaykla's grandmother instructions: "You take charge now," she said. "I must return to the warriors." She told the older woman to hurry to Salinas Peak, their "Sacred Mountain in the San Andres," taking only short stops along the way, and then to wait there for Nana. "We can spare no men," she explained, "but the young boys will obey your orders. . . . I go to join my brother."[16] The success of this escape relied on Lozen's skill with horses, her physical strength, the trust that the other Apaches placed in her, and her ability to move between the worlds of women and warriors.

Normally only married women could ride with the warriors. But Lozen was not a normal woman. "No," Charlie Smith explained, "she never married. But to us she was as a Holy Woman and she was regarded and treated as one. White Painted Woman herself was not more respected."[17] Kaywaykla agreed that although "she had not married, she went on the warpath with the men, which no woman other than the wives of warriors was permitted to do; and she was held in the greatest respect by them, much as though she were a holy person."[18] He also remembered Lozen participating in the council of leaders as they deliberated about whether to return to the reservation or continue their fight. Lozen's position indicates that, even if men usually controlled politics, a person earned a place at the council fire not by one's biological sex, but by being a successful warrior, which required physical prowess, intelligence, and integrity. "No other woman" was "bidden to the council, but that was because no other had the skill as a warrior that Lozen did."[19] Lozen's unusual position rested on a confluence of cultural, historical, and individual factors. Apache culture's flexibility allowed and even respected her unusual choice, and her physical and spiritual skills made her an asset to the beleaguered Chiricahuas, whose numbers in the 1870s and 1880s were depleted. Those skills were apparently extraordinary. "She could ride, shoot, and fight like a man; and I think she had more ability in planning military strategy than did Victorio," Kaywaykla recalled.[20]

While Apache girls and boys, men and women, were expert riders, horses were especially associated with men and their roles in hunting, raiding, and warfare. Lozen was a renowned raider, thanks in large part to her skills with horses. She likely was the woman that cavalry officer John C. Cremony remembered "as one of the most dextrous horse thieves and horse breakers in the tribe, [who] seldom permitted an expedition to go on a raid without her presence."[21] Ace Daklugie remembered her taking advantage of a melee between soldiers and Indians at San Carlos to grab some much needed ammunition. She and another warrior, Sanchez, "swooped down on the horse herd and drove a bunch off. They wanted especially the ammunition mules, for they had not yet been unloaded. . . . I do know that they got a good supply of ammunition."[22] Kaywaykla, too, emphasized her ability to catch horses. She "was expert at roping. . . . No man in the tribe was more skillful in stealing horses or stampeding a herd than she."[23]

One particularly dramatic example of Lozen's talent, and how she chose to use it, occurred during the summer of 1880 while the Warm Springs band made its way into West Texas and then toward Mexico, pursued closely by American troops. Lozen dropped out of the main group in order to help a pregnant Mescalero Apache woman who had gone into labor. The two women hid just out of sight of the cavalry, and then Lozen helped the woman deliver her baby. They had not taken any horses, fearing that the soldiers would notice the tracks and realize that someone had separated from the group. They had limited food and no water, and the distance between water holes was too great to make on foot. When they spotted a herd of cattle, Lozen killed a longhorn with her knife, "a feat that few men would undertake," but they still could not travel far without water. They hid alongside the Rio Grande and observed a camp of Mexicans on the opposite bank. Lozen decided to steal one of their horses. She cut a strip from the longhorn's hide to fashion into a bridle, waited for nightfall, and swam across the rushing river. The men slept around the fire, while one guarded the horses hobbled not far away. She waited until the guard started toward the fire and then "crept softly" to the "powerful steed" she had selected. "When she bent to cut the hobbles it snorted and plunged. She leaped to its back and turned it toward the river. Bullets whizzed past her head as the horse slid down the bank and plunged into the water." She was scrambling up the opposite bank before the men could follow. By the time the sun rose, the two women, the infant, and their new horse were far away.

Their ordeal, however, had not yet ended. The American troops had received reinforcements, who were guarding every water hole and had inadvertently cut off the women's path back to their band. Lozen guided the woman and her newborn by a stealthy and circuitous route back to the Mescalero reservation, which took several more weeks and involved stealing another horse on the way.[24]

Because Lozen was both a warrior and a woman, her cross-gender position made it possible for her to protect the Mescalero woman as a man normally would and to help her deliver her baby, which, because of the association with menstrual blood, would have been perilous for a man. Lozen, like many women, had ceremonial healing powers and may have known some of the ritual with which Apaches greeted a new life. At the same time, her skill as a warrior shielded the woman who was forced to give birth under particularly dangerous and unusual circumstances.

While Lozen and the new mother sneaked past enemy lines and made their way slowly to the Mescalero reservation, U.S. troops chased Victorio, Nana, and the rest of the band into Mexico. Previously, the Americans had not been able to follow them over the border, but Mexico and the United States had just instituted a treaty by which American troops were allowed to enter Mexican territory in pursuit of hostile Indians. The Apaches, low on ammunition, food, and water, camped on the slopes of a three-peak mountain range called Tres Castillos that rose out of the parched desert in the Mexican state of Chihuahua. Here their extraordinary ability to evade their pursuers finally failed. Mexican forces, who were the first to find them, attacked at dawn on October 15. At the end of this bloody battle, perhaps eighty Apaches lay dead and about seventy more, including Kaywaykla's grandmother, were captured and marched to the Mexican city, Chihuahua, where they were sold into slavery. Among the dead was Victorio.

"Many of the old Apaches," Ace Daklugie explained, "are convinced that, had [Lozen] been with Victorio at Tres Castillos, there would have been no ambush."[25] She was missed not so much for her fighting skills—the band was outnumbered and trapped among the boulders on the mountain slope, an impossible situation for the best warrior—as for her ceremonial power to locate the enemy. If she had been there, they believed, she would have anticipated the attack, and they could have escaped.

Lozen learned of her people's demoralizing defeat and her brother's death when she reached the Mescalero reservation. Leaving the mother and infant

there, she headed south to find the remnants of the band, which was still unwilling to return to reservation life. An older chief, Nana, had been on a raid
for ammunition during the battle and now led the group as it avenged Victorio's
death.

Meanwhile, other Chiricahuas, including Geronimo, were living restlessly
at San Carlos. There the "repugnant natural conditions" were exacerbated by
"intrigue, intertribal rivalries, incompetent and corrupt agents, and conflict
between civil and military officials."[26] Moreover, land-hungry, Indian-hating
white settlers ringed its boundaries. Tensions were already high when, in August 1881, the army tried to arrest a Western Apache shaman whose preaching
seemed to the officials to have dangerously antiwhite overtones. Fighting broke
out between the army and the shaman's followers, and the shaman, his wife,
and several other Apaches were shot and killed. Lozen may have been visiting
the reservation, as one Apache placed her theft of the ammunition laden mules
at this time. About seventy Chiricahuas, including Geronimo and other leaders, broke out and headed for Mexico.

They arrived in the Sierra Madre mountains, where the elderly Nednai
Apache leader, Juh, was now living. He welcomed straggling groups of recalci-
trant Apaches including Nana's Warm Springs band. Juh, too, had given up his
attempt to live at San Carlos and had escaped to the Sierra Madres where his
people had lived for generations. The mountains provided an impregnable
natural fortress. Various leaders from different Apache bands, local groups, and
tribes deferred to Juh. When he died suddenly, Naiche, the son of Cochise (a
respected Apache leader who had been killed some years earlier), assumed the
role of chief, but Geronimo, by virtue of his military leadership and stronger
spiritual power, increasingly became the most important leader.

The Apaches used their natural fortress as a base from which to launch
daring raids. In the spring of 1882 Geronimo led sixty warriors back to San Carlos
where they killed the police chief and enticed several hundred more Chiricahuas
to join them in Mexico. In response the American troops launched an all-out
offensive, led by General George Crook, to recapture and subdue the last of the
Apaches once and for all.

Crook was never able to administer a decisive defeat, but thanks to Apache
scouts working for the U.S. army, he was able to keep the "hostiles" on the
run. Constant pursuit and the coming winter made the reservation seem more
appealing. It was the summers at San Carlos that the Chiricahuas feared the
most, when the heat and malaria-carrying mosquitoes were most dangerous.
Winter in the mountains could be harsh, especially when they were so short
on supplies. And so, according to Apache memory, Lozen and Dahteste began

the negotiations for their people's return. The Apaches reached a deal by which about three hundred of the renegade Chiricahuas moved to an area called Turkey Creek near Fort Apache, on much more appealing land north of San Carlos. Kaywaykla, now old enough to be a young warrior himself, remembered his people settling happily at Turkey Creek and planting successful crops.

But the old reservation tensions resurfaced almost immediately. The agents heard whisperings of insurrection, and the Indians heard rumors that their leaders were to be arrested and imprisoned at Alcatraz Island in San Francisco Bay. Moreover, the military took it upon themselves to interfere more than ever before in the Apaches' family life, policing domestic conflicts normally regulated through the kin-based community structure. In May of 1885, fearing arrest, Geronimo and Naiche fled the reservation once again with approximately 140 followers including Lozen and about forty other warriors. The majority of Chiricahuas remained at San Carlos. Those who escaped headed back to the fortress of the Sierra Madres. And once again, they left in small groups, the women leading the children. Most of the soldiers pursued the warriors, but a number of women and children were shot or recaptured. General Crook, with his Apache scouts, pursued them for almost a year until a woman, probably Lozen, brought word that again they were ready to negotiate.

Crook met with them on March 25, 1886. Once again, he had administered no decisive defeat so the Chiricahuas were in a strong negotiating position. The Apaches' desire to restore ties of kin and community motivated them to reach an agreement. According to the new deal, the renegades would go to prison in the east for two years, after which they would be permitted to live freely with their families at Turkey Creek. The Indians retained their arms as they began to move north toward the border. But they remained suspicious. While the majority of the group continued on with the troops, Geronimo and Naiche changed their minds and took off again with a handful of their followers. Lozen, as usual, was at their side.

As it turned out, Geronimo and his followers were right to be suspicious of the terms of their surrender. Crook's superiors, General Philip Sheridan and President Grover Cleveland, repudiated the arrangements that Crook had made. They had no intention of releasing these infamous Apache warriors after two years. In anger and embarrassment, Crook resigned, while his replacement, General George Miles, led an augmented force of 5,000 soldiers against the thirty-six men, women, and children who had returned once more to the Sierra Madres. And, again, the American troops, despite their numbers and constant replenishment of supplies, could not defeat the Apaches.

In late August 1886, Lozen and Dahteste, for the final time, assumed the task of opening negotiations. For several days, Lieutenant Charles B. Gatewood, with whom the Apaches had dealt before, and two Apache scouts called Martine and Kayitah followed the women into the mountains, toward the hidden camp. The scouts, carrying a white flag, went ahead up the steep and winding trail. The warriors observed the scouts climb, first with field glasses and then, as the two men got closer, with bare eyes, and they recognized them. The fugitives debated whether or not to shoot them, but decided to admit them to the camp only because Martine was a Nednai and related to one of the warriors.

Geronimo and Naiche's band thought they were in a strong position to negotiate their return to Turkey Creek to join their families, but they were stunned by the news that all the Chiricahuas had been rounded up and sent to Florida. The prisoners included those who had remained in good faith on the reservation the whole time and even the Apache scouts who had served in the U.S. army. The very scouts who had found their hiding place and who had been promised land at Turkey Creek would, it turned out, be imprisoned in Florida. No Chiricahuas would remain in the Southwest. If they wanted to rejoin their kin, this last free group had to go east as well. They agreed to surrender personally to General Miles and, on September 3, 1886, laid down their arms for the last time. Five days later they were train-bound for Florida, and the Indian wars ended.

On the way to Florida, the train stopped near the Nueces River in Texas where a photographer captured a group of the Apaches sitting in front of a railroad car. Naiche, as the chief, sits in the center of the front row, with Geronimo in the place of honor at his left. Lozen is there too, in the only photograph ever taken of her. She is to Geronimo's left, a place reserved for one's second in command, but behind him as well, with women and girls on either side of her. Her face is calm, although her brow is furrowed. None of the captives betray their feelings to the photographer, but Lozen's stance, leaning slightly forward, seems a ready and restless pose, as though she remains prepared to protect either the girls who hide slightly behind her shoulders or to join the warriors in front of her.

Crowded into Florida's Fort Marion and Fort Pickens, accustomed to the dry climate of their homeland, the Chiricahuas suffered in Florida's heat and humidity. Tuberculosis, malaria, and smallpox took a heavy toll. By 1890, 119 of the 498 Chiricahuas who had been shipped to Florida had died. Their condition, especially the treatment of scouts who had served the American military faithfully, caused a public outcry led by General Crook. In 1887 and 1888, they were moved to the Mount Vernon barracks near Mobile, Alabama, which turned out to be just as miserable and unhealthy, and then, in 1894, to Fort Sill in Oklahoma. Finally, in 1913 the remaining Chiricahua Apaches were given their freedom and the choice of land near Fort Sill or a reservation in south-central New Mexico that they would share with the Mescalero Apaches. While some remained in Oklahoma, the majority returned to New Mexico, where their descendants still live. It was far too late, however, for Lozen. She had survived as far as Alabama, but there, like so many of those she had fought with and for, she succumbed to the "coughing sickness" and died of tuberculosis.

The story of the Apache Indian wars is often told as a heroic struggle among men with legendary names: Geronimo, Victorio, Crook, Miles. It is too easy to forget that at the heart of the wars lay the battle to preserve families, communities, and a culture—and that whole families and communities participated actively in the struggle and suffered immensely in the end. Apaches fought to live on land from which not only their sustenance but also their identity derived, an identity grounded in matrilocal extended families and a complementary sexual division of labor. Throughout this devastating period, Apache culture's strength lay in part in its flexibility. War parties continued to reflect traditional Apache social organization as they were structured around kin relationships and community bonds and called up in order to avenge the deaths of relatives. At the same time, the all-out warfare of the late nineteenth century meant that women had difficulty practicing their normal economic roles and instead followed, and sometimes joined, their husbands at war. As wives these women brushed against a permeable gender boundary that Lozen, an unmarried woman warrior, was able to cross.

Lozen forswore Chiricahua gender norms. But although she did not marry, did not have children, did not perform women's typical tasks and instead excelled at masculine pursuits, her community perceived her as neither a threat nor a deviant. Quite the contrary, it celebrated her powerful cross-gender position. Women warriors may have been unusual in Apache history, but they were also admired, even revered, and Lozen remains emblematic of that tradition. Almost invisible to the American authorities, her reputation and daring exploits survived in Chiricahua oral memory. That there was a place for such a woman within Apache society and that she was committed to using her exceptional position for the good of that society illustrate Apache culture's strength and complexity as it adapted to the dire circumstances of the late nineteenth century. When Lozen declined to live the life of a typical Apache woman, she did not deny the viability of her culture; instead, she spent her life defending it.

NOTES

1. Morris Edward Opler, *An Apache Life-Way: The Economic, Social, and Religious Institutions of the Chiricahua Indians* (1941; reprint Lincoln: University of Nebraska Press, 1996), 78.

2. D. C. Cole, *The Chiricahua Apache, 1846–1876: From War to Reservation* (Albuquerque: University of New Mexico Press, 1988), 35.

3. Eve Ball, with Nora Henn and Lynda Sanchez, *Indeh: An Apache Odyssey* (Provo, UT: Brigham Young University Press, 1980), 92.

4. Eve Ball, with James Kaywaykla, *In the Days of Victorio: Recollections of a Warm Springs Apache* (Tucson: University of Arizona Press, 1970), 15.

5. Ball, *Indeh*, 102–3.

6. Opler, *Apache Life-Way*, 416.

7. Ball, *Indeh*, 61–62.

8. Ball, *In the Days of Victorio*, 11, 15.

9. Ibid., 128.

10. Cole, *The Chiricahua Apache*, 57.

11. Opler, *Apache Life-Way*, 336.

12. Ball, *Indeh*, 104.

13. Ibid., 103.

14. Ibid., 37.

15. Ball, *In the Days of Victorio*, 50.

16. Ibid., 3–6, 9–10.

17. Ball, *Indeh*, 104.

18. Ball, *In the Days of Victorio*, 14.

19. Ibid., 21.

20. Ibid., 21.

21. John C. Cremony, *Life Among the Apaches* (San Francisco: A. Roman & Company, 1868; reprinted, Glorieta, NM: Rio Grande Press, 1969), 243, quoted in Donald E. Worcester, *The Apaches: Eagles of the Southwest* (Norman: University of Oklahoma Press, 1979), 53.

22. Ball, *Indeh*, 54.

23. Ball, *In the Days of Victorio*, 73.

24. Ibid., 116–19.

25. Ball, *Indeh*, 62.

26. Robert M. Utley, *The Indian Frontier of the American West, 1846–1890* (Albuquerque: University of New Mexico Press, 1984), 197.

7

MOURNING DOVE

Gender and Cultural Mediation

Dee Garceau

In a letter from Polson, Montana, dated October 21, 1916, Mourning Dove joked to her friend Lucullus McWhorter that the challenges of raising money to get her novel published might drive her to a life of crime. "My dear Bigfoot," she wrote, "I will tell you a secret":

> Since I have to raise $65.00 I decided either to rob some bank or start stealing cayuses. But an after thought and our Deer Lodge the State school for crooks came to my mind and I decided to go to work and earn honest money to pay for my first books and here I am . . . working for a family, 6 children all of the school age but the baby . . . and their old dad to cook for and keep house. . . . I am getting $1.50 a day and when he threshes I will no doubt reap $2.50 or three dollars a day, room and board.[1]

"I am so lonesome," she added. "But what is the use. I am just as tickled over the little Injun heroine coming to the front." The "little Injun heroine" to whom Mourning Dove referred was the central character in her first and only published novel, *Cogewea the Half-Blood; A Depiction of the Great Montana Cattle Range*.

This fragment of correspondence suggests the paradoxes in Mourning Dove's life. On the one hand, she lived on the economic margins of the inland Northwest, earning a wage as housekeeper, harvest cook, and migrant farm laborer.

On the other hand, she was an educated woman who wrote romance fiction and nurtured relationships with literary mentors such as McWhorter, who linked her to the publishing world. Her letter to McWhorter expressed both determination to bring her novel to fruition and the loneliness of her situation at that time and place. So, too, her letter crackled with humor, hinting that her economic struggle was symptomatic of a larger cultural struggle between membership on the margins and claiming a voice in the mainstream. Throughout her life, Mourning Dove would struggle between the demands of making a living and the demands of literary ambition. She would face condescension from white literary patrons and distrust from reservation Indians. She would negotiate multiple worlds and identities as an early twentieth-century mixed-blood woman who promoted Salish values through modern venues.

Mourning Dove was the pen name of Christine Quintasket,[2] a Southern Okanogan woman. A Salish-speaking people of the Columbia Plateau, the Southern Okanogan today are associated with the Confederated Colville Tribes of eastern Washington. Mourning Dove was born in 1888, among the first generation to grow up on a reservation. The Quintaskets homesteaded at Piya, near Boyds, Washington, where they raised horses. From 1895 to 1901, Mourning Dove sporadically attended the Goodwin Mission School of the Sacred Heart Convent in Ward, Washington. When her mother died in 1902, Mourning Dove returned home to keep house for her father and siblings. When her father remarried in 1904, she left Piya to pursue her education at Fort Shaw Indian School near Great Falls, Montana.[3]

At Fort Shaw, Mourning Dove met Hector McLeod, a Flathead Salishan. They married in 1909, and settled in Polson, Montana. This marriage did not last, and the couple separated in 1912. Mourning Dove headed for Portland, Oregon, in search of her own calling. There she began work on the novel *Cogewea*. In 1913, she moved to Calgary to study English composition, typing, and shorthand. With these courses completed, she taught school for a time on the Inkameep Okanogan Reserve in British Columbia. Visiting the United States in 1914, Mourning Dove met Lucullus McWhorter at a Yakima Frontier Days celebration. When she described the novel she had started, McWhorter was intrigued. The two began a literary partnership that would last her lifetime. In 1919, Mourning Dove married Fred Galler, a Colville of white and Wenatchi ancestry, and they settled in Omak, Washington. Their marriage produced no children and lasted until Mourning Dove's death in 1936.[4]

Mourning Dove's life spanned an era of intense assimilationist pressure on inland Northwest tribes. Before the reservation era, fur trading in the northern Rockies had generated a Euro-Indian culture of mixed-blood families, bilingual households, and blended customs. By the late nineteenth century, however, white settlers outnumbered Native residents and Northwestern tribes were confined to reservations. The world of Mourning Dove's childhood, then, hearkened to several generations of mixed cultural influences, but it was the reservation system that made systematic attempts to Anglicize Native American people. Federal Indian policy at the turn of the century mandated Christianization, patriarchal family organization, private property ownership, and subsistence farming. How Indian families translated these mandates into daily life is another story.[5]

Mourning Dove's childhood reflected the mix of cultural influences on Northwestern reservations at this time. Her mother and adopted grandmother, Teequalt, schooled her in Salish language and traditions; her father and adopted white brother, Jimmy Ryan, urged her toward English literacy. In keeping with Salish tradition, Mourning Dove went on puberty fasts; with Jimmy Ryan, she grew fascinated with "the mysteries of books." Mourning Dove's adult life would reflect both her belief in the value of Salish traditions and her desire to experiment with Anglo artistic forms—specifically books and movies—as vehicles for Native cultural expression. In 1927, Mourning Dove published *Cogewea*, the novel of contemporary Indian life she had begun in 1912. She followed with a collection of Salish legends, *Coyote Stories*, published in 1933. Mourning Dove also wrote portions of her own life story that were published posthumously as *Mourning Dove: A Salishan Autobiography*.[6]

Historians view Mourning Dove as a cultural mediator who tried to improve white understanding of Native Americans.[7] In an interview with the *Spokesman Review* in 1916, Mourning Dove explained that she wrote the novel *Cogewea* to dispel negative stereotypes about Indian people. "The white man does not know the Indian," she told the *Spokesman* reporter. "He thinks the Indian cold, emotionless, pitiless." But "my Indian girl heroine, Cogewea," she continued, "is intensely human, as am I. She craves for her place in the sun."[8] Eager to publish *Cogewea*, Mourning Dove hoped to reach white readers with an entertaining romance about Western life. She wanted to make visible to her white audience a Native perspective on Native Americans.

But if scholars agree that Mourning Dove chose the role of cultural mediator, they disagree about the nature of her published work. Some argue that Mourning Dove's white mentors distorted her voice by imposing their own political biases on her work even as they linked her with publishing contacts.[9] Chief among the culprits was Lucullus McWhorter, white advocate for the Yakama and Nez Perce tribes, collector and editor of Indian narratives, and literary mentor to Mourning Dove. According to literary scholar Allanna Brown,

McWhorter edited *Cogewea* with a heavy hand. A harsh critic of federal Indian policy, McWhorter rewrote portions of the novel to include his own polemics. The result is unevenness of voice, as the text veers between Mourning Dove's focus on developing plot and character, and McWhorter's political bombast.[10] In the following passage, Mourning Dove wrote the dialogue between Cogewea and one of her suitors, Densmore. Densmore, a white man from New York, is courting Cogewea because he secretly hopes to acquire her land; as her husband, he would claim title to her allotment. Cogewea is flattered, though wary of his motives. Each time he makes a declaration of love, she playfully changes the subject:

> Densmore whispered as his arm stole about her. "I love you! And yesterday you promised. . . .
>
> "It is late!" she exclaimed, slipping from the rock. "We had better go!"
>
> "But listen! My very own! I want to say so many things to you; that of which I wished to speak yesterday. Stay just a little longer! It is not late! Suppose it does grow dark? We can follow the trail. I must hear the ghosts!"
>
> "I don't believe they would be abroad when there is a Shoyapee [white man]. They would frighten you if they did come. Let's vamoose!"
>
> "Cogewea! Tell me that you care for me! That you . . ."
>
> "Aw! Let up! This love makin' is hell! Let's ride!"[11]

Implicit in Cogewea's distrust of Densmore's overtures is the larger story of tribal responses to powerful white reformers who offered their help. Cogewea's desire for love and acceptance make her vulnerable to Densmore's attentions, the same way that tribal needs for economic assistance moved them to consider strategies offered by Bureau of Indian Affairs (BIA) reformers. In both cases, an unequal balance of power jeopardized the relationship. Left to her own devices, Mourning Dove would have personified the uneasy relationship between tribes and white reformers through Cogewea's testing of Densmore's motives. McWhorter, however, overrode Mourning Dove's attempt to dramatize the uneasy dance of need and trust, partnership and exploitation. Instead, he reduced whites and Indians to oppositional stereotypes as villain and victim. Repartee between Cogewea and Densmore, under McWhorter's hand, became anti–BIA rhetoric. Contrast the dialogue above with the following diatribe, which scholars attribute to McWhorter: "'A nasty smear the Government escutcheon,' broke in the girl fiercely. 'A stagnant cesspool swarming with political hatched vermin! Stenchful with the fumes of avarice and greed; selfishly indifferent to the Macedonian cry of its victims writhing under the lash weilded by the hand of Mammon! Pitch is a fastidious cosmetic, compared with Bureau slime.'"[12]

Even more telling is the letter Mourning Dove wrote to McWhorter on the eve of *Cogewea*'s publication. In it, she referred to "the finishing touches . . . put there by you," final edits that she had neither seen nor approved. "Dear Bigfoot," she wrote, "I have just got through going over the book *Cogewea* and am surprised at the changes that you made. . . . I felt like it was someone elses book, and not mine at all."[13] One can only wonder at the meaning of her affectionate nickname for McWhorter, "Bigfoot." Was it a reference to his large shoe size, or to his weighty tread on her manuscript?

While some scholars hold that McWhorter distorted Mourning Dove's voice, others argue that her literary vision remained intact, insofar as *Cogewea* redefined the white, masculine, frontier narrative to make women visible and mixed-bloods central. Literary scholar Catherine Halverson observes that while the mythic frontier featured invincible white men in contests with Indians, Mourning Dove created a world where white men sought to get ahead through marriage to landed western women, mixed-blood as well as white. Halverson explains further that "if the frontier is the place at which white meets Indian, then the mixed blood who both literally and in spirit embodies that meeting is its most fit inhabitant and, indeed, is that which constitutes the frontier in the first place."[14] In *Cogewea*, the heroine is a mixed-blood woman; it is Jim, a mixed-blood man, who wins her hand in marriage; and it is the mixed-blood characters who are best prepared to bring the frontier into the twentieth century. Cogewea's everyday conversations include "standard English, Okanogan, Chinook, ranch slang, Latinate musings, and, perhaps most strikingly, her and Jim's slangy speech, with its [ironic] references to squaws, tomahawks, the war path, and other stereotypical Indian markers."[15] Unlike the taciturnity of the white male hero of frontier myth, Cogewea's and Jim's fluency with language represents the mixed-bloods' unique ability to navigate a diverse cultural landscape.

Cogewea, then, contains evidence for both arguments. Some passages ring with McWhorter's agenda, while others show how Mourning Dove repositioned mixed bloods from the margins to the center of Western life. If *Cogewea* is any indication, Mourning Dove's published work is, indeed, contradictory. Fortunately, Mourning Dove's unpublished work, a voluminous collection of letters written between 1914 and 1935, survives as well. These letters offer further clues to her positions within Okanogan and white society, and to her purposes and her self-definition as a mixed-blood woman. Correspondence between Mourning Dove and her literary mentors reveals her ambition to communicate Salish

values through new idioms borrowed from Anglo culture. Specifically, Mourning Dove wanted to affirm Okanogan tradition through romance novels and
films. By presenting elements of her Native culture through these forms of mass
entertainment, Mourning Dove sought to reposition Salish values from the
margins to the center, from the reservation to the mainstream.

Mourning Dove's syncretic ambition was complicated by both gender and
cultural identity. At times her goals foundered on the triple challenge of white
nostalgia about Native Americans, factionalism over cultural expression on
reservations, and lack of consensus about women's roles. At the turn of the
century, white nostalgia about the "Vanishing Red Man" gained momentum.
By the 1920s, Anglo artists, photographers, and writers were producing romantic
images of nineteenth-century Indian lifeways as paeans to a disappearing way
of life. Popular sentiment held that Native people on reservations were doomed
to extinction, culturally if not physically.[16] Mourning Dove's literary mentors,
McWhorter and J. P. MacLean, shared this nostalgic view. They urged Mourning Dove to transcribe her people's oral tradition before it "disappeared." But to
Mourning Dove, Okanogan tradition was neither static nor verging on extinction.
Throughout her career, she would challenge the white assumption that Native
cultural integrity went hand in hand with marginal status and nineteenth-
century lifeways. Indeed, the letters between McWhorter, MacLean, and Mourning Dove read like a power struggle over representations of Native identity and
tradition: McWhorter and MacLean tried to impose their vision of the "Vanishing Red Man" onto her work; and Mourning Dove countered with her own
vision of a flexible tradition.

McWhorter was locally renowned as a chronicler of inland Northwest tribal
history and lore. After reading a draft of Mourning Dove's novel in 1914, he vowed
to help her publish it. McWhorter wrote to MacLean, a friend with publishing
contacts in Ohio. MacLean and McWhorter came to value Mourning Dove as
another link to the inland Northwest tribes, but at times they treated her like an
exotic mascot. "I do not recall any instance of an Indian maiden writing a book,"
wrote MacLean to McWhorter. "The novelty of it will take."[17] Despite the fact
that Mourning Dove had been married for several years, MacLean referred to her
as an "Indian maiden" and to her literacy as a "novelty," formulaic markers consistent with romantic images of Native American women. Nor was McWhorter
immune to such sentimentality. Though sincere in his advocacy for Northwestern tribes, and though he developed a genuine, long-term friendship with Mourning Dove, McWhorter, too, fell prey to romanticism about Mourning Dove's
"Indianness." "Now, my dear MacLean," he wrote in 1916,

> I want to speak to you candidly and remind you that Mourning
> Dove is an Indian and that you will find her different from white
> people. . . . [S]he is an Indian and as you know from reading, an In-
> dian must be handled differently from White people. She has a tem-
> per, but she is not inclined to lift scalps. She has a Splendid idea of
> justice and I am sure that you will experience no trouble in getting her
> to do the things wanted of her from you.[18]

Here McWhorter re-created the image of a mysterious yet compliant Indian woman, a staple of popular lore about Indians reaching all the way back to Pochahontas.

Mourning Dove responded to her literary mentors' well-intentioned but stereotypical attitudes in two ways. Sometimes she challenged them directly; other times she played to their nostalgia, to disarm them when she raised diffi-cult issues. In one striking example, she resorted to both strategies in the same letter. In May of 1916, Mourning Dove had written to MacLean, asking what he thought of *Cogewea*. MacLean wrote back an equivocal reply, to the effect that he found the manuscript "natural." Mourning Dove distrusted the vague-ness of this response and confronted him. In June 1916, she wrote,

> My Dear Mr. Maclean,
>   . . . [Y]ou said the story is the most *natural* one you ever read. Well,
> a *toad* is natural, but I doubt if you like it as much as a songbird. The
> rattlesnake is natural and I bet that you do not like it. So I am wonder-
> ing and want your honest opinion of Cogewea. . . .
>   [A]ll I charge is that you tell me just what you think of the ro-
> mance. . . . If the story is not good, tell me and if it is good, tell me.
>   (Mourning Dove's emphasis)[19]

Here, Mourning Dove demanded forthright criticism. She refused to let MacLean retreat into nostalgia about how "natural" Indians and their stories were. In this way, she challenged MacLean to drop the Indian maiden trope, at least in his work with her. Two lines later, however, Mourning Dove playfully adopted the clichéd metaphors and terse speech of the mythic Indian as she drove home her point: "I am not working for words spoken by a forked tongue," she wrote. "I want true words from your heart."[20] Perhaps she hoped to defuse conflict through her own deliberate use of humor and stereotype, even as she held MacLean accountable for his unexamined use of stereotype.

By far, the most significant challenge Mourning Dove posed to her men-tors was her desire to adapt Okanogan tradition to new idioms, like popular fiction and film. Early in their acquaintance, MacLean and McWhorter tried to steer Mourning Dove into oral history collection and transcription. In November of 1914, MacLean wrote to McWhorter, saying, "Encourage her to write out in full . . . all the myths, folklore, and traditions of her people."[21] McWhorter took up the charge and persuaded Mourning Dove to forgo writing another novel in favor of recording oral tradition. Mourning Dove was only partly convinced by McWhorter's entreaties. Though she saw value in writing down oral traditions, or "folklores," she also saw Salish cultural tradition as flexible, adaptable to new venues. Repeatedly during her twenty-year correspondence with McWhorter, Mourning Dove spoke of writing a second novel or scripting a film. In April 1916, for example, Mourning Dove alluded to *Cogewea* taking cinematic form when she wrote, "Don't worry about the movies, Bigfoot. I will not likely forget my promise in regards to me giving you a ticket to the ten cents show—when "Cogewea" . . . becomes a success."[22]

In the winter of 1918–19, Mourning Dove and McWhorter posted a more revealing exchange. McWhorter wrote that a woman interested in producing a movie about Indian life had approached him. He had not followed up on it. Mourning Dove's response was immediate: "Dear Big Foot," she replied, "Since I got your letter about that movie woman, I have almost left off folklore thinking, and started a movie play—ha, ain't I a fickle folklore writer?"[23] McWhorter wrote back with renewed urgency about the need to preserve oral tradition before it disappeared. And so their tug-of-war continued. In November of 1921, Mourning Dove wrote, "Dear Bigfoot, . . . I outlined another novel of real Indian life the other night. . . . [T]he story is going to be a great movie story and I am going to send it to one of the greatest actresses of the day. And she will not say *no* . . . , so great is my confidence as I write this."[24] Despite Mourning Dove's fervor about writing a second novel or scripting a film, McWhorter offered no support in either of these directions. Still, Mourning Dove persisted. Some time in 1928, she appealed directly to a producer about turning *Cogewea* into a film. By then, however, McWhorter owned the copyright to *Cogewea*; thus he could block Mourning Dove's initiative to adapt *Cogewea* to the screen.

A letter from the producer, Harl J. Cook Investments, to McWhorter survives. "I had an excellent letter from our mutual friend, Mourning Dove," wrote Cook, "and she told me of her book [*Cogewea*]." He continued,

> I wrote to Mourning Dove at once, asking her if there was any chance for us to use this book by an amicable arrangement, and she replied that you [McWhorter] have the right to all the sales and the privilege of a movie.

She asked me to address you as to the idea and so I am doing that very thing. In case you have not made any arrangement for a good movie, I wish you would allow me to put this book up to him [Will Maylon of the Maylon Players in Spokane] and see if he would in any way consider such a production.

[If] . . . you give your consent for . . . an attractive and well-written movie, I will ask Mr. Maylon to go over the book with me.[25]

There is no record of McWhorter's reply; all we know is that a movie based on *Cogewea* never was made. These exchanges reveal Mourning Dove's and her literary mentors' conflicting agendas, with Mourning Dove wanting to communicate Native experience through fiction or film, and McWhorter and MacLean bent on preserving oral tradition. Mourning Dove depended on McWhorter and MacLean, however, for their contacts with publishers. Thus her syncretic ambition was refracted through the prism of her mentors' nostalgia about nineteenth-century Indian lifeways, and neither her second novel nor her movie script came to fruition.

A second factor complicating Mourning Dove's work was tribal factionalism. Adaptations to reservation life and their implications for cultural identity sometimes divided Native residents over issues of accommodation and resistance to federal assimilation programs.[26] On the early twentieth-century Colville and Flathead reservations where Mourning Dove lived and traveled, collecting oral stories, she met distrust toward the project. In a letter to McWhorter dated March 15, 1925, Mourning Dove wrote, "it seems out of style for the Indians around here to tell Indian legends. Whenever I ask any of them, they laugh and make fun of me, and say, 'We are not the old-timers [who] believe in them stories."[27] In a draft introduction to *Coyote Stories*, her published collection of Salish oral tales, Mourning Dove noted that the Indians' "well-founded distrust of the white man locks his bosom against . . . divulgence . . . of those ideals held to be sacred with the older tribesmen." She added that "Difficulties equally as serious are encountered when dealing with the young and school-instructed . . . this class in general are averse to delving into their ancestral folklore. This is, in part, [a result] of . . . ridicule on the part of teachers, religionists, and uneducated whites."[28] Given the pressures affecting cultural expression, Mourning Dove sometimes doubted her own compliance with McWhorter's goal of preserving oral tradition in writing. In the draft prelude to *Coyote Stories*, Mourning Dove added, "It has been with the greatest reluctance that I consented to . . . chronicling . . . the . . . oral philosophy of the Okanogans. . . . And now, on the threshhold of publication, there is a heart-shrinking from what I realize will be regarded by older members of my . . . tribe as irreverent sacrilege."[29] Mourning Dove feared misrepresenting Okanogan oral tradition because some stories had been altered to suit a white audience, while others were presented out of context. Was the result preservation or violation of Okanogan cultural heritage? Mourning Dove did not have the answers.

By the turn of the century, assimilation programs were not the only challenge to cultural identity. The language to describe Native identity was itself in transition, as blood quantum became conflated with ethnicity. "Indian blood" was a figure of speech that grew out of European ideas about race as a biological determinant of identity and behavior. In Euro-American culture, "Indian blood" not only signaled one's biological ancestry, it also placed one within a racialized hierarchy. Before this, when Native people inquired about a stranger's identity, they had asked, "What language do you speak?" rather than "What race are you?"[30] As the United States developed criteria for determining tribal membership in preparation for allotment, one's proportion of Indian blood became a measure of tribal identity. With the institutionalization of blood quantum requirements for tribal membership, racial lineage became synonymous with ethnic identity. In a letter to McWhorter about Native resistance to her attempt to collect oral stories, Mourning Dove reflected these transitions in the language of cultural identity. She attributed her outsider status to being a mixed blood among full bloods, yet the painful social distance she described had more to do with language differences than blood quantum. On September 4, 1916, Mourning Dove wrote,

> I cannot understand the Yakima language, and if they are not mixed-bloods like myself, I feel sadly out of place. . . . The same here [in Polson, Montana], I see Kootenais and Pend'Oreilles Indians and feel indifferent with them.
>
> I lived here [in Polson] ten years almost and I hardly know one full blood Indian from another because I don't understand their tongue and they only laugh at me when I talk to them. So you savey my position. It is h—— to be a half-breed.[31]

When she commented that it was "h—— to be a half-breed," Mourning Dove used blood quantum as a metaphor for language difference, reflecting the interplay between traditional and modern markers of tribal identity.

Whether separated by language or biology, Mourning Dove doubted her authority to record the oral traditions of those outside her own tribe. The Yakama, Kootenai, and Pend'Oreilles' distrust of a "preservation" project sponsored by white mentors, as well as Mourning Dove's perception of her own outsider status, spoke to the heightened sensitivity over cultural identity felt by reservation dwellers during this assimilationist era.

If Mourning Dove privately struggled with the issue of cultural authority as a mixed blood among full-bloods, she also refashioned herself as a full-blood for the white reading public. Early in 1916, McWhorter drafted a biographical sketch of Mourning Dove to preface the novel *Cogewea*. In it he described her as a mixed-blood woman of Okanogan and white ancestry. Mourning Dove asked McWhorter to omit her white ancestry from this description. In February 1916, she wrote, "I don't want mention about my Shewappee [white] blood. . . . if I let you mention of my blood, I know all honors will be cast to the white part of me. . . . I am plenty dark enough to pass as full blood to people that does not know the truth."[32] Thus Mourning Dove made sure that any prestige earned by her accomplishments as a writer would accrue to her full blood or Native persona, and thus raise the status of Native women everywhere. For Mourning Dove, blood quantum was a malleable concept, here a metaphor for ethnic difference, there a means to elevate Native women in the public eye.

Perhaps mixed-blood identity also functioned as a metaphor for experimentation in Mourning Dove's life, giving her license to explore new forms of artistic and cultural expression. Significantly, Mourning Dove never expressed doubts about her cultural authority to dramatize Okanogan values through fiction or film scripts. In short, Mourning Dove was drawn to artistic interpretation as a vehicle for cultural continuity, rather than exact transcription of oral traditions. To claim a voice in popular fiction or film would bring Okanogan values into the powerful currents of modern mass culture.

Mourning Dove's attitudes about adaptation and cultural continuity can be traced in part to her childhood training. In everyday life, her parents exposed her to a mix of Okanogan tradition and Anglo influences. Her father built a log cabin for the family, in accordance with Indian agency mandates. Her adopted grandmother, Teequalt, refused to live in it, insisting on a tipi next to the cabin for her residence. The rest of the family joined Teequalt in the tipi during the summer and returned to their cabin during the winter. Mourning Dove's mother embraced Catholicism, but continued to speak her Native language, translating Catholic catechisms into Salish each time she instructed her children. One of Mourning Dove's most vivid memories involved conflict between her mother and father over the issue of puberty fasts. Her mother and Teequalt had been training her in Salish spiritual traditions. When Mourning Dove had her first menses, they began preparing her for a traditional puberty fast. This was intended to guide her on a vision quest, in the hope that she might receive power from a guardian spirit. Her account of this incident is worth quoting at length, for it suggests the nature of conflict within families over strategies of acculturation.

> Mother . . . began to prepare me for my last ordeal of searching for spiritual guidance. . . . [S]he folded my braids and tied them with buckskin thongs so they would not come loose during my ten days of solitary fasting. Then she washed my face and painted it with a mixture of vermilion earth and tallow. . . . She dressed me warmly, tied a small woolen shawl around my shoulders, and put new moccasins on my feet. I was ready.
>
> It was almost noon when I was leaving. Father came home for lunch. He objected at once, and my parents argued. . . . He said our ancient customs were foolish, exposing children to cold and perhaps ruining their health. The modern world required that Indians be more like whites. Medicine women were no longer needed; the agency doctor was better qualified to treat the sick.
>
> I stood waiting at the door, faintly hoping that Father would get the best of my mother just this once. Mother did not say very much, but I could sense the disgust behind her stoicism. She waited for Father to finish. Then she waved her hand at me to leave. I closed the rough-hewn door and starting walking toward the mountains. [33]

Mourning Dove's puberty fast did not yield a vision, and she did not become a medicine woman as her mother and grandmother had hoped. But perhaps Mourning Dove bridged her mother's reverence for Salish spiritual tradition and her father's desire to engage the modern world by choosing as her life's work the communication of Okanogan values through modern forms like romance fiction and film.

If Mourning Dove's parents clashed over spiritual training, their argument was itself a disruption of inland Salish gender norms. During the nineteenth century, female elders oversaw the spiritual instruction of girls, and male elders, the spiritual training of boys. Mourning Dove's father's opposition to her puberty fast marked a departure from this tradition, for he was interfering with her mother and grandmother's responsibility for the spiritual training of female kin.[34] Indeed, the third factor complicating Mourning Dove's syncretic ambition was the lack of consensus about women's roles. Federal Indian policy promoted an Anglo ideal of female economic dependence and subordination to patriarchal authority within nuclear family households. This model of family relations did not square with Okanogan gender systems.

In nineteenth-century Plateau cultures, women's and men's roles had been complementary and "balanced in power." Frances Vanderburg and Dorothy Felsman, enrolled members of the Confederated Salish and Kootenai Tribes in Montana, described nineteenth-century Salish women as providers.[35] They dug camas and bitterroot, and gathered huckleberries, chokecherries, raspberries, and strawberries, as well as herbs and medicines. The foods Salishan Plateau women gathered provided from 50 to 70 percent of the nutrition in the nineteenth-century diet; the fish and game men hunted, 33 to 50 percent. Women owned their lodges and all food brought into the household. They also owned and traded their horses independently from men. In short, the work of both genders was judged equally valuable. "Good providers," male or female, earned political influence in council.[36]

Households were matrilocal, with kinship systems traced through the female line. Family members looked to the grandmother for advice and approval, one reason being that men frequently were away on hunting, trading, diplomatic, or military expeditions. Women suggested to the chief when to move camp and decided where to set up new camps. The *sku'malt*, or civil chief, was an elected position in which women sometimes served, hearing and mediating disputes. The wives of nineteenth-century Plateau chiefs advised them on major decisions, handled leadership responsibilities during a chief's absence, and nominated the chief's successor. In council, men and women alike discussed the issues until all sides of the question had been aired. Salishan women, then, traditionally held considerable social and political influence.[37]

Salish women also took active roles in the spiritual life of the community as healers. Female as well as male children vision-quested for guardian spirits. "Children," wrote Mourning Dove, "were continually sent out . . . to hunt for a guardian spirit. . . . Both boys and girls were obliged to undertake this search. . . . Finding a spirit gave a child a future career in medicine, with the ability to cure the sick."[38] In addition, women and men each practiced a spiritual cleansing ritual followed by ceremonial offerings and requests to appropriate powers before embarking on significant provider activities—women before their first root-digging expedition of the season and men before their first fishing expedition.[39]

Nineteenth-century Okanogan gender norms would be challenged and transformed by conditions on twentieth-century reservations. Extended family units fragmented under pressures to adopt nuclear family structure and patriarchal order. With fewer providers, households lost economic security, and survival became more precarious. Farming took hold unevenly, hindered by poor soils, arid climates, and land loss to "competency politics." The Dawes Act of 1887 had protected Indian land allotments from encroachment with twenty-five-year trust restrictions. By 1910, however, Congress lifted the trust restrictions for "competent" Indians, and authorized reservation superintendents to sell "unused land" belonging to "incompetent" Indians. Competency became a manipulable concept in the hands of some superintendents; by 1920, one million acres of trust land had been sold and another 4.5 million went under lease to whites. During Mourning Dove's youth, "competency politics" led to increasing outside control of Indian resources.[40]

At the same time, nineteenth-century methods of sustenance were undermined. Reservation borders interrupted the orderly round of seasonal migration to salmon runs, camas fields, bison grounds, and berry thickets.[41] Salish families developed new methods of economic support, including wage labor for adjacent ranching and timber interests, migrant farm labor, subsistence homesteading, and income from land sale or rent.[42] Like nineteenth-century Salish economic activity, these new strategies drew extensively on women's as well as men's work and resources. During Mourning Dove's lifetime, the demands of economic survival belied the Anglo ideal of husbands as sole breadwinners.

More important, Salish women's sense of economic responsibility persisted. As a married woman, Mourning Dove contributed equally to household support, sometimes side by side with her husband, sometimes in separate ventures. Mourning Dove and her second husband, Fred Galler, spent many seasons picking, thinning, and sorting apples. When Galler found work on his own away from home, Mourning Dove took in boarders, worked out as a housekeeper, or leased her allotment. Throughout her marriage to Galler, Mourning Dove remained an active economic partner.[43]

Despite the fragmentation of extended family households during this period, Mourning Dove's sense of responsibility to kin persisted. She regularly visited relatives scattered across Montana, Washington, and British Columbia. Periodically she took in adult sisters and their children, either to nurse them through illnesses or to help provide for them. Yet no matter how committed one was to family support, the road was difficult for Native people in the early twentieth-century inland Northwest.

Mourning Dove's work as field laborer, farm cook, nanny, and housekeeper demanded long hours for little pay. Galler, too, found no security and low wages as he traveled from the hop fields of the Yakima Valley to the lumber mills of northeastern Washington. In a rural economy characterized by seasonal work, the demands of supporting a household left Mourning Dove with little time to write. Her letters to McWhorter expressed this frustration.

As their friendship developed over the years, Mourning Dove gradually trusted McWhorter with her troubles. In February of 1920, she confided to him that she could not write until late at night when everyone was asleep, for those were her only unoccupied hours. "I am tired," she wrote. "I have care of my sister's children and . . . we have fourteen boarders. . . . I cannot get anything [writing] done."[44] Ten years later, her situation was little better. In the fall of 1930, she wrote, "I am packing apples . . . working ten hours each day but Sundays, and that will be my day to wash and clean my clothes."[45] Mourning Dove's arduous work history suggests that with the transition to reservation life, Salish women lost the relative economic security and balanced workload made possible by extended family households with multiple providers typical of an earlier generation. At the same time, Salish women maintained their responsibility for economic support of households and their sense of obligation to extended kin.

Continuity of responsibilities in an increasingly precarious economy challenged the ingenuity of Salish women during this period. For an artist needing time to write, the situation was nearly impossible. Mourning Dove's letters to McWhorter increasingly mentioned sick relatives, uneven income, and scant time or energy to devote to her manuscript. The following bulletin from Jennings, Montana, April 25, 1916, was typical:

> I came here as I told you before because my sister was quite ill, . . . she was so sick that we had to phone for the doctor and he came and gave her an operation and I hope for the best.
>
> Yesterday I heard from younger sister from B.C. Canada and her baby is very sick and she is in a delicate condition and wants me to come over as soon as I can. Oh dear I am just wondering Big Foot what is going to happen next. . . .
>
> I am half discouraged. I am wondering whether I will live through the writing of my Okanogan Sweat House [working title for the manuscript *Coyote Stories*]. I have not started yet but expect to as soon as I am able. At present I have my hands full with the children and my sister abed and housework.
>
> I have hardly time to think.[46]

In addition to caring for her adult sisters and their children, Mourning Dove struggled to make ends meet on intermittent income. During the 1920s, she and her husband grew hay on her allotment, and they sometimes leased acreage to local ranchers. But hay sales and lease payments were irregular, as suggested by the following excerpts from her correspondence with McWhorter: "Omak, Wash. August 28, 1925: We have lot of hay but there is no sale for it yet. Omak, Wash. July 28, 1926: Yesterday we rented our ranch for three years, and have made the lease. . . . We are not getting no cash rent till the first of the year."[47] If hay farming and land lease were no guarantee of income, wage work played a distant second. In an undated letter from the apple orchards in Naches, Washington, in 1930, Mourning Dove told McWhorter, "Wages are very meager this year, getting only 3 cents a box for packing. I think my work will last around four or five weeks." Again, she mentioned her difficulty finding time to write: "Oh I am so tired tonight, . . . I packed 133 boxes today in Yellow Newtons. . . . I am only telling you why I have been working so hard this summer so I could have the time to work on my book this winter if possibly [sic]."[48]

If the Anglo ideal of one male breadwinner per household was a far cry from Mourning Dove's family economy, so, too, the Anglo model of patriarchal authority took inconsistent and disruptive form in her family life. Galler sometimes wielded authority arbitrarily, typically when binge drinking. At these times, he was hostile to her literary ambition and imperious in the household. In May 1930, Mourning Dove wrote from Omak, Washington, that she and Galler had had "much quarreling and I went away sad and mad for three weeks." During her absence, Galler had gone on a bender with friends. "Big Foot," she continued, "I hate the class that he likes, and he is indifferent with my work and the class of people that I like."[49] Not only was Galler "indifferent to her work" when drinking, he chose those moments to rather pointedly assert his right to her housekeeping services. The couple decided to separate permanently, and Galler planned to leave for Oklahoma while Mourning Dove "went to Canada for a rest." She continued, "[W]hen I came home, behold he was home waiting for me, and all the grub gone in the house, and a dirty house and clothes. I was surprised. He told me 'possession was nine tenths of the law and he was staying home.'"[50] Galler's statement about "posession" is striking because Mourning Dove held legal title to their home.

Health professionals today understand alcoholism as a disease of addiction, not a moral failing. At the time, Mourning Dove experienced her husband's alcohol abuse as willful behavior that sabotaged their economic security. In 1933, she confided to McWhorter that "Fred got drunk last night . . . and wrecked the old Ford; spent all his months wages besides. . . . Big Foot I am too mad and grieved to cry."[51] Alcoholism created a skewed mirror of patriarchal family relations in Mourning Dove's household. For Mourning Dove, this compounded the stresses of making a living and finding time to write. The demands of meeting a Salish woman's responsibility to extended family across two states and one Canadian province, the economic struggle of a Salish wife as coprovider in a marginal arena of wage labor, and an erratic overlay of patriarchal norms signaled changes in Salish gender relations that intensified the challenges Mourning Dove faced.

The transitional nature of Salish gender systems; the questions about ancestry, ethnic identity, and cultural authority in an era of contested cultural expression on reservations; and the tug-of-war with her literary mentors over representations of Native culture all took their toll on Mourning Dove's life. She died relatively young, at age 48, in a Washington state hospital called Medical Lake. The records surrounding her death are contradictory, but all imply great stress at the time of her death. The death certificate listed "exhaustion from manic-depressive psychosis" as the cause. However, according to the Medical Lake admissions record, there were "old and new contusions all over Mourning Dove's chest and legs," suggesting domestic violence as the cause. In a third explanation, Medical Lake staff told Mourning Dove's family that she died of a "brain hemorrhage."[52] Thus, while her achievements as a writer against great odds are remarkable, we cannot be too sanguine about them. In the end, Mourning Dove's life, letters, and early death call for better understanding of both the promise and the costs of transforming gender and cultural identity.

NOTES

1. Mourning Dove to Lucullus Virgil McWhorter, 21 Oct. 1916. The letters cited herein are housed at the E. O. Holland Library Archives and Special Collections, Washington State University, Pullman, WA.

2. I have chosen to use Mourning Dove's pen name throughout this essay because this is the name by which she represented herself in the bulk of her adult correspondence.

3. Jay Miller, "Mourning Dove: The Author as Cultural Mediator," in *Being and Becoming Indian: Biographical Studies of Native American Frontiers*, ed. James Clifton (Chicago: Dorsey Press, 1989), 160–82; see 161–65.

4. Ibid., 165–70.

5. Jay Miller, "Introduction," *Mourning Dove: A Salishan Autobiography* (Lincoln: University of Nebraska Press, 1990), ix–xxxix. See also Sylvia Van Kirk, *Many Tender Ties: Women in Fur Trade Society, 1670–1870* (Norman: University of Oklahoma Press, 1980); Karen Anderson, *Changing Woman: A History of Racial Ethnic Women in Modern America* (New York: Oxford University Press, 1996).

6. Mourning Dove, *Cogewea the Half-Blood: A Depiction of the Great Montana Cattle Range* (1927 ed., Four Seas Press; reprint University of Nebraska Press, 1981); Heister Dean Guie, ed., *Coyote Stories*, by Mourning Dove (Lincoln: University of Nebraska Press, 1990); Jay Miller, ed., *Mourning Dove: A Salishan Autobiography* (Lincoln: University of Nebraska Press, 1990).

7. Miller, "The Author as Cultural Mediator," 160–82; Dexter Fisher, "The Transformation of Tradition: A Study of Zitkala Ša and Mourning Dove, Two Transitional American Indian Writers," in *Critical Essays on Native American Literature*, ed. Andrew Wiget (Boston: G. K. Hall, 1985), 202–11.

8. "Colville Indian Girl Blazes Trail to New Conception of Redmen in Her Novel, 'Cogewea,'" *The Spokesman Review*, 9 April 1916.

9. Allanna Brown, "Looking Through the Glass Darkly: The Editorialized Mourning Dove," in *New Voices in Native American Criticism*, ed. Arnold Krupat (Washington, D.C.: Smithsonian Press, 1993), 274–90. See also W. S. Penn, "Scylla or the True Spelling of Mourning," in *All My Sins Are Relatives* (Lincoln: University of Nebraska Press, 1995), 113–36. See 119.

10. Brown, "Through the Glass Darkly," 279.

11. Mourning Dove, *Cogewea*, 150.

12. Ibid., 145.

13. Mourning Dove to McWhorter, 4 June 1928.

14. Catherine Halverson, "Redefining the Frontier: Mourning Dove's *Cogewea, The Half-Blood: A Depiction of the Great Montana Cattle Range*," *American Indian Culture and Research Journal* 12 (1997): 105–24, quote from 108. See also Maureen Honey, "'So Far Away from Home': Minority Women Writers and the New Woman," *Women's Studies International Forum* 15 (1992): 473–85.

15. Halverson, "Redefining the Frontier," 112.

16. Brian Dippie, *The Vanishing American: White Attitudes and U.S. Indian Policy* (Emporia, KS: University Press of Kansas, 1982), 197–242.

17. MacLean to McWhorter, 1 Nov. 1914.

18. McWhorter to MacLean, 28 Aug. 1916.

19. Mourning Dove to MacLean, 10 June 1916.

20. Ibid.

21. MacLean to McWhorter, 1 Nov. 1914.

22. Mourning Dove to McWhorter, 1 April 1916.

23. Mourning Dove to McWhorter, 15 Jan. 1919.

24. Mourning Dove to McWhorter, 4 Nov. 1921.

25. Harl J. Cook to L. V. McWhorter, 14 Nov. 1928.

26. Anderson, *Changing Woman*, 37–66.

27. Mourning Dove to McWhorter, 4 Sept. 1916.

28. Mourning Dove, draft introduction to *Tales of the Okanogan Sweat House*, p. 3 (WSU Archives).

29. Mourning Dove, draft prelude to *Okanogan Sweat House*.

30. James Clifton, "Alternate Identities and Cultural Frontiers," in *Being and Becoming Indian*, 1–37, see 10–11.

31. Mourning Dove to McWhorter, 4 Sept. 1916.

32. Mourning Dove to McWhorter, 29 Feb. 1916.

33. Mourning Dove, *A Salishan Autobiography*, 3–48, quote, 42–43.

34. Interview, Frances Vanderburg by Dee Garceau, Missoula, Montana, 6 Aug. 1998; Interview, Dorothy Felsman by Dee Garceau, Arlee, Montana, 14 Aug. 1998. See also Mourning Dove, *A Salishan Autobiography*, 39–43.

35. Vanderburg interview; Felsman interview.

36. Lillian A. Ackerman, "Complementary but Equal: Gender Status in the Plateau," *Women and Power in Native North America*, ed. Laura F. Klein and Lillian A. Ackerman (Norman: University of Oklahoma Press, 1995), 75–99.

37. Ibid.; Vanderburg interview; Felsman interview.

38. Felsman interview; Mourning Dove, *A Salishan Autobiography*, 35, 37.

39. Vanderburg interview; Ackerman, "Complementary but Equal," 75–95.

40. See Frederick Hoxie, *A Final Promise: The Campaign to Assimilate the Indians* (University of Nebraska Press, 1984), 165–84.

41. Ackerman, "The Effect of Missionary Ideals on Family Structure and Women's Roles in Plateau Indian Culture," *Idaho Yesterdays* 31 (1987): 64–73.

42. Occupational overview of adult men and women, Flathead Reservation Census, 1910 (Missoula, MT: University of Montana Mansfield Library Archives).

43. Mourning Dove to McWhorter, 21 Oct. 1916, 12 July 1925, 28 Aug. 1925, 13 June 1930.

44. Mourning Dove to McWhorter, 9 Feb. 1920.

45. Mourning Dove to McWhorter, n.d. except 1930.

46. Mourning Dove to McWhorter, 25 April 1916.

47. Mourning Dove to McWhorter, 28 July 1926, 28 Aug. 1925.

48. Mourning Dove to McWhorter, n.d. except 1930.

49. Mourning Dove to McWhorter, 19 May 1930.

50. Ibid.

51. Mourning Dove to McWhorter, 12 Nov. 1933.

52. Brown, "Through the Glass Darkly," 287. According to Allanna Brown, "exhaustion from manic depressive psychosis" was "a commonly used diagnosis for patients who died at Medical Lake during the 1930s."

8

GERTRUDE SIMMONS BONNIN

For the Indian Cause

P. Jane Hafen

The image is indelible: a little girl dressed in buckskin and moccasins, running free across the plains, her long black hair loose and "blowing in the breeze . . . no less spirited than a bounding deer."[1] All too soon, the temptation of "red, red apples" and a ride far away on the "iron horse" disrupted the eight-year-old's paradise, and she was enrolled in a boarding school for American Indian children.[2] That is how Gertrude Simmons Bonnin, the Yankton Sioux woman who called herself Zitkala Ša, remembered her childhood. Succumbing to assimilationist pressures, she grew up to become a teacher, writer, orator, musician, composer, and political activist. Though she never forgot that little girl, she could not reclaim her. Gradually distanced from her own tribe, she became an advocate for all Indians.

By her own account, Gertrude Simmons was born on the Yankton Reservation in South Dakota on February 22, 1876, the same year the Sioux and other Indians defeated General George Armstrong Custer at the Battle of the Little Big Horn. She was the daughter of Ellen *Tat_Iy_hiwin* and a white trader named Felker. In her reminiscences of her life on the reservation, Gertrude described an innocent life on the plains. She listened intently to traditional stories told by elders: "As each in turn began to tell a legend, I pillowed my head in my mother's lap; and lying flat upon my back, I watched the stars as they peeped down upon me, one by one."[3] From her mother, she learned details of tribal life, essential practical and survival skills, appropriate social relationships, and proper behavior. Nevertheless, the excitement that boarding school promised led Gertrude to beg her mother to send her east.

When Gertrude arrived at the White's Manual Labor Institute at Wabash, Indiana, however, she encountered intense pressure to assimilate, common to Indian boarding schools of the time. School officials, determined to civilize the "savages," followed the admonitions of Colonel Richard H. Pratt, founder of the Carlisle Industrial Training School in Pennsylvania, to "kill the Indian and save the man."[4] The school began Gertrude's transformation by cutting her hair. She long remembered the anguish she felt:

> I cried aloud, shaking my head all the while until I felt the cold blades of the scissors against my neck, and heard them gnaw off one of my thick braids. Then I lost my spirit. Since the day I was taken from my mother I had suffered extreme indignities. People had stared at me. I had been tossed about in the air like a wooden puppet. And now my long hair was shingled like a coward's! In my anguish I moaned for my mother, but no one came to comfort me.[5]

In the oppressive atmosphere of the school, Gertrude asserted her individuality through minor acts of rebellion. Her teachers set her on a schedule of manual labor, such as cleaning or cooking, that they intended to inculcate in her the value of work. Gertrude lashed out by sabotaging a pot of turnips. She responded to Christian instruction by scribbling out the devil's eyes in a Bible storybook. Forbidden to speak her Native language, she learned to read and write English, and she used these new skills to celebrate her traditional culture. The pressure to assimilate gave resolve to Gertrude's resistance.

At the same time, home began to feel increasingly far away. Since she was at boarding school when she reached puberty, Gertrude did not participate in the rites that normally ushered young girls into adult Sioux society. At the same time, her new world was alien to her mother and older brother, David (Dawee), despite his own boarding school experience. Visits home became unpleasant, as Gertrude felt increasingly uncomfortable with her family. She later wrote: "The melancholy of those black days has left so long a shadow that it darkens the path of years that have since gone by."[6] Her acceptance to Earlham College in Indiana in 1895 only exacerbated the situation. Acclaimed for her musical and oratorical skills, she became a showpiece for Indian education: her teachers had transformed her from a "savage squaw" into an accomplished young woman.[7] Gertrude probably regarded her triumphs as public validation, but the positive reaction of some whites must also have presented a painful contrast to the prejudices she constantly battled.

In 1896 Gertrude won second place in a state oratorical contest with a speech entitled "Side by Side," but the experience "left little taste of victory."[8] She began her address with a stinging indictment of white society and hypocritical Christianity. She described the situation of her people as "pressed almost to the farther sea" and speculated on their prospects for the future: "Does that sea symbolize his death? Does the narrow territory still left to him typify the last brief day before his place on Earth 'shall know him no more forever'?" She subtly challenged the morality of U.S. Indian policy that had reduced Native people to these desperate circumstances: "Shall might make right and the fittest alone survive?" Gertrude also appealed to Christians by couching her rhetoric in biblical rhetoric and urging whites to "Look with compassion down, and with thine almighty power move this nation to the rescue of my race."

At the age of twenty, however, Gertrude was not a pessimist. Despite her bitter experience, she had come to believe that education was the salvation of her people, and she endorsed the Indian policy that promoted schools:

> Within the last two decades a great interest in Indian civilization has been awakened; a beneficent government has organized a successful system of Indian education; training schools and college doors stand open to us. We clasp the warm hand of friendship everywhere. From honest hearts and sincere lips at last we hear the hearty welcome and Godspeed.

Indians, she suggested, welcomed efforts to change them:

> We come from mountain fastnesses, from cheerless plains, from far-off low-wooded streams, seeking the "White Man's ways." Seeking your skill in industry and in art, seeking labor and honest independence, seeking the treasures of knowledge and wisdom, seeking to comprehend the spirit of your laws and the genius of your noble institutions, seeking by a new birthright to unite with yours our claim to a common country, seeking the Sovereign's crown that we may stand side by side with you in ascribing royal honor to our nation's flag. America, I love thee. "Thy people shall be my people and thy God my God."[9]

Some in the audience, however, challenged Gertrude's plea for racial harmony. Before that vast ocean of eyes, college rowdies threw out a large white flag that bore a drawing of a forlorn Indian girl. Under this caricature, they had printed in bold black letters words that ridiculed the college that was represented by a "squaw."[10] Racism had marred her academic triumph. Surely she questioned whether her dreams of a "common country" would ever be realized.

An unidentified illness prevented Gertrude finishing her degree at Earlham, but she taught at Carlisle Industrial Training School in Pennsylvania from 1897 to 1899. She had bitter disagreements with Carlisle's founder, Colonel Pratt, which stemmed from her growing opposition to his crusade against Native culture. She acknowledged her alienation from her own culture and the profound sense of loss that she felt: "For the white man's papers I had given up my faith in the Great Spirit. For these same papers I had forgotten the healing in trees and brooks. . . . At last, one weary day in the schoolroom, a new idea presented itself to me. . . . Thus I resigned my position."[11] But instead of renewing her ties to Sioux culture, Gertrude left Carlisle to study violin at the New England Conservatory of Music.

Although she did not return to Yankton, Gertrude began to reclaim her Sioux heritage by publishing articles and short stories in periodicals such as *The Atlantic Monthly* and *Harper's Magazine*. These writings included her memoirs of her "Indian Childhood," "School Days," and teaching experiences. She also assembled a collection of Sioux myths, *Old Indian Legends*, in which she recounted the stories she had heard as a child.[12] Consisting largely of socializing tales about the Sioux trickster, Iktomi, the compilation was illustrated by fellow Carlisle teacher Angel De Cora from the Winnebago tribe. All of these public writings appeared under Gertrude's self-given Sioux name, Zitkala Ša, which means "Red Bird." Of her name, she explained that when her mother became disaffected with her father, Felker, she took her brother's surname of Simmons. She reinvented herself by declaring her traditional language.

> My brother's wife—angry with me because I insisted upon getting an education said I had deserted home and I might give up my brother's name "Simmons" too. Well—you can guess how queer I felt away from my own people—home-less—penniless—and even without a name! Then, I choose to make a name for myself—& I guess I have made "Zitkala Ša" Known—for even Italy writes it in her language![13]

Gertrude revealed this information in a letter to Carlos Montezuma, a well-known Yavapai physician who practiced medicine in Chicago. In all likelihood, Gertrude met Montezuma when he visited Carlisle while she was teaching there, and they became engaged after she went to Boston. For over a year they corresponded, and Gertrude's letters were full of emotional intensity. Although she was studying classical music, Gertrude had an intense desire to reclaim her Sioux heritage, and she decided to return to the Yankton Reservation. She implored Montezuma to close his profitable urban practice and join her on the reservation. Montezuma had already endured several miserable experiences in the field, however, and he refused. She angrily broke off the engagement and lost the ring he had given her.

Contributing to Gertrude's distress, Montezuma impugned her honesty and threatened to sue her for the price of the ring. In her emotional reply, she accused him of hypocrisy: "You are neither a follower of Christ nor of Love—as *you* professed." Gertrude asserted her right to equality: "I am proud—fearless and as independent as *you* are. Man that you pose to be. I can walk into the Realm of the Muddy Waters—defying your feeble forces any day." She demanded of him: "Speak to me as I deserve to be spoken to. And I will show you what stuff I am made of. I then would make every effort to satisfy your mercenary demands."[14] This letter reflected little of the reticent "squaw" image so ubiquitous in popular culture at the time. Nor did it embody the Victorian propriety in which Gertrude had been schooled. Instead, she projected self-confidence and insisted on respect and tolerance, demands that became hallmarks of her life.

Gertrude put the unhappy affair behind her. On August 10, 1902, she married Raymond Bonnin, a fellow Yankton Sioux. The following year their only child, a son named Ohiya, was born, and the family took up residence in Utah where they lived from 1903 through 1916. Raymond worked as a clerk for the Indian Bureau on the Uintah-Ouray Reservation; Gertrude worked intermittently, teaching and assisting Ute women with domestic skills. Like Gertrude, Raymond had been educated in boarding schools. Appreciative of the advantages education had brought them, they also valued their Sioux identity and attempted to mediate between the two.

In December 1902, Gertrude published "Why I Am a Pagan" in *The Atlantic Monthly*. In this essay, she privileged traditional Sioux ideals over Christian ideologies, reveling in nature and criticizing Christian practices that conflicted with Native cultures. Her allegiance seemed clear:

> I would not forget that the pale-faced missionary and the hoodooed aborigine are both God's creatures, though small indeed their own conceptions of Infinite Love. A wee child toddling in a wonder world, I prefer to their dogma my excursions into the natural gardens where the voice of the Great Spirit is heard in the twittering of birds, the rippling of mighty waters, and the sweet breathing of flowers.[15]

Within months of the publication of "Why I Am a Pagan," however, Gertrude and Raymond became Catholics. In 1910, she hardly sounded like a "pagan" when she lamented the lack of Christians in Utah in a letter to the Bureau of Catholic Indian Missions:

I long for these Utes to have the opportunity to learn of God as our Catholic Church teaches. I appeal to you in their behalf. The Episcopal Church has been represented here for more than ten years: yet these Utes still continue their Annual dances—"The Bear Dance" in the early spring and the "Sun Dance" the first of July.

Sunday is not observed by the Indians, for it is usually a Dance day. I firmly believe only the Catholic Church can reach these benighted Utes.[16]

A few years later, Gertrude was a practicing Mormon, and she ultimately had a Mormon funeral in Arlington, Virginia, but not before she had spent several years involved with Christian Science.

Gertrude's religious perambulations provide us with a rare glimpse into her Yankton consciousness. Her education in boarding school and estrangement from kin may have muted that consciousness, but her response to religion implied deeply embedded attitudes. Unlike Christianity, Native religions were not generally exclusive. Indeed, they welcomed additional sources of spiritual power. Instead of standing in opposition to her "paganism," Christian doctrines simply became additional layers of beliefs that her Sioux worldview enabled her to mediate. Consequently, Gertrude felt no need to reject Christianity totally in favor of "paganism" or to belong exclusively to one Christian denomination; her spiritual world had room for all. She exhibited this inclusiveness in 1921 when she collected the periodical articles she had written at the turn of the century into an anthology, *American Indian Stories*. For this volume, she retitled "Why I Am a Pagan" as "The Great Spirit," thus mitigating the diametrical opposition of "paganism" and Christianity implicit in the original title.

In rural Utah Gertrude and Raymond met and befriended a young music teacher, William F. Hanson. The popularity of Wild West shows, Indian cultural performances at fairs, and local Mormon pageants led Gertrude and Hanson to decide to compose an opera with an Indian theme. First they considered the life of Chipeta, widow of Ute leader Ouray, as the plot for the opera. But after seeing the Utes' Sun Dance, in which participants sought spiritual purity through self-sacrifice, they settled on that subject.

Their selection of the traditional Sun Dance for public performance was somewhat bizarre. At this time, the federal government, as part of its drive to assimilate Indians, had forbidden many indigenous religious dances and practices, particularly the Sun Dance. Furthermore, this subject presented problems for many Native people who regarded the public revelation of sacred practices as a sacrilege. The composers attempted to alleviate these concerns by focusing on an intertribal love triangle set against Sioux ritual practices rather than on the Sun Dance itself. The Sioux hero, Ohiya, vows to win the love of Winona over his rival, the evil Shoshone, Sweet Singer.

Complicating the cultural dimensions of the opera were the questions of Gertrude's familiarity with the Sun Dance and the role of Native people in the opera's production. Of all the groups in the Sioux nation, only the Yankton did not practice the Sun Dance, which meant that Gertrude had no personal tribal knowledge of the ritual. Gertrude and Hanson insisted on the cultural validity and accuracy of the opera, however, and they cited the authenticity of the Sioux melodies in arias, which Gertrude had first played for Hanson on her violin, as well as the use of the Sioux wedding flute that Raymond had given Gertrude. The marginalization of Indian culture carried over from the script and score to the performance. Classically trained, non-Native performers played the primary roles. At various times, the opera paused for traditional songs and dances performed by local Utes and led by a Sioux centenarian, known as "Old Sioux" and "Bad Hand," who lived with the Bonnins.

Equally problematic was Hanson's colonial role in the composition and production of the opera. A non-Indian, Hanson appropriated a sacred ceremony for his own use. By removing the Sun Dance from its cultural context—which certainly was not a love triangle—he distorted its purpose and demeaned its significance, about which Gertrude may have been unclear. In 1935 Hanson revived the opera at Brigham Young University, and his former associate, John Hand, who had become director of the New York Opera Guild, chose *The Sun Dance Opera* for performance in spring of 1938 as opera of the year. Hanson claimed the opera as his own and simply acknowledged Zitkala Ša's collaboration in the program notes. The revival received poor critical notices; Gertrude apparently had no involvement and died before the New York performances.

The Sun Dance Opera, as well as her essay "Why I Am a Pagan," revealed many of the cultural conflicts Gertrude played out in her life. Often she seemed caught between validating her indigenous beliefs and seeking public approval. Such a position is not always oppositional, but part of the complex mediation in which all Native peoples engage in order to survive in the twentieth century. In the next phase of Gertrude's life, she seemed even farther removed from her tribal origins, yet her public role became more entrenched in an aboriginal persona as she worked tirelessly "for the Indian cause."

In 1913 Gertrude reconnected with Carlos Montezuma. He had been a primary organizer of the Society of American Indians, a political, pan-Indian group founded in 1911. The membership of the society included Indian professionals, like Dr. Charles Eastman (Sioux) and Reverend Sherman Coolidge (Arapaho), who had endured the boarding school experience. As well-educated Native people who spoke English fluently, members of the society chafed at the prejudice and discrimination they encountered in the dominant white society. Seeking an end to Indians' second-class status, the society promoted Indian education and advocated U.S. citizenship for Native Americans. Many members of the society also opposed the Bureau of Indian Affairs (BIA), which they believed kept Indians in a subordinate state of pupilage by supervising most aspects of their lives from child rearing to administering their trust funds. Given the opportunity, Indians could manage their own affairs and improve themselves without government bureaucracy. In Utah Gertrude did fieldwork for the society by teaching homemaking skills to the Utes. After reporting details and budgetary accounts, she concluded:

> Our Community Center work is non-sectarian and non-partisan. For this reason we are in a position to lend unobtrusively, very beneficial aid toward uniting and welding together the earnest endeavors of various groups of educators and missionaries.
>
> Our chief thought is co-operation with all constructive uplift work for humanity. Therefore, in our attempt to do our very duty to our race, we [do] so with a full appreciation of all kindnesses and gratitude for all that good people have done and are still doing in behalf of our race.[17]

Gertrude intentionally did not mention BIA programs in this summary. Only U.S. citizenship and autonomy from government programs, she believed, offered protection of both individual and tribal rights.

Gertrude attended the national conferences of the society, joined the advisory board in 1914, and in 1916 became its secretary. As an officer of the national organization, Gertrude felt compelled to relocate to the society's headquarters, so she and Raymond moved to Washington, D.C. As secretary, she edited and contributed articles to the Society's publication, the *American Indian Magazine*.

In her new public political career, Gertrude immediately took up the cause of Indian citizenship. Ten thousand Indian servicemen had fought for the United States in World War I although they were not American citizens. These soldiers included Raymond Bonnin, who achieved the rank of captain. Gertrude editorialized about their contributions to the war effort:

> The black night of world war has served to bring out the brilliant stars of Indian bravery and heroism. . . . Now in demobilization, our Indians in khaki do not lay aside with their military uniforms these telling

qualities of heroism which have won so much "undistinguished collective acclaim." They continue to be clothed with that divine courage which some have called "Indian stoicism;" and in their company we realize that each and every one of us possess the attributes of heroism, as our divine heritage![18]

The society's campaign ultimately succeeded in 1924 when Congress extended citizenship to Native Americans.

As editor of the *American Indian Magazine,* Gertrude addressed issues such as education, treaty rights, and land claims on which members agreed, but also some that were controversial within the society, like the use of peyote. Gertrude vehemently opposed peyote, a mild hallucinogen that many Native people ingested in their quest for spiritual understanding and power. Her stance brought her into an unusual alliance with her former adversary, Colonel Pratt, but placed her in opposition to many defenders of Native sovereignty as well as several prominent cultural anthropologists.

Gertrude used the *American Indian Magazine* as a forum to promote her views on peyote. In one article, she recounted her visit with Chipeta, the widow of Ouray. She had heard that Chipeta and her brother "had been deceived into the use of a dangerous drug and that they were being fleeced by the mercenary traffickers in peyote buttons." Gertrude vividly described to the elderly woman "the inevitable degeneration that follows the habitual and indiscriminate use of narcotics." Chipeta replied that "peyote eased her brother's rheumatism and hers," but she admitted, "I have noticed that the pains return when I stop the use of the drug."

Gertrude believed that peyote prevented Native people from paying proper attention to education and religion because it clouded their minds; "in their abnormal condition," drug users were "helplessly unable" to learn. Gertrude's views on peyote mirrored the attitudes of many white reformers, and she linked her campaign against peyote to the struggle of the National Women's Christian Temperance Union and Federated Women's Club against drugs and alcohol. Such substances presumably corrupted industrious citizens and jeopardized the nation. Therefore, reformers believed, the federal government had a responsibility to take action, a sentiment that led to a constitutional amendment prohibiting alcohol in 1920 and a series of federal laws banning marijuana and other drugs. Gertrude pointed to that course of action: "What do civilized communities do with their drug victims? Do not they legislate for the protection of society and for the protection of the drug user?" She urged the federal government to protect Indians in a similar fashion:

> A great longing filled me for some message from the Great White Father telling his red children that peyote was bad for them and asking them to refuse to use or sell it. Federal action is needed. Chief Ouray, friend of the white man, would that your old friends might befriend your aged widow and the people whom you loved. Would that federal action might be taken before it is too late.[19]

The antipeyote campaign posited Gertrude against fundamental tribal and civil rights. Her appeal to the federal government for a ban compromised both tribal sovereignty, that is, the power of tribes to regulate the activities of its members, and freedom of religion, guaranteed to non-Indians under the U.S. Bill of Rights.

Gertrude opposed peyote on religious as well as social grounds. During testimony to the House of Representatives' Subcommittee on Indian Affairs in February 1918, she recounted tales of sexual excess and suicide as a result of peyote use among the Utes. She testified that she was a Christian and that her Christianity was the basis for her fervent opposition to peyote. Despite the urging of many Indian agents and reformers, the federal government declined to enact an outright ban on peyote. This refusal offered protection to the newly chartered Native American Church, a fusion of Christianity and peyote, when the state of Oklahoma outlawed its use. Nevertheless, some tribal governments, whose actions took precedence over the Bill of Rights, did heed the warnings and make peyote illegal.[20]

The Society of American Indians was a pan-Indian organization, but the Native people who belonged to it did not always reach consensus. Some issues like peyote use and the role of the BIA deeply divided them. Furthermore, tribal allegiances sometimes had divisive effects, and elections often were bitterly contested. At the eighth annual conference in 1919, Raymond ran unsuccessfully for president of the society, and after his defeat, Gertrude resigned her position. By 1920, the influence of the Society of American Indians had diminished, largely because of internal disputes rather than the Bonnins' departure, and the group eventually disbanded.

The Society of American Indians was not the only organization committed to Indian welfare in which Gertrude was involved. When it served her purpose, she allied with the Indian Rights Association, founded in 1882, and the Lake Mohonk conferences, started in 1893. These organizations, made up largely of non-Indians, focused on assimilation. They regarded the communal landholdings of Indian tribes to be an impediment to assimilation, and they advocated allotment, the assignment of tracts of land to individual owners, and the extension of state laws over Native people, which essentially ended Indian tribal governments. They accomplished their goals with Congressional enactment of the Dawes Act in 1887 and the Curtis Act in 1898.

Allotment was a disaster for most Native people, as Gertrude learned first-hand during a trip to Oklahoma. Following allotment, oil was discovered in Oklahoma on Indian land, and unscrupulous people preyed upon Indians for their oil riches.[21] Gertrude accompanied representatives of the Indian Rights Association and the American Indian Defense Association to Oklahoma where they examined the conditions that these frauds had created among the Osage, Cherokee, Chickasaw, Choctaw, Creek, and Seminole tribes. The investigation revealed rampant corruption, demonstrated the failure of federal policies, and precipitated a change.

In 1926 Gertrude and Raymond organized the National Council of American Indians (NCAI), a pan-tribal group that lobbied Congress on Indian issues. Gertrude served as president and Raymond as secretary/treasurer. The NCAI claimed to be the only Indian welfare organization comprised solely of Indians. During the summers, Gertrude and Raymond traveled west among various Indian peoples, and when they returned to Washington, they presented the concerns of the people they had visited to NCAI members. To keep in touch with Indians who joined the council, Gertrude sent out newsletters encouraging activism. In one of these, she described the nature of the United States government to Native people who had been citizens for only a few years:

> "THE GOVERNMENT OF THE UNITED STATES IS NOT IN ANY SENSE FOUNDED ON THE CHRISTIAN RELIGION." are words of George Washington, our first President of the United States. The government is founded upon the Constitution of the United States. Don't let yourself be confused between the two. One says "THOU SHALT NOT KILL." The other provides for MAKING WARS. Religion deals with Spiritual Laws; Government deals with man-made laws.

She explained how these new citizens could play a role in making laws, and she urged her readers to participate actively in the national government:

> Citizen Indians, Get busy. Citizens owe it to their Senators and Representatives to inform them of desirable [sic] legislation. Since Congressmen are not mind readers WRITE LETTERS to them. There is no-law prohibiting Indians against writing letters. . . . You have a mind, a heart and a life. Make USE of them daily. Our stay on Earth is short, after all. Make use of life wherever you are. *ACT!!*[22]

The activism Gertrude encouraged was true to her own credo. However, Gertrude's intense personality often led to conflicts. In 1928 the NCAI shared offices with the American Indian Defense Association, and disagreements led to her running battle with that organization's secretary, John Collier.

In 1933 Franklin D. Roosevelt appointed Collier commissioner of Indian affairs. Collier wanted to promote the tribal governments and communal values that previous federal policy had tried to subvert. Following his lead, Congress in 1934 passed the Wheeler Howard/Indian Reorganization Act, the basis of what has become known as the Indian New Deal. This legislation ended allotment and provided for the incorporation of tribes and the establishment of constitutional governments. Gertrude and Raymond opposed both Collier and the legislation, which they regarded as "eating the very vitals out of the future."[23]

In 1935 the Bonnins embarked on a road trip to encourage tribes to organize their own governing structures independent of the Wheeler Howard Act. When Gertrude and Raymond arrived at the Yankton Reservation, they were disappointed by the Yanktons' reluctance to accept their views of the Wheeler Howard Act, and they blamed unfair BIA tactics:

> Discussion of the WHA was the main subject. Bureau employed men under the direction of Supt Robert, is driving night & day in car & gas [is] Govt furnished—crowding the Inds. to accept the Charter & byLaws drawn up by the Bureau. Employees, not lawyers, got up before assembled Inds & grossly misconstrued the WH act.

Gertrude lamented her fellow Yanktons' lack of respect for her broad experience: "I mentioned [that] I too [was] a little reinvested in [the] tribe thru my work & now I am excluded."[24] The exclusion and frustrations Gertrude felt were part of the price she paid for her early removal from tribal society and her education in the non-Indian world. She had sacrificed her tribal, communal self to the larger purposes of Indians in American society.

Gertrude spent the last few years of her life in poverty and despair. The Bonnins' son, Ohiya, was diabetic, in poor health, and unable to care for his own children. The two older grandchildren came to live with the Bonnins in Virginia. In the spring of 1937, Ohiya's poor health brought him, his wife, and their other two children to live with the family as well. Ohiya unsuccessfully looked for employment. Raymond, who had legal education but was never formally admitted to the bar, worked to secure contracts to represent Western tribes in Washington. The Bonnins' debts mounted, and Gertrude's health began to decline. She died on January 25, 1938, and was buried, as the wife of a veteran, in Arlington National Cemetery. Raymond died in 1942 and was buried next to her. They have no known living direct descendants.

Gertrude Simmons Bonnin led a complex life at a crucial time for American Indians in this country. Her early writings recounted the injustices of assimilative practices. Gaining the attention of reformers with her eloquence and passion, she ultimately came to advocate many aspects of assimilation. Assimilation for her did not mean that she became less Indian. When that eight-year-old left the reservation for boarding school, she began a process in which her tribal self—her identity as a Yankton Sioux—became subsumed by a broader identity as Indian. She used the skills she had learned in the non-Indian world to fight for Indian rights, a commitment that stemmed from her memories of those long ago days on the plains. She remained, as she always signed her letters, "yours for the Indian cause."

NOTES

1. Zitkala Ša, *American Indian Stories* (Washington, D.C.: Hayworth Publishing House, 1921; Lincoln: University of Nebraska Press, 1985), 8. Other studies of Zitkala Ša include Susan Bernardin, "The Lessons of a Sentimental Education: Zitkala Ša's Autobiographical Narratives," *Western American Literature* 32 (1997): 121–39; Martha J. Cutter, "Zitkala Ša's Autobiographical Writings: The Problems of a Canonical Search for Language and Identity," *MELUS* 19 (1994): 31–45; Diana Vanessa Holford, "'Hanging in the Heart of Chaos': Bi-Cultural Limbo, Self-(Re)presentation, and the White Audience in Zitkala Ša's *American Indian Stories*," *Cimarron Review* 121 (1997): 154–73; Dexter Fisher, "Zitkala Ša: The Evolution of a Writer," *American Indian Quarterly* 5 (1979): 229–38; P. Jane Hafen, "Zitkala Ša: Sentimentality and Sovereignty," *Wicazo Ša Review* 12 (1997): 31–42, and Hafen, "A Cultural Duet: Zitkala Ša and the Sun Dance Opera," *Great Plains Quarterly* 18 (1998): 102–11; Doreen Rappaport, *The Flight of Red Bird: The Life of Zitkala Ša* (New York: Dial Books, 1997); Jeanne Smith, "'A Second Tongue': The Trickster's Voice in the Works of Zitkala Ša," in *Tricksterism in Turn-of-the-Century American Literature: A Multicultural Perspective*, ed. Elizabeth Ammons and Annette White-Parks (Hanover, NH: University Press of New England, 1994), 46–60; Ruth Spack, "Revisioning American Indian Women: Zitkala Ša's Revolutionary *American Indian Stories*," *Legacy* 14 (1997): 25–43; Mary Stout, "Zitkala Ša," in *Handbook of Native American Literature*, ed. Andrew Wiget (New York: Garland Publishing, 1996), 303–6.

2. *American Indian Stories*, 41–42.

3. Ibid., 15.

4. Judith Nies, *Native American History* (New York: Ballantine Books, 1996), 291.

5. *American Indian Stories*, 55–56.

6. Ibid., 67.

7. While "squaw" was common usage in Gertrude's era for a female Native, currently it is considered derogatory by many because of its etymology as a vulgar term of Algonquian origin for female genitalia.

8. *American Indian Stories*, 79.

9. *The Earlhamite* 2.12 (16 Mar 1896): 179.

10. Ibid., 79.

11. *American Indian Stories*, 97–98.

12. Zitkala Ša, *Old Indian Legends* (Boston: Ginn and Co., 1901; reprint Lincoln: University of Nebraska Press, 1985).

13. Letter to Carlos Montezuma, June–July 1901, Carlos Montezuma Papers, Division of Archives and Manuscripts, State of Wisconsin.

14. Letter to Carlos Montezuma, 10 July 1902.

15. *American Indian Stories*, 107.

16. Letter to Father W. H. Ketchum, May 25, 1910, Archive Collection, Bureau of Catholic Indian Missions, Marquette University, Milwaukee Wisconsin.

17. *American Indian Magazine* 4 (1916): 310.

18. *American Indian Magazine* 7 (1919): 62–63.

19. *American Indian Magazine* 5 (1917): 168–70.

20. Because they retain sovereignty, tribal governments take precedence over the Bill of Rights. See John Wunder, *"Retained by the People": A History of American Indians and the Bill of Rights* (New York: Oxford University Press, 1994), 85.

21, For a fictionalization based on fact, see Linda Hogan, *Mean Spirit* (New York: Atheneum Books, 1990).

22. National Council of American Indians, *Newsletter*, 22 Feb. 1932.

23. Gertrude Simmons Bonnin Diary, Special Collections, Brigham Young University, Provo, Utah.

24. Ibid.

9

LUCY NICOLAR

The Artful Activism of a Penobscot Performer

Bunny McBride

Lucy Nicolar always had more than her share of self-confidence. In January 1900, the seventeen-year-old Penobscot Indian from Maine visited the Women's Debating Society in New York City. At the end of a lively discussion about immigration, the debaters resolved that it was "dangerous and threatening to all true Americans." According to a journalist who wrote about the event, Lucy—also known as Princess Watahwaso—took their conclusion as her cue:

> She arose to speak, her stately form commanding instant recognition. . . . "I believe I am the only true American here. I think you have decided rightly. Of all my forefathers' country, from the St. John [River] to the Connecticut, we have now but a little island one-half-mile square. There are only about 500 of us now. We are very happy on our island, but we are poor. The railroad corporations, which did their share of robbing us of our land, are now begrudging us half-rate fare. But we forgive you all." There was a long silence, and the subject was laid on the table. The president said that the musical feature would have to be omitted as the pianist was sick, and "would someone please volunteer?" No one had the courage to try an impromptu before that large audience. At last who should beg to be allowed to try but Wah-Ta-Waso, who played some selections from Chopin with the greatest ease and sang a plaintive air which touched the hearts of all those present and made them feel like doing anything in the world for her.[1]

Such juxtapositions of art and politics were the hallmark of Lucy Nicolar's life as an Indian entertainer and activist. Time and time again, she used artistry as a means to a political end—to win public school access for Penobscot children, to convince the state to build a bridge linking her island reservation to the mainland, to gain voting rights for her tribe. Moreover, she used it to squelch public assumptions that Indian cultures should and would melt into mainstream society. In 1942, her artful activism prompted one local journalist to write, "It is a recognized fact that, wherever any move is afoot on the reservation for public betterment, Princess Watawaso, well known Penobscot singer and actress, is involved somewhere."[2] Lucy's life story is fascinating in and of itself, but in a larger sense, it is a bold-faced example of how Native women responded to turn-of-the-century socioeconomic challenges and opportunities. It helps us understand why American Indians and "Indianness" have survived despite relentless pressures of assimilation.

Lucy Nicolar's life began June 22, 1882, on Indian Island, 315 acres of reservation land lying in the Penobscot River opposite Old Town, Maine. In the century leading up to her birth, Penobscot territory had been whittled down from hundreds of thousands of acres to just 140 small islands in the thirty-mile stretch of river between Old Town and Mattawamkeag. Hunting, the mainstay of her forefathers, had diminished greatly due to new game laws, the destruction of forests, competition from white hunters (settlers and lumber crews), and declining fur markets. Pressed by these changes, Penobscots sought other livelihoods. Most, anxious to retain a measure of their traditional liberty, avoided the miserable confines of factory jobs requiring long hours for paltry wages. Some acquiesced to farming small plots, which yielded crop bounties paid by a government hoping to settle and assimilate the Native population. Many younger men labored seasonally as river drivers. Both men and women made the moosehide moccasins used in logging camps and the sturdy woodsplint baskets that settlers needed for harvesting and household storage.

But, more than anything else, nineteenth-century Penobscots began to capitalize on mainstream society's romantic fascination with primitive naturalism, largely a reaction to industrialization. Coupled with society's "ambivalent racism," this fascination created a ready audience for Indians willing to act out cliché versions of tribal traditions, prompting a handful of Penobscot men and women to become entertainers in vaudeville and medicine shows.[3] As the naturalist ideal lured summer tourists and sport hunters to Maine, quite a few Penobscot men became hunting and fishing guides, and many women began making fancy woodsplint and sweetgrass baskets designed specifically to suit the Victorian tastes of well-to-do visitors. Usually, men cut the ash trees and transformed them into weavable splints, and women gathered the sweet-grass and wove the baskets. Men and women alike ventured to Maine's coastal resorts to market their wares.

By the time Lucy was born, Penobscot women had stepped forward as major cash earners by producing and selling crafts and in a few cases performing in road shows. This was a striking shift. Traditionally, women in Maine's several tribal groups (collectively known as the Wabanaki) had significant roles in the economic well-being of their communities, but little power beyond the domestic sphere. Their expanding sphere of influence is evident in the fact that by 1900 two-thirds of the households on Indian Island depended on the sale of baskets as their primary source of income—and women were the major makers and marketers of the craft.

Lucy, along with her older sister Emma and her younger sister Florence, landed in the arms of remarkable parents. Their father, Joseph Nicolar, was a keen-witted and much-respected man whose reputation reached well beyond the shores of Indian Island. Born to Tomer Nicola and Mary Malt Neptune in 1827, he hailed from a notable line of Penobscots. His maternal grandfather, John Neptune, was one of the most impressive Penobscot chiefs of all time. And his paternal great-grandfather was the famous "Half-Arm" Nicola, who survived the 1724 English attack on the Indian village of Norridgewock—but minus part of a limb. Joseph, intellectually ambitious from childhood, attended school in several Maine towns and was said to have "the best education of all the Indians of his time."[4] At age thirty-one he served his first term as tribal representative to the state legislature, an elected position he won more often than any other Penobscot. People on and off the reservation referred to him as the lawyer of the tribe. They also called him the tribe's scribe, for he wrote newspaper articles about Penobscots and authored a book, *The Life and Traditions of the Red Man*, published in 1893. A handsome and compelling speaker, Joseph frequently received invitations to lecture about Penobscot life. In addition, he did a bit of land surveying and proved highly successful at farming. For a while, he served as the tribe's state-appointed superintendent of farming. Moreover, like most Penobscot men of his day, Joseph hunted and fished "for the pot" and helped market baskets made by his wife and daughters. Lucy saw him as "the grandest man who ever lived."[5]

Lucy's mother, Elizabeth Josephs Nicolar, was twenty-one years younger than her husband. Described by a local newspaper as "respected," "intelligent," and "superior in many ways," Lizzie was considered "a power for good" in "all the doings" of her people.[6] As skilled at public relations as she was at basketry, she traveled throughout New England to market her craft. A born leader, she

organized social and charitable events on the reservation. In 1895 she helped
found the Wabanaki Woman's Club of Indian Island, which gained membership in the State Federation of Women's Clubs in 1897. As the club's first vice
president, she played a key role in its mission "to collect and preserve the history and legends of the aboriginal inhabitants of Maine and to establish an
industrial union to which each member shall contribute her own work, the sale
of which shall form a fund to be used as the society directs."[7] Lizzie, as much as
Joseph, was a role model for Lucy.

Lucy and her family lived on the southeast side of the island in a comfortable, two-story house with clapboard siding and a mansard roof. Home life
centered on the big wood stove in the kitchen, where the heady odor of pipe
tobacco smoke mingled with the tempting smell of roasting venison and the
sweet scent of grass and ash strips used for basketmaking. Lizzie knew how to
weave an array of baskets and passed the skill on to her three daughters. They
participated in sweetgrass braiding parties with other women and girls on the
island, and each summer they traveled by train to the coastal resort town of
Kennebunkport where they set up camp and sold their wares. Basketmaking
demonstrations helped promote sales, as did dressing in Indian garb and having the children perform for tourists. Even as a child, Lucy was always eager to
offer a dance or a song. When she realized that customers especially enjoyed
her singing, she began charging a nickel for a song.

As an economic mainstay, baskets figured in many aspects of Penobscot
life. When a family hit upon hard times, women got together to weave a batch
of salable baskets to help the family get by. The sale of donated baskets also
financed church renovations. And every year Penobscots celebrated May Day
by decorating each other's doors with beautiful May baskets. At home and in
the public eye, baskets became a symbol for Penobscot culture; as they gained
prominence, so did the women who made them.

In Lucy's youth, impromptu house concerts were common at parties and
sweetgrass braiding get-togethers. Many Penobscots played musical instruments
and sang traditional Penobscot music, as well as a variety of Western music
picked up in lumber camps and taught at the Catholic mission school on the
island. Often, they played for events at the reservation's community hall, such
as minstrel shows, dramatic presentations, and lectures. At least once a year,
Penobscots invited folks from the mainland to a grand ball or a big wedding
dance, where island musicians played a musical potpourri.

Across the river, a parade of entertainers passed through the white settlement of Old Town during the summer months of Lucy's childhood. Circuses
and menageries remained popular, vaudeville shows were on the rise, and at

least one Indian medicine show came to town each year. A variety of other entertainments appeared year-round at Old Town City Hall, and in 1892 Lucy's father hired the hall with fellow tribesman Frank Loring for a performance of Penobscot customs. The event, which Lucy surely saw, is of special note. Loring, a celebrated showman known as "Big Thunder," had left Indian Island as a boy in the 1830s, looking for work. After a stint with the great P. T. Barnum, he spent half a century producing, directing, and acting in "Indian entertainments" throughout New England. His life echoed that of many other Indians who, in the course of the nineteenth century, resorted to commodifying their cultures to make a living. Despite a life on the road, Loring was never a stranger to Indian Island, and in 1890 he settled there as a sort of entertainer-in-residence. He maintained a small museum, marked by a birchbark sign that read: "Big Thunder, Indian Relics and Traditions Told." And he lived out an old friendship— and slight rivalry—with his contemporary Joseph Nicolar.[8] In their twilight years, both men still commanded attention—Nicolar as a dignified presence accustomed to writing seriously about Penobscot traditions and speaking on behalf of his people in the halls of state government; and Loring as a seasoned entertainer who could package any tradition and bring it to life for public consumption. Their joint City Hall performance, described in the local paper, showcased their contrasting skills and personalities: "Mr. Nicolar" gave an "articulate" lecture, and "Big Thunder" quickened everyone's pulse with his "very amusing" enactment of Indian customs.[9] We can assume Lucy's father appeared in a suit and tie, while Loring donned an Indian costume, including his signature ostrich plume headdress. In the years that followed, echoes of that evening resounded in Lucy's performances as she gave audiences something between the decorum of her father and the flamboyance of Big Thunder.

At age fourteen, three years after her father's death in 1894, Lucy determined to become the first girl from her reservation to attend high school in Old Town. A zealous student, she had attended primary school with the Sisters of Mercy, who founded the school on Indian Island in 1878. Along with the three R's and catechism, the nuns taught music—piano playing and singing, in particular—and the children performed in school concerts tied to religious holidays. Making the leap from the reservation school to the high school required special preparation, and Lucy worked diligently with a tutor to catch up to her peers on the mainland.

The nuns and Lucy's father may have been the force behind her early formal education, but her mother provided her and her sisters with practical knowledge, making sure they knew how to make baskets and market them in sophisticated ways. Under her tutelage, the girls graduated from entertainers of tourists

at their summer basket stand in Kennebunkport to participants in major sports-
men's shows from Boston to New York to Baltimore. These grand exhibits touted
the pleasures of "rusticating"—the special sort of tourism for which Maine had
become famous—and featured displays that promoted wilderness equipment.
No show was complete without an Indian encampment to conjure up romantic images of life in the wilderness. And no encampment was complete without a cast of real Indians. Lizzie and her daughters spent many days at such
sites, making and selling baskets and snowshoes. Some showcases featured a
miniature lake where visitors could enjoy being paddled about in a canoe by
lovely Indian maidens. To these events Lucy brought a rare flair, born of natural beauty and charisma enhanced by a mix of traditional and formal education. She had "black snapping eyes—so bright and dark that you couldn't see
the pupils."[10] Those eyes, her flow of sable hair, and her lively engaging personality began to captivate journalists. At age fourteen she appeared in an
article titled "Belle of the Penobscots." It included two full-length portraits of
her—one depicting her wearing an "Indian costume" and holding a rifle Annie
Oakley–style, the other showing her dressed in modern clothing and comman-
deering a bicycle. The text read, in part:

> Lucy is a young miss of marked beauty, and wherever she goes with
> baskets or Indian exhibits, many a young American who looks upon
> the Indian maiden feels that the land of the Penobscots must be "the
> land of handsome women." Just now Lucy is receiving private instruc-
> tions that she may enter Oldtown High School. Her instructor tells me
> that she is bright in her studies and that mathematics is her forte. Lucy
> is perhaps the most proficient piano player on the island, being the
> owner of an instrument. She also sings pleasantly. But the skill of the
> tribe is not forgotten by this young member, for she can make baskets,
> etc. etc., as well as some of the older ones.[11]

Among those charmed by Lucy was Montague Chamberlain, an administrator at Harvard College. A naturalist by avocation, Chamberlain had a keen
interest in the traditions of American Indians, especially Lucy's people, because
a Penobscot had saved his grandfather's life. After his first visits to Indian Island in 1897, he wrote a sympathetic article about contemporary Penobscot
life for the *Cambridge Tribune*.[12] Becoming an advocate for the education of
young Penobscots, he gathered books and funds to set up a library on the reservation, hosted picnics and sports competitions for youngsters, and sought
scholarships and other educational opportunities for them. Lucy met Chamberlain while preparing for high school on the mainland, and by 1899 she had

moved into his household in Boston. With his help she received the best in educational and musical advantages. Chamberlain also offered Lucy on-the-job training by hiring her as an assistant. His Harvard connections opened doors for her in Boston and New York; and when she walked through those doors, people took notice. While showing herself to be comfortable with the manners of white society's cultural elite, she played into their romantic notions of what it meant to be Indian and began introducing herself as "Princess Watahwaso," ("Bright Star"). By 1900, as one journalist noted, "Wah-Ta-Waso, an educated and refined girl, is often the pet of New York society."[13]

Around 1901 Chamberlain left Harvard and became an accountant. Lucy continued working for him, bragging that she was better at numbers than he was. At age twenty-three, she married a wealthy Boston doctor and later moved to Washington, D.C., with him. Little is known about this marriage, but in 1913 Lucy turned thirty-one, divorced her first husband, and moved to Chicago, where she began to study advanced piano at the Music School of Chautauqua. By then she had developed a concert program of Indian songs, legends, and dances, and she had performed for various audiences at schools, women's clubs, and benefits. But a man named Tom Gorman had a bigger vision for her talents. A lawyer whose real calling was theater, Gorman offered to become Lucy's manager—and her husband. She said yes to both. Before long, successful bookings in numerous midwestern cities led to a contract with the Redpath Lyceum Bureau as a performer on its prestigious Chautauqua Circuit.

This entertainment circuit had its roots in two popular forms of nineteenth-century adult education: lyceums and Chautauquas. Lyceums, which in the United States date back to the 1820s, were institutions that organized weekly lectures, debates, and other secular educational events. Chautauquas sprang from a summer camp for religious teachers founded in 1874 on the shores of Lake Chautauqua in New York. Aiming to keep participants alert, camp founders punctuated religious classes with recreational activities, musical offerings, and lectures by authors, explorers, and political leaders. The concept spread swiftly. Soon, hundreds of communities nationwide offered such programs of "constructive entertainments," usually combining local talent with features acquired through lyceum bureaus.[14]

The standard-bearer among lyceums was the Redpath Bureau, and when Lucy stepped into the Bureau's Chicago office, its director recognized the Penobscot princess as "a find."[15] Her first contract with Redpath marked out a thirty-week tour at a fine salary: $75 per week in 1917, with a possible renewal at $112.50 the following year and $150 the year thereafter. Her performances were memorable. Forty years after seeing her onstage as part of the "Deluxe Seven Day Circuit," the bureau's former treasurer wrote: "As the days went on the programs became even better. The fourth night opened with The Spanish cellist, followed by beautiful and aristocratic Princess Watahwaso. She Was a full-blooded Penobscot Indian from Maine, 'flower of one of the last pure Indian families,' the program said. She sang tribal songs, told tribal legends, and danced in tribal costumes, including a feathered war bonnet."[16] Circuit itineraries were grueling, with shows in nearly thirty towns a month. Lucy selected her own accompanists and often appeared with composer-pianist Thurlow Lieurance, noted for transcribing and recording Indian melodies, chants, songs, and prayers. It is a measure of Lucy's stature that she earned $15 more per week than he did.

Like other Indian performers, Lucy succeeded, in part, because she played into popular notions of romantic exoticism.[17] She did not really have a choice, but she knew exactly what she was doing, and therein lay her strength. Seeing herself as an ambassador for all American Indians, she pointed out distinguishing aspects of the songs, legends, and dances of the various tribes represented in her program. But she also adjusted her presentations to suit popular taste, aware that Chautauqua's white audiences were curious about other cultures, but would not tolerate anyone who challenged their "civilized" biases. Bicultural and broadly educated, the Indian princess from Maine was both alluring and safe to circuit crowds. She fulfilled the noble savage ideal dictated by popular stereotypes of the day, while making it clear that she was well versed in the cultural etiquette of her hosts.

Lucy joined Redpath as a self-assured and accomplished woman, and her work with the bureau made her all the more so. She shared the bill with a rotating cast of celebrated opera singers and illustrious speakers. Women supplied at least half of the talent in the circuit, and they must have been emboldened seeing one another crisscross the country hauling luggage, dealing with strangers, and negotiating all the details and difficulties of life on the road. Since its inception in 1868, the bureau had gained a reputation for booking lecturers whose views matched the liberal opinions of its founder, James Redpath. They included women's rights advocates such as Susan B. Anthony and Elizabeth Cady Stanton. The tradition continued with the bureau's Chautauqua Circuit, which featured such leading suffragists as Carrie Chapman Catt and Anna Howard Shaw. Indeed, the fight for women's rights waxed eloquent and passionate in Chautauqua tents. This was especially true during Lucy's 1917–19 stint with the circuit, which marked the final run toward the passage of the nineteenth amendment. Typically, local women raised a suffrage tent within a stone's throw of the Chautauqua tent and thrust literature into the hands of every passerby.[18] Their demands resonated loudly with Lucy, for American Indians had neither citizenship nor the right to vote. In the years ahead she would become one of the strongest advocates for correcting these injustices.

Lucy left the Redpath Circuit in the spring of 1919 just before her thirty-seventh birthday. She and Tom moved to New York City, where he set up an office in the Hippodrome and worked as a liaison between entertainers and top vaudeville houses. Lucy, preparing for a recording contract, took classes at a voice studio, where she befriended opera celebrities Rosa Ponselle and Anna FitzHugh. A year later, both divas attended Lucy's debut at Aeolian Hall. Billed as a "song recital in costume" by the "Indian Mezzo-soprano Princess Watahwaso," the concert featured an Italian aria and a variety of Indian songs adapted by Thurlow Lieruance and other noted composers. It was timed to coincide with the release of several Victor Record Company recordings of Lucy singing Lieruance's compositions, including "By the Waters of Minnetonka" (her most popular recording) and "By the Weeping Waters" (her favorite). After the concert, the company sent Lucy on a nationwide promotional tour.[19]

In June 1921 Lucy went home to participate in a big celebration on Indian Island, an event that foreshadowed the great pageants she would help organize in years to come. Penobscot spokesman Newell Francis told the *Lewiston Evening Journal* that his tribe staged the event "to renew old times and customs so the ways of our fathers will not be forgotten by our children." Some 2,000 visitors flocked to the gathering, which featured traditional dance performances and canoe races and foot races, as well as displays of tribal "treasures that had been passed down through the generations." The Penobscot band, dressed in beads and feathers, played much of the day, and in the afternoon Lucy gave one of her grand solo "entertainments" for the crowd.[20]

During the 1920s, Lucy performed on numerous vaudeville circuits, no doubt booked by Tom. Now in her forties, she gathered up younger Indian performers and took them on the road. In 1927 she organized a troupe that included herself, Penobscot dancer Molly Spotted Elk (embarking on her own road to fame), and five other budding performers—a Comanche, Onondaga, Pawnee, and two Kiowas. Setting out on a two-month tour on the renowned Keith-Albee-Orpheum Circuit, they played major theaters in Ohio, Michigan, and New York. Lucy's various numbers included one with Bruce Poolaw, a twenty-four-year-old Kiowa rodeo star from Oklahoma. Promoted as "Chief Poolaw" ("Prairie Wolf"), Bruce sang "Indian Love Call" with Lucy in front of a painted backdrop of a tepee in a forest clearing. This unlikely duet between the Penobscot matron and a cocky young Kiowa proved to be providential.

Lucy and Bruce met earlier in 1927 at one of the Wednesday night dinners she hosted for Indians in New York. According to Bruce's niece Linda Poolaw,

"Everyone had to bring food, and those who didn't had to sing for their meal." Bruce, fresh out of Oklahoma and struggling to get by, sang for his supper along with fellow Kiowa Tommie Little Chief. "They sang some Kiowa song," said Linda, "and it made them so lonesome that tears started rolling down their cheeks. But after that Lucy signed them up and dragged them around" on the vaudeville circuit.[21]

By the end of the decade, vaudeville had fizzled under the weight of the Great Depression and competition from the new "talkies" that superseded silent films. In response, Lucy and Bruce developed a new act for schools, summer camps, and clubs. Crisscrossing the nation by car, they stopped at Indian reservations in their path, picking up Native costumes, props, and ideas. Meanwhile, soon after the Wall Street crash of 1929, Tom Gorman grabbed most of his and Lucy's assets and took off to Mexico.

For Lucy, all roads led home to Indian Island. Since leaving the reservation as a teenager, she had visited at least once a year, even after her mother's death in 1924. Sometimes she came to Maine to perform, and sometimes when she came to see family, she ended up performing. Reports of her return usually made it into Maine newspapers. On June 26, 1930, a page-one headline in the *Old Town Enterprise* announced: "Princess Watawaso, Famous Penobscot Tribe Daughter in Old Town on Visit." The article noted that "the princess" had come home to rest "after an extensive tour of the south and southwest" and announced that she would give a concert in the reservation's community hall "in response to the urgent request of her friends on the island reservation, as well as many others in Old Town and the surrounding vicinity. . . . The princess has done much for the uplift of her people during her public career, both locally and nationally." This visit turned into a permanent move back to the island. By the end of the year Lucy had settled into a new abode next to the ferry landing. Indicative of her worldliness, she had bought a modular house in Chicago and had it shipped by train to Old Town and hauled to the island on a raft.

Soon after Lucy moved into her new house, so did Bruce. Some say their relationship was strictly business; others call it a unique love affair. According to Lucy's grandnephew Robert Anderson, who lived with the couple as a boy from 1935 to 1944, Lucy "went for" Bruce because "she liked young men and she got caught up in that show biz thing." More significantly, they needed each other. Bruce lacked Lucy's formal education, social finesse, and cross-cultural scope, but he could sing and dance and captivate an audience. In short, Lucy educated Bruce and he, in turn, assisted in her shows—driving her from one venue to the next and adding distinct spice to her act.[22]

When Lucy returned to Maine and resettled on Indian Island, she brought with her worldly experience and a reputation that helped her hold her own with the state's movers and shakers, whether politicians, businessmen, or scholars. She had come to a point in her life and a place in the world where she had an opportunity to make a more lasting mark. As she saw it, there was much to do on the home front: Penobscots were in an economic slump, compounded by the Great Depression. The only primary school education option for Penobscot children was the reservation school, which was falling short. Indian Island residents couldn't register to vote in Old Town. And, without a bridge to the mainland, the community was too isolated for its own good. Lucy determined to do something about these problems and allied her efforts with her sister Florence.

Florence had walked a very different path than Lucy. Several years after graduating from Old Town High School at age twenty-two, she had married Leo Shay, a bright, hard-working Penobscot six years her junior. For a time they had lived on the reservation, but in 1923, as their son Bill recalls, they had moved to Connecticut "for economic opportunity and to put us kids in school some place other than with the nuns."[23] By 1930 the Depression had chased them home, and now, for the first time in thirty years, Florence and Lucy both lived on the island.

The sisters brought contrasting strengths to their endeavors. Lucy's flair and fun-loving spirit caught one's eye, and her gift for gab grabbed one's ear. A powerful presence, she could be intimidating to anyone who crossed her. Florence was a quiet but firm presence, a careful thinker more likely to voice her views with pen than tongue. Lucy called her the "tribal scholar."[24] Joining forces with Florence's sister-in-law Pauline Shay, they revived the Wabanaki Woman's Club (cofounded by their mother thirty-five years earlier) and committed themselves to promoting "Indian welfare, education and social progress."[25]

The first item on the women's agenda was state legislation that would give Penobscot parents the option of sending their children to the public schools of Old Town instead of to the reservation's Catholic school. As they saw it, the nuns offered too much catechism and too little standard education. Within a year they achieved victory, but it came at a price: "expulsion" from the church.[26] Consequently, with twice-divorced Lucy leading the way, they set out to establish a Protestant church on the island. After a mighty struggle, they succeeded—becoming Baptists by fire.

Meanwhile, Lucy's entertainment work with Bruce continued. On February 2, 1931, they staged an Indian pageant in the tribe's community hall. Two weeks later they rented Old Town City Hall for a powwow and dance, open to anyone who had the 50-cent entry fee. That summer they went back on the road for engagements at several Maine camps. A journalist caught up with them in Lewiston. As usual, Lucy used the interview to expound upon her causes. She mentioned the educational and cultural preservation efforts of the Wabanaki Woman's Club. She discussed her plans to assemble a "representation of Maine Indian craftsmanship" for the National Indian Exposition in New York at the end of the year. And she promoted the upcoming "Inter-tribal Ceremonial," which cosponsors from the Penobscot Valley Club and the Maine Development Commission touted as "an event of entertainment, education and historical value to preserve the customs and crafts of our Maine Indians and to bring real financial benefits to the State."[27] Some forty Penobscots and Passamaquoddies showed up at the pageant in Bangor, Maine, along with their Kiowa "guest," "Young Chief Poolaw." They presented an elaborate melodrama—a sort of hybrid Pocahontas/Hiawatha story—featuring numerous traditional dances and songs, including cameo performances by Lucy and Bruce. Basketmakers and local businesspeople promoted their wares, and everyone involved garnered accolades.[28]

The following year the Old Town Chamber of Commerce determined to profit from its proximity to Indian Island by hosting a spectacular Indian pageant that would outdo the Bangor event. In early May the chamber's secretary came up with a basic script for the August pageant, as well as what he considered a catchy name for it: "Shadowy Sachem." Two weeks later, spurred by Lucy and Bruce, the Penobscot tribe pledged its cooperation. In late June the *Old Town Enterprise* announced that Princess Watahwaso, Chief Poolaw, his brother, and their helpers have been "industriously at work" constructing the "Princess Wattawasso Indian Village" at the edge of Old Town. Designed to be the pageant's center point, the village featured bark tepees, a sweat lodge, and an archery range, plus a "large workshop tent," where tribespeople would make Indian crafts in public view, and a "commodious" gift shop tent for the selling of "baskets, bows & arrows, bead work, Navajo blankets, etc."[29]

Largely due to Lucy's theatrical experience and the rigorous rehearsal schedule she imposed, the pageant drew thousands and surpassed everyone's wildest expectations. The local paper described the three-day event in detail. On the first day "gorgeously arrayed" Indians canoed to the Old Town ferry landing. From there, a mounted "Shadowy Sachem" led Princess Watahwaso and "scores of Indian braves, squaws and children" to the newly constructed traditional village, which Chief Poolaw consecrated with a prayer song and pipe ceremony. Then came an array of demonstrations and performances. Men built a canoe and carved paddles. They made bows and arrows and showed white youngsters how to use them. And they pounded an ash log to make wood strips for baskets. Women wove baskets, rocked "papooses" in cradle boards hanging

from low tree boughs, and prepared a midday feast. Boys and girls played traditional games and sports. That evening a crowd overflowed the bleachers for
a program of dances, songs, and legends led by Princess Watahwaso who "covered herself with glory as the conductor of the program." Day two featured a
dramatization of colonial conflict: A band of Passamaquoddy Indians came to
the village carrying wampum and seeking approval for a marriage between one
of their braves and a Penobscot maiden. A grand wedding ceremony began, only
to be interrupted by the sound of guns and the arrival of a group of white men
who drove the Indians from their village to the reservation. The final morning
of the pageant belonged to Old Town citizens and their parade of some two
dozen floats decorated by local merchants and organizations. Then came a
Native show of swimming and canoe races and other water sports, held in the
stretch of river in between Old Town and Indian Island. Festivities concluded
that night with a curious cultural combination: a Grand Colonial Ball with music
by the Indian Orchestra.[30]

If Lucy had mixed feelings about commodifying Penobscot culture, she
did not show it. The following year, she outdid the 1932 pageant, adding to
the program three dramatizations: a legend about the origins of the Red Man,
a story about star-crossed Indian lovers, and a historic reenactment of "The
Norridgewock Massacre." The last was a graphic portrayal of the devastating
English attack of 1724 that gave Lucy's forefather his name, "Half-Arm" Nicola.
Putting this gruesome piece of Maine history onstage brought damning speci-
ficity to the previous year's generic presentation of Indians being driven away
by white settlers. In blatant understatement, the Old Town paper described this
daring piece of political theater as simply "a fine performance."[31]

The Penobscot pageant never became an annual event after the great pro-
ductions of 1932 and 1933, but similar events did take place every few years,
and Lucy and Bruce directed or participated in the gatherings throughout their
lives. Although these galas played into Indian stereotypes, they also offered
Penobscots a cultural ritual for preserving a measure of ethnic distinctiveness.
Certainly they gave Lucy the high profile she needed to make a living and boost
her causes.

Sometime in the early 1930s, Lucy divorced Tom, and in 1937 she married
Bruce. But before she and Bruce made their vows, he had an affair with Margaret Ranco, another woman on the island, who gave birth to his daughter, Irene.
In the years that followed, Lucy reached out to the child and treated her "like
a daughter."[32] Like many children on the reservation, Irene eventually spent
time working in Lucy and Bruce's Indian novelty store. They started the business sometime in the early 1940s, selling baskets from a tent in Bar Harbor and

then from a green clapboard building next to their home by the ferry landing. In 1947, when Lucy was sixty-five and Bruce forty-four, they decided to expand the operation. They hired a couple of men on the island to tear down the green building and use the scrap lumber to build a two-story tepee alongside their house. Painted white with deep red trim, the structure was highly visible from the mainland, and it quickly became a destination point for tourists. Inside one could buy everything from baskets, rattles, war clubs, and beaded moccasins to miniature tepees, toy birchbark canoes, and balsam pillows. And one could meet and chat with the shop's famous owners. To keep up inventory and attract buyers—and to provide jobs for tribal members—Lucy and Bruce hired basket-makers to weave at their shop for about $3 a day. They also encouraged Penobscot children to come by and dance, outfitting the youngsters and guiding their perfomances. By the end of the day, the kids had won a few coins, and Poolaw's Tepee had won a few more customers.

Lucy and Bruce were masterful promoters of anything they decided was worth promoting, from Indian cultures and political causes to themselves as entertainers and sellers of Indian novelties. A classic example of this occurred in 1943 when First Lady Eleanor Roosevelt came to Maine to celebrate the launch of a mine detection boat at Camden Shipyard. Lucy and Bruce talked their way into the event and made Mrs. Roosevelt an honorary member of the tribe. The Penobscot naming ceremony nearly eclipsed the boat launching. First, Lucy's grandnephew kindled a "council fire." Then Bruce lit the "pipe of peace" and sang to the "Great Spirit" of the four directions, asking protection for the "big war canoe." Next, Lucy sang the "Woman's Song," and three Penobscot children danced. Finally, Penobscot governor Ted "Bear" Mitchell, proclaimed, "I, the Bear, deem it a great privilege to make you, Eleanor Roosevelt an honorary member of our tribe. I will ask Princess Watawahso to place the band of wampum upon your head. Your name in the tribe is *Owduleesul*—"Many Trails." Press photos of the event show Lucy and Bruce with a smiling Mrs. Roosevelt clutching a Penobscot basket and wearing a band of wampum around her hat.[33]

The Poolaws often included Penobscot children in their programs around the state, rewarding them with modest (some say stingy) payment. Those who performed with Lucy and Bruce all remember riding with them in their "BIG Cadillac." The couple's ostentatious cars and personalities, along with their relative prosperity, rankled many on the island, as did Lucy's relentless drive to found the Protestant church. But many others were drawn to the showy duo, especially to Lucy. As Bruce's daughter, Irene, put it, "To kids, Lucy was like a pied piper. She would organize plays and use them to teach us things. She gave you a feeling that there wasn't anything you couldn't do."[34] Beyond this, there is no doubt that Lucy and Bruce's presence—especially their tepee store—helped put food on the table of Penobscots who made baskets and other crafts.

Controversy was nothing new on the reservation and barely bothered Lucy. She was far more troubled by the social and economic gap between tribal members and white dominant society. In her eyes, living on an island exacerbated the problem, and she set her mind on getting the state to build a bridge to the mainland. Her niece recalls that Lucy wanted the bridge because "she wanted people to get to work and young people to get out and see the world, especially to go to school."[35] Beyond this, a bridge would solve the problem of dangerous river crossings and drownings caused by sudden freezing or thawing, running ice and shifting currents and water levels. Also, although Lucy didn't mention it, a bridge certainly wouldn't hurt business at Poolaw's Tepee. Lucy and Bruce spoke about the bridge so often in her public appearances that some people thought they were raising money to build it. Ultimately, politicians listened and took action. On November 29, 1950, Lucy stood on the newly erected bridge, along with various dignitaries and island residents, for the dedication. As program committee chair for the event, she acted as master of ceremonies, introducing speakers, including Maine's Governor Frederick Payne, who became an honorary tribal member that day and received a Plains Indian war bonnet to mark the occasion.

Three years later Lucy presided over another political victory: voting rights for Indians in Maine. In 1924 American Indians had gained U.S. citizenship and with it the right to vote in federal elections. However, in Maine, Indians living on state reservations still could not register to vote and therefore had no voice in state and federal elections. This stemmed from their legal position as "wards of the state"—an ambiguous status that also exempted them from paying taxes. Many Penobscots were wary of a change, quite willing to surrender voting to avoid state taxation. As Lucy saw it, her people should have the right to vote and to be tax free. After 1924 both she and Florence had voted freely when living off the reservation. But, as Florence later wrote, when they moved back home and tried to register as citizens in Old Town, they "met with a distinct refusal [because] an obsolete law of the State of Maine forbids the registration and voting by Indians, and in that law we are classed with criminals, paupers and morons."[36] The sisters made several other attempts to vote in Maine and for three decades pressed state legislators for an Indian suffrage bill. Florence wrote letters, while Lucy did her lobbying face-to-face, no doubt inspired by the suffragists she had heard during her Chautauqua days. She couched her argument in issues of the moment. For instance, during the war years she told anyone who would listen that Penobscots were "as patriotic as any Americans," pointing out that thirty-three men from Indian Island were in the armed services.[37] Eventually, the sisters and a small band of other Penobscot activists prevailed, and in 1953 Maine law changed, giving reservation Indians the right to vote without altering their tax status. The following year, at least one Maine newspaper ran a photograph of Lucy, then seventy-two years old, dropping her vote into the ballot box. The caption read: "INDIANS VOTE FOR THE FIRST TIME—Princess Watawaso of the Penobscot Indian Tribe at Old Town casts the first vote of an Indian on a reservation in Maine."[38]

Lucy stayed active throughout her life, although she traveled less in her final years. Beyond maintaining Poolaw's Tepee with Bruce, she remained devoted to the island's Baptist church. She served as church pianist and organist for twenty-five years, always singing as she played. On March 27, 1969, three months before her eighty-seventh birthday, Lucy sang her last note. Newspapers near and far reported her death. The *New York Times* noted that "Princess Watawaso had lectured and sung the songs of her people in most of the United States" and recounted the many venues of her artistry.[39] The local paper reached beyond her stage career to chronicle her role in the church and her service as a tribal council member and officer in various organizations. To accommodate a large and varied crowd, her family held funeral services in Old Town's Baptist church. But they laid Lucy to rest in the tribal cemetery on Indian Island—beneath a headstone that had Bruce's name etched next to hers. Despite this engraved invitation, Bruce never joined her there. Several years after her death, he packed up most of their belongings and returned to Oklahoma. In 1984 he passed away among his own people, and they buried him there.

When Bruce left Indian Island, Irene and her husband moved into Lucy's house and ran Poolaw's Tepee. In 1988 they relocated the business to a storefront building on Old Town's main avenue. Ten years later, a terrible fire consumed the new shop. Ironically, that same year one of Lucy's nephews completely restored the original tepee, revitalizing its landmark status.

In Lucy's vaudeville days, folks who really knew her may have chuckled when they saw her play the role of a delicate forest maiden singing "Indian Love Call," since, in fact, she was a strong, independent self-provider. She shared these traits with many other turn-of-the-century women in the Penobscot community, but there was something—in addition to her bold personality—that made Lucy's life particularly memorable and significant: At the time of her birth, most people, including Penobscots, assumed her small tribe would vanish through assimilation, but Lucy never accepted that idea. Deeply rooted in Penobscot traditions, she could probably recount them more accurately than anyone else of her generation, and she spent a lifetime making sure they stayed in the public eye. The young Watahwaso who addressed the Women's Debating Society in 1900 might have forgiven her white audience for trespasses against her people, but she had no intention of letting them forget that Penobscots existed. An artful pragmatist, Lucy altered traditions to win over audiences and politicians, but she also kept an essential core alive within the armor of theatrical packaging. Without her efforts to keep Native concerns and cultural hallmarks in the spotlight, it is doubtful that Penobscots could have brought so much cultural vitality to their successful political moves to reclaim lost lands and rights in the 1970s and 1980s. In this sense, "Bright Star" has continued to shine.

NOTES

I wish to thank several Penobscots who helped me piece together this story: Lucy's nephews, Charles and Bill Shay, her grandnieces, Caron Shay and Emma Nicolar (all of Indian Island), and her grandnephew Robert Anderson of Lincolnville, Maine, as well as Bruce's daughter, Irene Ranco Pardilla of Indian Island, and his niece Linda Poolaw of Anadarko, Oklahoma. Others who helped include Carol Binet and the late Glenn Starbird, keepers of Penobscot genealogical information, James Neptune at the Penobscot Museum, Jean Archambaud Moore, my Penobscot hostess and friend and a storehouse of information, and my husband, Harald Prins, whose depth of knowledge on Maine Indian history has strengthened all I have written in this area.

1. "Penobscotbelles," *Bangor Daily Commercial*, 12 January 1900:1.
2. "Little New Church Starts with Courage and Faith," *Bangor Daily News*, 9 February 1942. (Note: The year of publication is approximate, as that part of the date was clipped off this article before it was placed in the church's scrapbook.)
3. The term "ambivalent racism" comes from Harald E. L. Prins, "Chief Big Thunder (1827–1906): The Life History of a Penobscot Trickster," *Maine History* 37.3 (Winter 1998): 154, 156. For a close look at American Indians in the entertainment industry, see Bunny McBride, *Molly Spotted Elk: A Penobscot in Paris* (Norman: University of Oklahoma Press, 1995), especially 41–46, 52–53, 64–69, 97–125, 145–46, 211. For a discussion on the concept of primitivism, see Harald E. L.Prins, "The Paradox of Primitivism: Native Rights and the Problem of Imagery in Cultural Survival Films," *Visual Anthropology*, 1997: 243–44. Rayna Green, "The Pocahontas Perplex: The Image of Indian Women in Popular Culture," *Massachusetts Review* 16 (Autumn): 698–714.
4. Fannie Hardy Eckstorm, *Indian Place Names of the Penobscot Valley and the Maine Coast* (Orono: University of Maine Press, 1978), 237.
5. John R. Wiggins, "Indian Princess," *Down East*, November 1966: 28–30.
6. "Belle of the Penobscots," unidentified Lewiston, Maine, newspaper, 11 December 1897, in M. A. Little, "History and Biography of Maine" (scrapbook in Maine His-

torical Society collection, Portland); "Old Town Island," *Old Town Enterprise*, 9 February 1889; "Old Town Island: Home of the Progressive Penobscots," ibid., 1 January 1910:1; "Died: Mrs. Elizabeth Nicolar," Ibid., 11 December 1924:5.

7. Jennie June Croly, *The History of the Woman's Club Movement in America* (New York: Henry G. Allen & Co., 1898), 575–76.

8. The most complete account of Frank Loring's life is Prins, "Chief Big Thunder."

9. "City Items," *Old Town Enterprise*, 5 March 1892: 2.

10. Emma Nicolar, interview by Bunny McBride, Indian Island, Maine, 21 May 1998.

11. "Belle of the Penobscots."

12. "The Penobscot Indians: A Brief Account of Their Present Condition," 8 February 1898; reprinted in the *Old Town Enterprise*, 4 March 1899: 1.

13. "Penobscotbelles."

14. Joseph E. Gould, *Chautauqua Movement* (New York: State University of New York, 1961), 3–12; Harry P. Harrison, *Culture Under Canvas* (New York: Hastings House Publishers, 1958), 39–49; John E. Tapia, *Circuit Chautauqua* (Jefferson, North Carolina: McFarland & Co., 1997), 19–24.

15. Redpath's treasurer, Harry P. Harrison, 6 January 1917 letter to A. Fisk, among papers in Box 248, Redpath Chautauqua Collection, Special Collections, Maine Library, University of Iowa, Iowa City.

16. Harrison, *Culture Under Canvas*, 7.

17. Other American Indian women on the Chautauqua circuit include Cherokee-Creek singer Tsianina Blackstone and Chickasaw folklorist-performer Te Ata (Mary Frances Thompson). See McBride, *Molly Spotted Elk*, 81–82; Tapia, *Circuit Cahutauqua*, 100.

18. Harrison, *Culture Under Canvas*, 217–28.

19. In Wiggins, "Indian Princess," Lucy dates this recital April 19, but a program from the event says April 7, Box 248F, Redpath Chautauqua Collection.

20. "Chief Newell Francis . . . on Indian Island," 30 July 1921.

21. Linda Poolaw, telephone interview by Bunny McBride, Anadarko, Oklahoma, 13 Dec. 1999.

22. Robert Anderson, interview by Bunny McBride, Lincolnville, Maine, 17 May 1998.

23. Lawrence "Bill" Shay, interview by Bunny McBride, Indian Island, Maine, 16 May 1998.

24. William H. Clark, "Penobscot Tribe Has Few Men Left at Oldtown, Me.," *Boston Sunday Globe*, 23 August 1942.

25. Florence Nicola Shay, *History of the Penobscot Tribe of Indians* (Old Town: Florence Shay, 1941), 15. According to Lawrence "Bill" Shay, the woman's club was formed "for political pull."

26. Shay, *History of the Penobscot Tribe of Indians*, 6–9.

27. "Penobscot Indians Visit Lewiston, Princess Watawasa and Kiowa Chief," unidentified newspaper clipping (perhaps *Lewiston Journal* or *Maine Sunday Telegram*), 15 July 1931.

28. Program of the "Intertribal Indian Ceremonial" (Bangor: Penobscot Valley Country Club and the Maine Development Commission, 1931).

29. "Indian Village in Progress of Construction," *Old Town Enterprise*, 23 June 1932:1.

30. Title missing, ibid., 11 August 1932:1.

31. Several 1933 articles in ibid.: "Governor of Penobscots Announces Present Plans: Indian Pageant in August," 20 July; "Putting Finishing Touches on Indian Pageant," 27 July; "Pageant Next Wed., Thurs., Fri.," 3 August; "Indians, Outnumbered 3000, Entertain Paleface Horde with Singing and Dancing," 10 August; "Shadowy Sachem Pageant . . . Scores Triumphant Success," 17 August.

32. Irene Ranco Pardilla, telephone interview by Bunny McBride, 27 July 1998.

33. Barbara F. Dyer, *"Grog Ho!" The History of Wooden Vessel Building in Camden, Maine* (Rockland, ME: Courier-Gazette, Inc., 1984), 104.

34. Pardilla interview.

35. Nicolar interview.

36. Shay, *History of the Penobscot Tribe*, 12.

37. Clark, "Penobscot Tribe Has Few Men Left."

38. This photograph appeared in an unidentified newspaper clipping saved by Emma Nicolar.

39. "Mrs. Bruce Poolaw, Singer of Penobscot Indian Lore," *New York Times*, 21 March 1969.

10

MARIA MONTOYA MARTINEZ
Crafting a Life, Transforming a Community

Terry R. Reynolds

When Maria was born in 1887, her parents could not have foreseen that
she would be a major catalyst in changing their centuries-old village. They could
not have known her future would bring her fame, fortune, travel, and powerful
friends. They would teach her to care for others in the village, not because she
was a female, but because they wanted her to become a good community member. They would have been satisfied for her to concentrate on her family, relatives, and neighbors with little thought to or activity beyond these spheres of
village life. Maria, however, was caught up in the winds of change blowing
throughout the southwestern United States at the turn of the twentieth century.
With talent and skill in a traditional craft of women in her village, pottery making, and her thoughtful approach to living a good life in village terms, she, along
with her husband, brought the village to the nation's attention. She also helped
to create an economic strategy through which her family, as well as other villagers, could enter the national economy and prosper. At the same time, Maria crafted
a life based upon her ancestors' traditions and service to others.[1]

Like generations before them, Reyes Peña Montoya and Tomas Montoya,
Maria's mother and father, lived in San Ildefonso Pueblo of northern New
Mexico. Their adobe house sat on a slight rise at the north end of the village,
overlooking the plaza lined by their neighbors' houses. In addition to the new
baby, Reyes and Tomas were parents of two-year-old Maximiliana. In another
two years, they would have Desideria, and then Juanita and Clara would arrive

eleven and twenty-two years later. From their home, the Montoyas could see cottonwood trees lining the banks of the Rio Grande west of the plaza. Beyond the river rose the steep-sided Pajarito Plateau where their Tewa-speaking ancestors had settled centuries before.

Despite its setting, the history of the village was not idyllic. Since contact with Spanish colonists at the end of the sixteenth century, villagers had mounted two major insurrections against Spanish control of the Pueblo's affairs. People fled from their homes, and epidemics decimated the remaining population. People of Spanish descent moved into the community so that by the late eighteenth century, two-thirds as many people of Spanish descent lived there as did Tewa. By 1887, less than 150 Tewa lived in the village.[2]

At the beginning of the decade in which Maria was born, railroads reached New Mexico and ran near the Pueblo. Some of the village men worked on its construction, which provided large-scale wage labor to San Ildefonso men for the first time and drew them into the U.S. cash economy. The village, however, maintained its agrarian way of life. Many of the village men, including Maria's father, continued to grow crops on widely scattered valley fields watered by irrigation ditches. Tewa women, including her mother, processed foodstuffs, such as cheese, and traded them to other villagers for cash and goods. Some women also produced pottery for family use and trade, but Maria's mother, like many other San Ildefonso women, was not a potter. Since the 1820s, traders had brought metal buckets and enameled dishes over the Santa Fe Trail from St. Louis, and the need for handmade pottery by the villagers had dwindled. Just a few women produced all the pottery that the Pueblo's inhabitants needed for domestic and ceremonial uses.

The railroad could have stimulated an exodus from the Pueblo where an agricultural subsistence was precarious and few opportunities for wage labor existed, but village and family were central to the lives of the Tewa, particularly Tewa women. Leaving home was not only difficult personally, but the village council usually denied women permission for long absences. The railroad, however, opened a potential market for women's pottery and other crafts— the tourist market. Tourists traveled to the West in the late nineteenth and early twentieth centuries in order to experience the grandeur of deserts and mountains and also to observe ways of life presumably left behind in the industrial development of the eastern United States. The railroad provided relatively easy access to Native villages, and the tourists' desire to return east with souvenirs from their trip gave women an opportunity to supplement their families' income without leaving the Pueblo. Maria was to become a major force in the production and marketing of San Ildefonso pottery to non-Indians.

Although her mother was not a potter, Maria was born into a close-knit community of women, some of whom were potters. Following Tewa tradition, village women visited Maria and her mother during her first three days.[3] They brought gifts of food and clothing, and each symbolically cast out all the illness, laziness, and misfortune that might beset her in the future. On the fourth day her mother's sister presented her to the sunrise and gave her the name *Po've'ka,* or Pond Lily. For the rest of her life, other people in the village knew her by this name. Tewa people, however, lived in a complex world of many cultural traditions and so, on April 10, 1887, five days after her birth, she received baptism in the Catholic Church and her Spanish name of Maria Antonia. Outside the Pueblo, people knew her as Maria, and she used the name throughout most of her life in signing her pottery, although at one point she also added the name *Poveka.*

Maria's childhood memories included two experiences that she felt pointed her in the direction that her life eventually took. One of these memories involved selling her mother's cheese to other villagers and receiving in return buttons, cornmeal, and coins. From this experience she wanted to become a storekeeper and sell things to others, a dream that she realized as an adult. The second of her experiences provided the basis for her fame and fortune as a potter. When Maria was about eight, she and her younger sister Desideria tried to make little dishes for their playhouse on the banks of the irrigation ditch. They made these dishes of mud from the ditch bank, but they cracked as they dried. The girls went to their mother's sister, Nicolasa, to learn how to make pottery that did not crack, but Maria's mother warned her not to bother her aunt. Rather, her mother told her to watch her aunt and other potters and to learn from what they did.

Nicolasa told the girls the secret of tempering the clay with sand so that it would not crack when it dried and was fired. She made a small saucerlike base upon which to build a bowl through adding coils of clay. She showed them how to blend the coils together by first smoothing the sides of the bowl with wet fingers and then scraping the bowl with a sharp piece of a dried gourd. She then applied the slip to the outside of the vessel. Eventually, Nicolasa taught them how to lay the fire, how to place the pottery on the grating, and how to put sheets of scrap iron around the pottery to protect it from the fire. They watched her sprinkle sacred cornmeal and heard her say a prayer before she lit the fire's kindling. In later years Maria remarked that no one formally taught her how to make pottery but that she learned through the examples of women like Nicolasa.[4]

During her childhood years, Maria also learned appropriate behavior from her parents and other relatives. She used these lessons to craft a good Tewa life for herself and her children. More than anything else, they provided a touchstone to which Maria returned when she faced new and unexpected situations. Most of what she learned focused on providing her family and village with love, generosity, protection, guidance, assistance, and care. The Pueblo's inhabitants valued harmony, which both men and women sought through nurturing one another. Maria learned to seek balance in her own life and in her relations with others, as well as to promote harmony among all members of the community. Like all Tewas, her goal was to find what was best for the community, not necessarily what was best for her, and to give freely to those who asked for help. As a woman, she centered her thoughts and activities primarily on nurturing her family, and her family—parents, grandparents, aunts, and uncles—provided constant examples of how to live a good life.[5]

Maria learned more formal lessons at the local day school. After four years, the San Ildefonso village council sent Maria and her sister Desideria, along with other San Ildefonso children, to Catholic boarding school in Santa Fe that Reyes and Tomas had attended when they were young. Even though the council was willing to send all three of Reyes and Tomas's daughters to school, the parents decided that Maximiliana would stay at home to help them. For two school years Maria and Desideria attended St. Catherine's where they perfected their English and received confirmation in the Catholic Church. The girls brought honor to their family and community by excelling; Maria won a prize for her sewing and Desideria for her writing.

After returning to San Ildefonso from St. Catherine's, twelve-year-old Maria thought about what she wanted to do with her life. Her old day-school teacher suggested that perhaps she would like to be a teacher in an Indian school, so with her parents' approval, she agreed to be the school's housekeeper. Maria kept the school building clean and orderly, in return for additional lessons to prepare her for continuing her education as a teacher. At the day school Maria began to see Julian Martinez, who chopped wood for the school and was a couple of years older than Maria. In the late afternoon, as Maria cleaned and scrubbed, they talked. He then walked her home and returned to the schoolhouse to chop wood. When wood was not needed, he helped Maria finish her chores before walking her home.

Julian was the son of Luisita Peña Martinez and Santiago Martinez. His father was a craftsman who made flour sifters and saddles, and while Julian helped him, there was not enough demand for both of them to work full-time. His mother tended a garden, but unlike most men in the Pueblo, the Martinez men did not farm. Consequently, Julian had only limited prospects in a community reliant on agriculture because he lacked farming skills and steady work in the fields. Therefore, Maria's parents worried about Maria's developing relationship with Julian, whom they feared could not provide for a family. They wanted their daughter to have a secure future. Furthermore, they were concerned about propriety. The two young people had been seeing each other regularly for three years, but Julian's parents had not visited Reyes and Tomas to arrange a marriage with Maria, according to the custom of San Ildefonso. Another young man's parents already had visited them to propose their son as a husband for Maria, who at fifteen was considered to be of a marriageable age. Reyes finally asked Maria if she intended to marry Julian or was willing to marry another young man.

Maria spoke with Julian about her parent's concerns. Within a day his parents arrived at the Montoyas' home to arrange the marriage of their children. The marriage took place in 1904 when Maria was sixteen years old, a year after Maria and Julian's son Adam was born. The Tewa attached no stigma to premarital sex or births outside wedlock. Maria's parents provided the young couple with a small house in the village where Tomas's mother had lived, and Julian asked Tomas for permission to work with him in the fields so that he could learn to farm.

San Ildefonso customarily celebrated two marriage ceremonies for young couples. The first, the traditional Tewa ritual in which the couple's parents blessed them and a Tewa religious leader spoke to the couple about their responsibilities, was held at the Montoyas' home. Everyone from the village attended the ceremony and a feast that followed. Aunt Nicolasa gave Maria a wedding jar she had made for this ceremony. The next day the couple's immediate families attended the Catholic marriage mass in the church at San Ildefonso where Julian had arranged for the priest from Santa Cruz to officiate. The Tewa ritual held at the woman's house reflected the prominent role of the community in Tewa society; the Catholic mass arranged by the man embodied European society's emphasis on the individual.

Following more feasting and dancing, Maria and Julian left San Ildefonso for a trip to the Louisiana Purchase Exposition in St Louis, a journey that presaged the economic transformation in which this young couple would participate. Julian's uncle had hired them to go to the exposition to present Tewa singing and dancing to visitors for several months. They received transportation, food, accommodation, and fifty dollars a month. Maria and Julian, therefore, began their married life selling traditional crafts and demonstrating aspects of Tewa life to non-Indians.

Including people from the Tewa villages in an international exposition gave fair visitors access to traditions and handicrafts that differed from their own. Some visitors probably thought about the "progress" industrial America had made from the life represented by the Tewa exhibit. Others, more inclined toward reflecting on what industrial America had lost, saw fabled American Indians who presumably lived closer to the natural world, maintained the social ties of a close-knit community, and made things with their hands rather than with machines. Most visitors thought that the Tewa represented a way of life soon to be lost in the continuing industrialization of America. Their introduction to Native people in the secure environment of the exposition probably encouraged many to consider a rail trip west to visit Native villages while they still could.

While Maria participated in some dances along with Julian, she found that fair visitors were more interested in watching her make small polished-red bowls and ollas. Many of those who met the young couple purchased Maria's pottery, bringing the family additional income. In the Tewa world, men dealt with outsiders, so Julian began to learn English so that he could talk with visitors while Maria worked.

With the money they earned, Julian and Maria purchased presents in St. Louis for their families, clothing and personal items for themselves, and things they needed to begin their married life when they returned to the village. Their village was not prosperous, and the young couple had a difficult time when they returned. While Maria learned housekeeping and cooking, Julian went to work in the fields. Subsistence from farming, however, was becoming increasingly difficult as non-Tewas acquired land and cut timber from hills above the village, destroying the watershed and causing fields to flood and irrigation ditches to silt up. Without enough good land on which to grow crops, there was not enough food. Some young people had to find work away from home. One or two young unmarried women became housekeepers in Santa Fe. Some young men worked for the railroad or harvested beets in Colorado. Nevertheless, Julian began to learn farming from his father-in-law, but he was not very good at it. More interested in the patterns the plow made in the soil, he told Maria that he would rather look at the fields than plow them.

In 1907 the prospect of nearby wage labor appeared for some men in the village. Dr. Edgar Hewett, director of the new School of American Research in Santa Fe, proposed archaeological excavations on the Pajarito Plateau and needed laborers for the excavation. The village council gave permission for the work to take place, and the archaeologists hired Julian to help them. Because the excavation was too far from the village for the workers to go back and forth, Julian lived at the work site. Maria took Adam and an infant daughter named Pond Lily back to her parents' house. That summer an epidemic struck the village, and a number of children died, including Pond Lily. The baby's death was hard on Maria, but she had the support of her family around her. Her father went to the excavation to tell Julian, who was very upset by the news and wanted to leave his job, but Tomas convinced him to remain employed.

At the end of the summer, Julian returned home and, as was customary in Tewa society, turned his earnings over to Maria. She gave Julian a dollar, and then she split the rest among her parents, his parents, and themselves. Julian spent his money on wine from a local Hispanic merchant and arrived home quite drunk. This incident marked the beginning of Julian's lifelong battle with alcohol. As a result, Maria began to consciously craft her marriage with Julian's alcoholism in mind. She took their share of his earnings and hid it for future household use. The following summer, the archaeologists again hired Julian to work, but this time Maria and Adam accompanied him to the excavations. She hoped to prevent her husband from drinking liquor as well as to protect their son from further epidemics in the village.

At the excavation site, Maria found she had time to explore the old ruins. She found four polishing stones used by ancestral potters, which she prized and kept for her own use. She also began to look at the broken pieces of pottery scattered about the site and developed an interest in the older techniques of pottery making. That summer, the archaeologists had Julian copy ancestral wall art and discovered that he was quite good at it. At Hewett's request, he also painted pictures of Tewa dancers. Influences from outside the village, there-fore, motivated both Julian and Maria to develop their artistic and craft skills.

At the summer's end, Hewett asked Maria to produce some pottery like the beautiful potsherd he gave to her. It was of thin construction with a dark, shiny gray surface decorated with fine black lines. She was intrigued by the task of physically producing the old pottery, but protested that she could not paint the design on it. Maria already had been making for her own use some undeco-rated, polished redware vessels as well as decorated polychrome pottery like other villagers made. The designs on the polychrome ware were done in black and red on a white or buff background. Maria's older sister, Maximiliana, and her husband, Crescencio Martinez, decorated Maria's pottery because Maria never felt that she had any design talent and was content to shape the pottery, apply a slip, and polish its surface. Hewett suggested that, with his design skills, Julian could do the decorating. Maria agreed to try to make pottery according to Hewett's specifications during the winter.

During the winter she searched the countryside for the right kind of clay and sand with which to make the old pottery. She brought it home in bags and then learned to sift both clay and sand through various kinds of cloth in order to achieve a fine-grained quality. Julian prepared yucca paintbrushes with which to decorate the pottery. Maria's aunt, Nicolasa, helped the young couple in their preparations by pointing out a place in which to find fine sand for tempering the pottery. She also provided dried *guaco* syrup that she had made by boiling Rocky Mountain beeweed, which Julian could reconstitute for his decorative black paint. Maria also asked her to help with the firing of their first pieces of pottery for Hewett.

That winter tested Maria's strength as a caregiver. Her mother and father moved in with the young couple because Reyes, not a young woman, was pregnant and found it difficult to do her work without help. In her last moments while dying giving birth to Clara, Reyes asked Maria to look after her youngest sister, which she did for the rest of her life. After his wife's death, Tomas invited Maria and Julian to move into the larger family home with him. Maria thereby added her father to the number of people for whom she cared. Julian's response to grief and new responsibilities was to turn to the bottle.

Nevertheless, Maria and Julian found time to work on the pottery commissioned by Hewett, and, the following summer, the young couple's first pieces so impressed him that he purchased them all. He promised to find buyers for everything that they could produce. Maria decided to spend that summer in the village making pots so that Julian could finish them when he returned from the excavations in the fall and had little else to do. Often helped by her sister, Juanita, who assisted in smoothing and polishing the bowls, Maria worked hard on the pottery. By the time Julian arrived, there were about two hundred pots for him to decorate that winter. Maria intended to do the firing in the spring and sell the pieces the following summer.

But unbeknownst to her, Julian had accepted a job for the winter as a janitor in the new Museum of New Mexico in Santa Fe where Hewett served as director. Maria was worried that he would do a lot of drinking in town, and she arranged with Hewett for Julian to decorate her pottery when he was not needed for museum tasks. One of Hewett's assistants brought decorated pots back to Maria for firing and carried newly coiled pots into Santa Fe for Julian to paint. Maria also began to send fired pottery to the museum for Julian to sell. Unfortunately, Julian used some of the pottery money to buy alcohol. Hewett asked Maria to move to Santa Fe because he thought Julian would be less likely to drink if she were there, so Maria packed up the children and her pottery supplies and tools and moved to the city.

During the years they lived at the museum, Maria never really felt at home. Home for her was the Pueblo, where she was surrounded by her family and neighbors. To fill her time as well as Julian's at the museum, Maria made pottery, and he decorated it. They fired it in the museum's backyard and sold it to museum visitors. Eventually, shopkeepers in Santa Fe asked them to make pottery and sell it to them wholesale. Maria agreed since she wanted to buy a cooking stove for their home in the village. She also arranged for them to sell her sisters' pottery. The museum paid Maria to give demonstrations and classes in making redware and polychrome pottery.

During this time at the museum both Maria and Julian refined their respective skills in making pottery. The quality of Maria's work began to surpass that of other potters in her village. Made with traditional techniques and her ancient polishing stones, her pottery was exceptionally thin-walled and well fired, with smooth, highly polished surfaces. Julian carefully executed his decorative designs with yucca brushes. By studying a variety of old designs from various traditions throughout the Southwest at the museum, Julian compiled a notebook of designs that he liked. His sense of design was superb, and he developed designs based upon traditional motifs. Two of these, the feather design from Mimbres pottery and the water serpent from Tewa designs, became integral to his work.

After three years Maria could no longer justify living at the museum. It was time to return to the Pueblo. She needed the nurturing community in which she had grown up. She also feared that the Pueblo could not survive if its young people moved away. Tewa population had declined to the point that villagers who worked and lived elsewhere had to return to the Pueblo so there were enough people for various village religious rites. Maria was a member of the women's ceremonial society in her Pueblo and the drummer for the women's dances, while Julian belonged to a medicine society in the village. Not only did Maria and her family need the village's stability, but the Pueblo needed them. To subsist, they knew that they needed to have income beyond that brought in by agriculture. Pottery was their way to produce cash. Maria thought they could sell some from their home to the tourists who came to visit the village in increasing numbers. They also continued to sell to the museum and to storekeepers in Santa Fe.

They also expanded the types of pottery they made for sale. In response to a shop owner's insistence on getting more shiny black pottery, which they had accidentally made in an early firing, Julian figured out how to produce this color consistently by smothering the fire with powdered manure. Maria further perfected her skills at the 1915 Panama-California Exposition in San Diego. She, Julian, and her cousin, Ramoncita Gonzales, were hired to make large pots to serve as chimneys on the pueblo-type building being constructed at the fair. Maria had never made any really large jars. With Julian's design assistance, Maria and Ramoncita learned to construct the large vessel's walls so that they would not cave in as they coiled the vessel higher and higher. While the fair's visitors watched, Maria and Ramoncita also made smaller pieces to sell. Julian was very adept at talking and joking with the visitors while he painted designs on the pots, his gregarious personality helping to market the pottery. From this venture they made a lot of money, which they split equally.

The exposition wages plus the pottery cash allowed Maria, now twenty-eight years of age, to fulfill some of her dreams. She purchased a cooking stove as well as a sewing machine. Maria and Julian also built an additional room on to their house to serve as a store where they could market their own pottery, as well as the work of other women, to tourists. They also sold general store merchandise to villagers. Maria saw the store as an additional way to help her family, other families, and the community as a whole.

For the next decade, Maria and Julian prospered economically and were able to save money. They made an adequate living from their pottery, store, and garden. They purchased a cow as well as a wagon and team, and their children were well clothed. Their family was growing as well. Three more sons were born to the couple: John (Juan Diego) in 1915, Anthony (Antonio) in 1921, and Phillip (Felipe Carmelito) in 1925. Maria was often busy with household chores and child-care tasks, and Julian tended the garden and animals. Maria continued producing a supply of pottery for Julian to decorate. She made bowls, jars, and plates, a form suggested by a Santa Fe shopkeeper. San Ildefonso potters did not traditionally make plates, but the shopkeeper thought they would sell well, and so Maria made them like the old storage jar lids with which she was familiar. Julian painted pottery every day in the store where he also could help customers, and he spent his evenings packing mail-order shipments of pottery. He also painted some watercolor pictures for sale to tourists. Periodically, he left the store in Maria's care while he collected the clay and sand needed for pottery production.

During this period Julian made two discoveries regarding pottery manufacture that catapulted Maria to national fame. The first occurred when he decided to try using Maria's polishing slip, rather than *guanco*, as paint for decorating their pots. This produced a dull black against the shiny black of Maria's polished surface after the vessel was fired. Julian experimented with dull and shiny aspects of design until by the mid-1920s it was clear that the shiny background with dull design was the most satisfying. Julian also discovered that sheep manure produced the most smoke when used to smother the pottery fire. With the clay slip as decorative paint, the pottery fired with sheep manure was as good a black color as could be produced. This decoration and firing perfectly complemented Maria's finely wrought pots. Julian and Maria's elegant black-on-black ware became the most sought-after type of American Indian pottery, and Maria became the most famous potter in the United States.

When it became clear to other villagers that Maria and Julian's pottery sold well, her cousin, Isabella, and her brother-in-law's sister, Tonita, asked Maria to teach them how to make the black pottery. Maria did not hesitate. She and Julian had always felt that pottery making was a Pueblo activity and that what they had learned was to be shared. Consequently, they taught pottery making to any villager who asked for instruction. Maria also offered to sell other potters' ware to traders and shopkeepers when she sold her own pieces. The outside world had influenced Maria and Julian in many ways, but they remained firmly rooted in the communal values of the Pueblo. After a couple of years, several other potters and their husbands decided to set up shops in their homes. Maria welcomed what outsiders might have considered competition because she believed that any activity that improved the economic situation helped the Pueblo. She also felt relieved because other pottery shops in the village would take the pressures of growing tourist trade off her operation. She and Julian could concentrate on their mail orders and inventory for Santa Fe shops, where they were the only Indian artists selling pottery on a commission basis.

As the demand for San Ildefonso pottery increased, a government official in 1923 convinced Maria that she should sign her pottery. He pointed out that the practice was common in the United States and that customers wanted to know who made each piece. The practice of signing a single name on a pot countermanded the ethics and process of making pots at San Ildefonso. For Maria and the other potters, it had been important that the pottery was from the village, not who the individual potter was. In fact, a number of people might work on any particular piece of pottery. Maria would mold a number of vessels and leave them to dry, and several women would come to help slip and polish them. These women earned $1.00 a day, the going wage at the time. Eventually, Julian painted the designs, but sometimes an assistant filled in the outline that he had applied. Pots, therefore, represented a group effort and reflected the community-oriented culture of the Pueblo.

When Maria learned that the pottery would probably sell more easily if signed, she agreed to put her name on the bottom of vessels with a polishing stone. Because she was gaining a national reputation, she and Julian worried that people might buy her signed pieces and ignore those of other potters. Therefore, Maria offered to sign the pottery of any potter who asked her to do so. She also showed Julian how to write his name so that he could begin signing the pictures he painted. Because signatures meant little to them, Maria signed Julian's name to the pottery he decorated because he did not feel comfortable writing with a polishing stone, and someone else might, in fact, write both their names on their pots. The signature was a sales mechanism for Maria. She still saw herself and villagers as members of a Pueblo that produced pottery and paintings and their success as important to the village. But signing each pot or painting was the final step in transforming Maria and Julian into individual artists in the eyes of the rest of the country.

While Maria's life was economically successful, she still had to deal with situations that tested the strength of her ability to nurture and to be a good member of her Pueblo, faithful to the Tewa way of life. When her sister Clara was about twelve years old and attending boarding school in Santa Fe, she began to do poorly in school. Apparently, Clara had had an infection that had left her largely deaf. Maria brought her home and incorporated her into the pottery business. Clara kept sales records and, eventually, became a highly skilled polisher of pottery. She assisted Maria and her other sisters in finishing their pottery. She also began to take over Maria's household tasks as Maria spent more time making pottery.

In the 1920s and 1930s, Julian's drinking problem worsened. Unable to cope well with stress, Julian might have been reacting to strife in the village. For years a major dispute brewed over whether or not to relocate the village. Some villagers attributed epidemics, poor crops, and other hardships to the Pueblo's site, and they constructed a new plaza to the south. Others, including Julian and Maria, wanted to remain where they were. Despite their attempts to share their success, the dispute brought to the fore deep resentment of the couple in some quarters. In a community that placed such a high premium on harmony, this kind of personal feeling, as well as the broader dispute, made life difficult for Maria and Julian. Maria found solace in family and work, but these did not suffice for Julian.

Julian's situation deteriorated when alcohol became easily available in nearby bars owned by Hispanics. Maria tried to eradicate his sources of alcohol by reporting illegal purveyors of liquor to law enforcement officers. She even purchased property at the edge of the village owned by Julian's primary supplier in order to curtail his drinking. But her efforts met with only momentary success, and then she found herself taking care of him until he recovered from his latest binge. As Julian's drinking worsened, he could not be trusted to attend to business or to farming. Maria turned to Adam, who married in 1926, to assist her with these activities. Slowly, Adam took over his father's business and farming activities, although Julian still painted pottery and pictures. To protect the younger children from his drinking, Maria received permission of the village council to send them to boarding school in Santa Fe. Eventually, with the council's permission, Maria sent John, the most academically inclined of the boys, to military school in Georgia and then to Stanford University to study engineering.

The superintendent of the boarding school in Santa Fe suggested that Maria might help Julian if she took him away from the village. Therefore, in 1934, at the age of forty-seven, she reluctantly agreed once again to travel and to demonstrate pottery making at the Chicago World's Fair. Maria and Julian were more successful than ever. They made a lot of money, which Maria sent home to Adam. Julian was sober while in Chicago, and Maria was so pleased that she entertained the idea of additional travel. She agreed to go on a government-sponsored trip of Indian artists to the East Coast. Julian collected clay from each state through which they traveled, and when they returned home, they made pottery from it. They visited Washington, New York, and Atlanta, where they met powerful people and saw famous places, but Maria was glad to return home, especially since John was to be married.

After the wedding, Maria returned to making pottery. Occasionally she taught classes at the Santa Fe Indian School. Julian continued to decorate her pottery, but he began drinking again. Consequently, Maria agreed to go to San Francisco in 1939 to do pottery demonstrations at the Golden Gate International Exposition on Treasure Island. While they were gone, Anthony married a girl from the village of San Juan without his parents' knowledge or permission. Maria was very upset, and she vowed not to travel again.

To Maria's surprise, the village council in 1940 chose Julian to become governor. The council usually did not choose someone who had such obvious character flaws and who had behaved improperly, but Julian had skills that balanced his defects. The governor had the authority to work with people outside of the Pueblo in the interests of the town, and so he needed to be someone who was able to speak with outsiders. Julian certainly was experienced in talking with people from all over the country. He was very conscious of his responsibilities and very proud to be governor. He hung the silver-headed cane that was the symbol of his authority on the shop wall. Their salesroom now became the governor's office, where people came to consult with him. He settled disputes, organized the cleaning of the irrigation ditches, and, when World War II came, worked with people organizing the draft. Julian did not drink when he was governor.

When his two years as governor of the Pueblo ended, however, Julian began to drink again. He was no longer a young man, and his health declined. In the late fall in 1943, when Julian was fifty-eight years old, he went out in the cold and snow to drink and did not return home. He was found four days later dead on a hill not far away. Maria did not cry. They had been together a long time. When she looked at him to say good-bye, he seemed young again and at peace. She felt it was a good way for his life to end.

Julian's body was taken away to the hills by village men for a traditional burial. They removed his belongings, including his design notebook, from the house and disposed of them in the river. Most of the villagers attended a feast and comforted the family, and on the following day, a mass was said in the church. Maria went home, where she and Clara now lived alone.

Maria decided to continue to make her pottery and sell it. She was not, however, a storekeeper, and in time she did away with the salesroom in the house. Santana, Adam's wife, replaced Julian in decorating her pottery. For the next thirteen years Santana's name appeared with Maria's on the bottom of each piece.

Anthony also was a skilled artist. Before World War II, he studied with Dorothy Dunn at the Santa Fe Indian School. When he returned from army service, he became interested in pottery and began to help Maria gather clay and sand and assist in the firings. In the late 1940s, he and his wife established a studio of Indian art at San Ildefonso to display Maria's better pieces and her awards. He also formally abandoned "Anthony" for a Tewa name, Popovi Da. From the studio he sold the work of his mother, family, neighbors, and American Indians from elsewhere. In 1956 he took over decorating his mother's pottery from Santana, but he also made his own pottery. He was responsible for developing refinements of and new techniques in the firing process. He created new colors, finishes, and color combinations for the pottery and first used turquoise for decoration. He was village governor for six two-year terms and served as the chairman of the All-Pueblo Council.

Anthony's premature death in 1971, when he was fifty years old, greatly saddened Maria. She had already lost John and Philip in 1966. She and Clara moved in with Adam and his family, and she gave her house to one of her grandsons. She made less and less pottery since it had become increasingly difficult for her to form the vessels as well as she once had. From time to time, she demonstrated making a small pot and talked about pottery making. With visitors she often talked about all the fascinating people she had met and the places she had been. On July 20, 1980, Maria passed away at home in San Ildefonso Pueblo at the age of ninety-three.

During her long life, Maria received many awards for her artistry, but some, such as the Jane Addams Award for Distinguished Service in 1959, looked beyond her skill as a potter to the woman who had also crafted a good life. Maria's life was in many ways undistinguished and common. She lived according to principles, long held by her Tewa village, of how people should treat one another. With her husband's assistance and her ability to adapt to forces outside her Pueblo, she not only won worldwide acclaim but she also helped her neighbors accommodate to enormous change without surrendering the values they held dear. Maria always understood her success in terms of the community: she learned how to make pots from others, and she happily shared her own skill, marketing tactics, and even her signature with her neighbors. With an identity so fully embedded in the community, success would have been meaningless if she had acted otherwise. Crafting an ethical life meant as much to Maria as creating the magnificent pottery on which her reputation rests.

NOTES

1. For other works on Maria Martinez, see Alice Marriott, *María: The Potter of San Ildefonso* (Norman: University of Oklahoma Press, 1948); Susan Peterson, *The Living Tradition of Maria Martinez* (Tokyo: Kodansha International, 1981); and Richard Spivey, *Maria* (2d ed., Flagstaff: Northland Publishing, 1989).

2. Sandra A. Edelman, "San Ildefonso Pueblo," in *Handbook of North American Indians: Southwest*, v. 9, ed. Alfonso Ortiz (Washington: Smithsonian Institution, 1979), 308–16; William Whitman, "The San Ildefonso of New Mexico," in *Acculturation in Seven American Indian Tribes*, ed. Ralph Linton (New York: D. Appleton–Century Co., 1940), 390–462.

3. Elsie Clews Parsons, "Tewa Mothers and Children," *Man* 112 (1924): 148–51.

4. Ruth Bunzel, *The Pueblo Potter: A Study of Creative Imagination in Primitive Art* (New York: Columbia University Press, 1929); Carl E. Guthe, *Pueblo Pottery Making: A Study at the Village of San Ildefonso* (New Haven: Yale University Press, 1925).

5. Alfonso Ortiz, *The Tewa World: Space, Time, Being, and Becoming in a Pueblo Society* (Chicago: University of Chicago Press, 1969); Rina Swentzell and Tito Naranjo, "Nurturing: The *Gia* at Santa Clara Pueblo," *El Palacio* 92 (1986).

11

ALICE LEE JEMISON

A Modern "Mother of the Nation"

Laurence M. Hauptman

No woman in the twentieth century was as bold, courageous, strident, or fanatical in her defense of the Seneca Nation of Indians as Alice Mae Lee Jemison, the most prominent American Indian journalist in the United States from the early 1930s to her death in 1964.[1] Although she was viewed by the Interior Department and the FBI as a dangerous subversive and put under surveillance because of her unyielding criticism of U.S. government Indian policies, Jemison's political activism was well rooted in Seneca culture and history. Despite being falsely labeled at various times as an unrepresentative "mixed-blood," a Nazi, a fascist, and a communist, Jemison was a much more representative voice of Seneca women than her enemies ever acknowledged. Beginning in the late 1920s, Jemison set the tone and stage for a new generation of outstanding women to transform women's roles: they emerged from behind the scenes to assume a more visible position in Seneca Nation politics. Jemison's relentless commitment to Iroquois sovereignty-minded views and her willingness to take extreme measures, even at all costs to her reputation, made her a formidable opponent of Washington- and Albany-directed Indian policies from 1930 to her death in 1964.

At the time of Alice Mae Lee Jemison's birth in 1901, Seneca women were primarily homemakers. Although a few women worked as domestics in nearby white communities, most wage laborers were men employed by the railroads. Although their failure to produce visible income may have devalued women in the eyes of non-Indians, Seneca women continued to contribute to their families' subsistence in traditional ways: they cultivated gardens, collected wild plants for food and medicine, and made various household goods. Seneca society in the precontact and postcontact periods had been organized around complementary gender roles. The Iroquois village with its horticultural focus was the world of the women, matrilineal descent, and matrilocal residence. The world beyond the village was the arena where men absented themselves to conduct diplomacy, go on the hunt, or take the warpath. Although men were more politically visible, women possessed considerable power, including the right of clan mothers to depose chiefs. With the process of Euro-American colonization came vast disruptions in Seneca existence. Seneca culture underwent significant change: housing arrangements went from extended longhouse residences to nuclear households, and a patrilineal naming system compromised traditional matrilineal descent. Following a series of fraudulent land cessions, the Seneca Nation of Indians (different from the separate Tonawanda Band of Senecas) adopted a written constitution with elected officials in 1848, creating a republican form of government that broke with the traditional Iroquoian chieftanship system. Under the 1848 constitution, only men over the age of twenty-one could vote, although Seneca clan mothers continued to have voting rights on land issues.

Throughout the nineteenth and well into the twentieth centuries, the Seneca Nation accommodated Euro-American culture, religious traditions, and values, and with them, certain restrictions on the role of women in its society. Despite not having the right to vote or seek public office until 1964, women relied on their roles as mothers in a matrilineal society to exert influence on major political issues. Insisting that they had the right to speak for seven generations to come, women petitioned the federal government to accept the results of the Seneca revolution of 1848. Reflecting traditional practice, Seneca laws continued to recognize that husbands and wives each kept control of their own property. Women still served as clan mothers and faithkeepers, and the Nation acknowledged that women were traditionally protectors of the Seneca lands and, with it, identity. To this day, only children of Seneca women can achieve tribal enrollment. Seneca women are, therefore, the mothers of their nation politically, socially, and culturally as well as biologically.[2]

Born at Silver Creek, New York, near the Cattaraugus Reservation of the Senecas, Jemison was the daughter of Daniel A. Lee, a cabinetmaker of Cherokee descent, and Elnora E. Seneca, a member of a prominent Seneca family, whose brother Cornelius Seneca would serve as president of the Seneca Nation in the 1940s and 1950s. Her parents met while attending Hampton Institute. Her youthful ambition to become an attorney was frustrated by her family's poverty. Her formal education ended with her graduation in 1919 from Silver Creek High School, where she had studied debating and journalism. That same year she married Le Verne Leonard Jemison, a local Seneca steelworker. Nine years later they separated as a result of Le Verne's chronic alcoholism, and thereafter, as a single parent, Jemison had to support her mother and her two young children. Living on the Cattaraugus Reservation through the 1920s, she struggled to provide for her family, working in a factory and as a clerk, peddler, dressmaker, practical nurse, stone and gravel hauler, and as a legal researcher for a Buffalo attorney. In 1929 she became the secretary to, and researcher for, Ray Jimerson, then president of the Seneca Nation. The next year Jemison worked for the U.S. Bureau of the Census, gathering information on the reservation.

By 1930, Jemison's worldview had already been firmly shaped as a woman growing up in Seneca society, with the omnipresence of powerful women. Moreover, as the head of household after the collapse of her marriage, Jemison was forced to be even more self-reliant. As a hardworking woman from a proud and distinguished Seneca family lineage, she believed that officials in Washington and Albany fostered Indian dependence and welfare. As an Iroquois traditionalist, she insisted that what was needed was the carrying out of United States-Iroquois treaties, most specifically the Canandaigua Treaty of 1794, the only federal accord that returned lands to the Senecas. Any other course of action was wrong, she avowed, repeatedly pointing out that the Indians did not need any more reforms such as the Indian Reorganization Act (IRA) that only added new levels of bureaucracy and benefited only government workers. To her, a bloated and corrupt Bureau of Indian Affairs (BIA) in Washington and New York State programs that delayed Indian land claims settlements or did not recognize Indian hunting and fishing rights were hardly beneficial to the Indians.

As a disciple of the famous Yavapai journalist and physician Carlos Montezuma, Jemison could easily find fault with both federal and state Indian policies. Like Montezuma, she condemned the BIA, an agency that had done little to prevent the alienation of over 90 million acres of the Indian land base since the passage of the Dawes General Allotment Act of 1887. By 1933, Indians retained approximately 48 million acres, much of it arid, unusable land. Moreover, 49 percent of the Indians on allotted reservations were landless. Even before the onset of the Great Depression, 96 percent of all Indians earned less than $200 per year, and only 2 percent had a per capita income greater than $500 per year.

Jemison's worldview had been shaped by other factors. In the 1920s, she witnessed a growing resurgence of Iroquois nationalism. During and after World War I, a renewed Iroquois land claims movement arose. In 1922, a New York

State legislative committee, the Everett Commission, insisted that the Iroquois actually held legal title to millions of acres of New York State taken from the Indians in the six decades after the American Revolution. At approximately the same time, in response to an earlier favorable ejectment case, *United States* v. *Boylan*, involving Oneida lands in New York, a Six Nations land claim arose, fostered by Laura Minnie Cornelius Kellogg, a charismatic, spellbinding Oneida orator. Although this Six Nations case, *Deere et al.* v. *State of New York,* was eventually dismissed, the so-called Kellogg movement stirred Iroquois nationalism. Other claims followed. Cayuga efforts at securing justice led to a United States–Canada arbitration commission in 1926. Iroquois assertions of vocal expressions of their sovereignty included sending delegations to the League of Nations in Geneva, Switzerland, and to Great Britain's Board of Trade in the 1920s under the leadership of the great Iroquois nationalist, Chief Deskahe.

Alice Lee Jemison's Senecas were not idle in this regard. During World War I, their attorney, George Decker, later the attorney for Chief Deskahe, was hired to assert the Seneca claims to the Niagara River, a claim that remains active today. More importantly to Jemison, Congress in 1927 ignored Seneca insistence that they had the right to fish on their own tribal lands without a New York State license and "awarded" Senecas and New York State joint jurisdiction on Indian reservation lands. Moreover, in the same act, as a result of lobbying by New York's attorney general, Congress retroactively confirmed the state's "take" of Seneca lands at the Oil Spring Reservation, an illegal state move that had been made in clear violation of the federal Trade and Intercourse acts and one that had never been approved by the United States Senate.[26] This act, known as the Seneca Conservation Act, was a major turning point in Jemison's political awakening.

Another turning point in Jemison's life came with the Marchand murder case of 1930, the most notorious event to take place in Buffalo since the 1901 assassination of President William McKinley. Two American Indian women were accused of killing a white woman, Clothilde Marchand, the wife of noted artist and museum designer Jules Henri Marchand. Jemison moved to Buffalo to work with Iroquois leaders who sought federal intervention in the case. To challenge disparaging portrayals of the accused women and Indians in general, Jemison wrote letters to public figures and articles for the *Buffalo Evening News*. The two women were convicted, but, after serving time in prison, they were freed because of legal questions involving the fairness of the trial. The experience Jemison gained in lobbying and publicity and the contacts she made in the journalistic world became her springboard for a new career. By 1932 her articles were syndicated by the North American Newspaper Alliance and reached a wide audience. As a result of her work for the Senecas, she was nominated by the Seneca Nation Tribal Council for positions in the Indian service on at least two occasions.

In 1934 Jemison moved to Washington, D.C., and began writing for the *Washington Star*. She also served as a lobbyist for the Seneca Nation and monitored congressional activities on Indian affairs. She soon became the major publicist-lobbyist for a new nationwide Indian organization, the American Indian Federation (AIF). Cutting through its extremist right-wing language of protest that was as much rhetoric and tactic as ideology, the AIF was a loose umbrella-like organization that was composed of many strands of Indian thinking: the Indian National Confederacy of Oklahoma, which included members of the Five Civilized Tribes; the Mission Indian Federation of California; the Intertribal Committee for the Fundamental Advancement of the American Indian, based in Buffalo and Detroit and largely dominated by Iroquois Indians; and the Black Hills Treaty Council, which included a substantial number of Sioux Indians opposed to the IRA. Hence, the organization was as diverse as Native America itself, with Indians coalescing in a national lobbying effort largely because of local reservation grievances, some of which preceded the New Deal.

Throughout the debate over the "Indian New Deal," Jemison served as spokeswoman for the AIF. She edited the federation's newspaper, *First American*, and served as the organization's major lobbyist on Capitol Hill. From 1934 until her resignation from the federation in 1939, Jemison appeared at more congressional hearings on Indian affairs than any other Native American. In addition to her objection on principle to the BIA, Jemison criticized federal reformist policies and the IRA, proposed by Franklin Roosevelt's commissioner of Indian affairs, John Collier, and supported by secretary of Indian affairs Harold Ickes, both of whom she believed did not understand the diverse world of American Indians. The IRA, passed by Congress in June 1934, provided for the establishment of tribal elections, constitutions, and corporations; a revolving loan fund to assist organized tribes in community development; and preferential hiring in the Indian Service, namely, waiving civil service requirements for Indians in order to encourage their employment. The act also created an educational loan program for Indian students seeking a vocational, high school, or college education. Moreover, the act directly related to Indian lands, ending the land allotment policies of the Dawes Act and providing for the purchase of new lands for the Indians. Unallotted lands were to be returned to tribal councils. Conservation efforts were also encouraged on existing Indian lands by the establishment of Indian forestry units and by herd reduction on arid land to protect range deterioration.

Jemison viewed this far-reaching IRA as a growth of bureaucracy in Indian life and as an intrusion on tribal sovereignty since the approval of the secretary of the interior was required for nearly every provision of the act. She challenged Commissioner Collier by insisting that no act or uniform program dictated by Washington could do justice to the diverse needs of Native Americans across the United States. Many Indians, too, objected to the provisions for tribal plebiscites, a vote of members, required with the acceptance of the terms of the IRA. Jemison furthermore accused the BIA of manipulating congressional hearings on the legislation by looking more favorably on requests for travel funds from the act's supporters than from its opponents.

To Jemison's own Senecas, who already operated under an elected system, IRA provisions calling for a new constitution and a new elected system were superfluous. With over 50,000 acres of tribal lands remaining in their hands, many Senecas feared that the reform was merely a new scheme to get at their land base. One contemporary of Jemison wrote Commissioner Collier: "We have been fooled time after time that most of the Indians have lost faith in the Saxon race we certainly have had some raw deal in back history we have never had a square deal" [sic].[3] Much like Alice Lee Jemison, President Ray Jimerson viewed the forty-eight-page IRA as "too long and complicated . . . full of new rules and regulations . . . and subject to Bureau interpretation."[4] Hence Jemison, as a mother of the nation, defined her mission to save her people and her people's homeland at all costs.

Jemison's activism was also prompted by the terrible conditions found on her reservation. Since most Senecas worked off the Cattaraugus Reservation in factories in or near Buffalo or were employed as structural ironworkers, they were not insulated from the devastating effects of the Great Depression. Unemployment was high, and many Indians depended on work relief to survive. Throughout the period after 1929, these Indians frequently complained that state, and later federal, programs designed for their needs—including road work and school construction projects—discriminated against the Indians by hiring only non-Indians or requiring American citizenship, voter's registration cards, and loyalty oaths that ran counter to Iroquois beliefs in sovereignty. The worst conditions at Cattaraugus were in the area of public health. In 1934, the death rate caused by tuberculosis on the reservation was six times higher than in the non-Indian world. The continued pollution of Cattaraugus Creek, which traverses the reservation, was a major source of the spread of disease.

To vocalize these and other Indian complaints against the New York State Department of Conservation, the Seneca Nation Tribal Council appointed Jemison as their lobbyist in Washington. From January 1933 to June 1935, she actively campaigned to overturn the Seneca Conservation Act of 1927. Working with President Ray Jimerson and Robert Galloway, the attorney for the Seneca Nation, she convinced New York Congressman Alfred Beiter to introduce legislation to revoke New York State Department of Conservation jurisdiction on hunting and fishing on Indian reservations. She argued both that the law violated Iroquois rights as guaranteed under the Treaty of Canandaigua and that state officials were harassing the Indians. In June 1935, just after Iroquois rejection of the IRA, President Roosevelt, a former two-term governor of New York State, vetoed the Beiter Bill, much to the anger of the Senecas. In reaction, Jemison wrote a four-page letter of protest in which she criticized Roosevelt's action, claiming his veto was motivated by Iroquois opposition to John Collier and their voting down the IRA. She insisted that he reread the Canandaiga treaty of 1794 and fire the commissioner of Indian affairs:

> I know that my people will be deeply grieved at your attitude. Having been Governor of New York State you are in a position to know that the New York State Indians are now and always have been in the status of "quasi dependent nations"; that their lands have been held by the Highest Courts to be "extra territoria"; and that they have always enjoyed the rights of self-government free from any outside direction, under the provisions of the Treaty of Canandaigua made in 1794 with George Washington. Up until you became President of the United States this popularly termed Conservation Act constituted the only existing legislative violation of that treaty.[5]

The failure of this campaign to overturn the Seneca Conservation Act contributed to Jemison's increasing activism in the mid- and late 1930s and to her overwhelmingly negative reaction to Commissioner Collier, the IRA, and the Roosevelt administration as a whole.

Indeed, despite her national focus in her work for the AIF, Jemison was primarily an Iroquois woman, a political disciple of Montezuma as well as an evangelical abolitionist. She feared an omnipotent federal government and was suspicious of all non-Indian governmental authority, be it Washington- or Albany-based. Although her remarks before congressional committee hearings echoed much of her organization's right-wing rhetoric of protest and represented much of the sentiments of the Oklahoma faction within the AIF, Jemison's protests also reflected much of the Iroquois thinking of the period. Her belief in Iroquois treaty rights, coupled with an Iroquois vision of sovereignty that never wavered, came into conflict with Commissioner Collier and his views throughout the New Deal years.

At a congressional hearing on February 11, 1935, Jemison affirmed her belief in the sanctity of the Treaty of Canandaigua, insisted that the "situation in New York State is entirely different from any other Indians in the United States," and concluded that, under the terms of this and other treaties with the federal government, "we [have] always had self-government among the New York Indians."[6] At the same hearing, Collier totally dismissed this interpretation of the Iroquois as independent sovereignties who "never came under the jurisdiction of the United States." After all, Collier argued, the Supreme Court has repeatedly held that the "sovereignty in an Indian group is dependent on the will of Congress, and that Congress may invade, modify, regulate, or abolish it."[7] Hence, two divergent belief systems, one subscribed to by Jemison and a significant number of Iroquois and the other held by the non-Indian world and its legal institutions, clashed throughout the New Deal.

It should also be noted that by 1937 the Indian New Deal, as well as the New Deal as a whole, was in serious political trouble. The conservative coalition in Congress began to assert the power that it had relinquished during the economic emergency of President Roosevelt's first term. The "court-packing" fight of 1937 also undermined the administration's influence on Capitol Hill. Commissioner Collier and Secretary Ickes, never liked by many congressional leaders, had also begun to face the wrath of a newly assertive Congress. Most of the major pieces of legislation of the Indian New Deal had been introduced and passed during Roosevelt's first administration. Equally significant, Senator Wheeler, who by 1937 led the opposition to Roosevelt's court packing, introduced a bill to repeal the IRA, the very piece of legislation he had sponsored into law. Just as the president had purged his foes in the congressional primaries of 1938 and 1940, Collier and Ickes, now under attack by Congressman Dies's House Committee on Un-American Activities Committee, began to retaliate against their enemies. It appears as no coincidence, then, that the day after Jemison testified about communism in the Interior Department before Dies's committee, Ickes first alleged that Jemison, code-named "Pocahontas," was a Nazi go-between. The FBI file on Jemison also reveals that her two major accusers of alleged Nazi activity were the Secretary of the Interior and the commissioner of Indian affairs, the same two administrators subjected most to Jemison's attacks.

Jemison's attacks were frequently overblown and extremist in tone. Sometimes branding her opponents as communists or atheists, Jemison herself was accepted by right-wing critics of the Roosevelt administration, ranging from the Daughters of the American Revolution to William Dudley Pelley, the extremist leader of the Silver Shirts of America. In her relentless war against the BIA, she was willing to appear at the same hearing with self-styled fascists, as she did in

1938 and 1940 before the House Committee on Un-American Activities. Such tactics allowed the Interior Department to portray her as an Indian Nazi, a charge belied by the fact that she passed every loyalty check made by the FBI and was able to secure government employment in the Bureau of the Census during World War II. The Interior Department's portrayal of Jemison as a subversive was furthered by her own actions in defense of Iroquois sovereignty. Another thorny and volatile issue was whether or not the federal government could draft Iroquois into the armed forces. Once again, although her stand labeled her as unpatriotic, it was Jemison who led the opposition to the Selective Service Act of 1940, based on her insistence that only the Iroquois Confederacy and/or each nation's tribal council had the ultimate authority to make decisions for war.

Because of family economic necessity, federal limitations on government employees' political lobbying, and the climate of the country after Pearl Harbor, Jemison muted her outspoken stance through World War II while working for the Bureau of the Census. After the war, Jemison remained in Washington and continued to call for the BIA's abolition, while opposing the transfer of criminal jurisdiction over Indians in New York from federal to state government that occurred in 1948. In 1948, when Senator Arthur Watkins of Utah suggested that a lump-sum monetary payment replace the symbolic treaty cloth that the Iroquois annually receive under the Treaty of Canandaigua, a practice the senator considered to be anachronistic, Jemison angrily responded: "We have kept our shares of the treaties, and we are here to ask that you keep yours. The little amount of calico [treaty cloth] for which the money is appropriated each year by this Congress doesn't amount to very much per person, but it is the significance of that calico which means something to all of us."[8]

The ultimate irony of Jemison's political activism over three decades was that her work for self-determination of Indian nations was distorted by the Congressional policy of termination established in the 1950s. It had the opposite effects on Native Americans than what she had intended. She wanted to help American Indians by abolishing the BIA; however, her arguments for its abolition added fuel to a policy that proved more of a detriment than a cure. Termination, the policy of removing the BIA's role in administering Indian programs by ending the separate legal status of American Indians guaranteed by treaties, was applied in the 1950s and 1960s. Congress "turned certain Indian tribes loose" from federal authority, for reasons not simply related to BIA mismanagement or because of its faith in the ability of Native Americans to rule themselves, as Montezuma and Jemison had maintained. Masking their motives in self-determination rhetoric, conservatives in Congress, such as Senators Arthur Watkins and Karl Mundt, urged termination for cost-saving reasons, anti–big government sentiment, antiwelfare statism, and basic laissez-faire attitudes. Liberals, such as Senator Hubert Humphrey, viewed the Indian world in a civil rights context against the backdrop of the milestone *Brown* v. *The Board of Education of Topeka, Kansas* and remained largely unaware of the cultural separatist nature of much Native American thinking. Consequently, they urged termination as a means of freeing the Indians from oppression.

Although one is tempted to label Jemison a "terminationist," this over-generalization is as misleading as the labels given her by Collier. She was an Iroquois woman, a political disciple of Montezuma, an evangelical abolitionist, an individual who, until her death in 1964, had complete faith in Native American peoples' right and ability to rule themselves. She consistently agitated in the 1950s for the abolition of the BIA, just as she had in the 1930s. Although Jemison's arguments were used by congressional critics of the bureau and proponents of termination in the early 1950s, she and other activists among the Iroquois saw the dangers of the legislation proposed during the Truman-Eisenhower administrations. In February 1954, Jemison predicted with startling accuracy the dangers facing the Indians. She insisted that the "present proposals will accomplish only one thing with any certainty—the termination of Federal expenditures for the benefit of the Indians, and will leave the Indians suspended in a twilight zone of political nonentity, partly tribal, partly State. And twenty years from now another Congress will be considering measures to correct the mistakes of this experiment."[9] In 1973, nearly twenty years after the passage of the first termination bill, Congress restored the federal status of the Menominee Nation of Wisconsin.

Jemison's activism inspired other women to take a more active role in Seneca politics. By the 1960s, in a conscious attempt to rebuild the Seneca Nation of Indians after the flooding of over nine thousand acres of their lands with the construction of the Kinzua Dam, Seneca women resurrected their image as mothers of the nation. During the Kinzua crisis, Seneca women refused to remain passive victims; they became forceful activists. As a result of the Kinzua crisis and the lobbying efforts of Genevieve Plummer, Reva Barss, and George Heron, Seneca women finally achieved the right to vote and hold political office. With the election of Martha Bucktooth to the council in the mid-1960s, women have been frequently elected and/or appointed to key positions within the tribal government, although no woman has yet been elected president of the nation.

Women emerged in even more visible roles by the mid-1970s. Faced with a major health crisis, land loss in the final completion of New York State Route 17, the ending of the ninety-nine-year lease to the City of Salamanca, and a bitter tax struggle with New York State, Seneca women were no longer detached from politics or played politics from behind the scenes in the traditional way, but were active participants in the events that transpired. As a result of a highly organized group of women, the Seneca Nation Health Action Group, led by Hazel Dean John, Norma Kennedy, Wini Kettle, and others, the Senecas established two modern Indian Health Service facilities at the Allegany and Cattaraugus Reservations. After raising support for a tribal commemoration of the twenty-year anniversary of the Kinzua Dam tragedy in 1984, numerous young Seneca women actively pro-tested the completion of New York State Route 17 the following year. Between 1985 and 1991, Seneca women such as Loretta Crane, Cheryl Ray, and others played key roles in the final settlement of the Seneca Nation–Salamanca lease controversy that had lingered for a century. Indian women have been among the key organizers of the resistance to New York State's efforts to collect sales taxes on Indian reservations, and their efforts sometimes brought them into face-to-face confrontations with heavily armed state troopers.

Alice Lee Jemison was a modern woman of the Seneca Nation of Indians, but she reflected the ancient values of her people. Instead of swaying her people in behind-the-scenes negotiations as in the past, she was an especially outwardly combative person espousing a most traditional message, namely, respect for Iroquois sovereignty and treaty rights, although she used a twentieth-century weapon—the mass media—to fight back. No longer relegated to the world of the clearing as in olden times, Jemison realized that the Senecas were in a state of crisis. Because the Senecas were a powerless people, she attempted to appeal beyond the reservation, using the power of her journalism to grab headlines and often scurrilously attack her enemies. Her willingness to sacrifice everything for her cause, which she interpreted as her people's survival, was often viewed by outsiders as extreme and even fanatical, and in many ways she might be considered the harbinger of Red Power politics among the Iroquois. She, how-ever, saw herself as a mother of the nation, protecting and ensuring Seneca survival into the future. Following Jemison's example, successive generations of Seneca women have resurrected the image of women as mothers of the nation, guardians of tradition in the face of overwhelming odds and crises.

NOTES

1. I have written about Alice Mae Lee Jemison before. Besides brief accounts in the *DAB, ANB,* and *Notable American Women,* see my "Alice Lee Jemison: Seneca Political Activist, 1901–1964," *Indian Historian* 12 (1979): 15–22; *The Iroquois and the New Deal* (Syracuse, NY: Syracuse University Press, 1981), chap. 3; "The American Indian Federa-tion and the Indian New Deal: A Reinterpretation," *Pacific Historical Review* 52 (1983):

378–402; *The Iroquois Struggle for Survival* (Syracuse, NY: Syracuse University Press, 1986); "The First American," in *American Indian and Alaska Native Newspapers and Periodicals, 1925–1970*, ed. Daniel F. Littlefield, Jr., and James W. Parins (Westport, CT: Greenwood Press, 1986), 28. My research is based on extensive fieldwork as well as archival holdings. More extensive documentation of my sources can be found in those works.

2. The following studies deal with women in Iroquois culture and history: Elisabeth Tooker, "Women in Iroquois Society," in *Extending the Rafters: Interdisciplinary Approaches to Iroquoian Studies*, ed. Michael K. Foster, Jack Campisi, and Marianne Mithun (Albany: State University of New York Press, 1984), 109–23; Nancy Bonvillain, "Iroquoian Women," in *Studies on Iroquoian Culture*, ed. Bonvillain (Rindge, NH: Occasional Publications in Northeastern Anthropology, No. 6, Dept. of Anthropology, Franklin Pierce College, *Man in the Northeast*, 1980), 47–58; Judith K. Brown, "Economic Organization and the Position of Women Among the Iroquois," *Ethnohistory* 17 (1970): 151–67; Nancy Shoemaker, "The Rise or Fall of Iroquois Women," *Journal of Women's History* 2 (1991): 39–57, and Shoemaker's "From Longhouse to Loghouse: Household Composition Among the Nineteenth Century Senecas," *American Indian Quarterly* 15 (1991): 329–38; Joy Bilharz, "First Among Equals? The Changing Status of Seneca Women," in *Women and Power in Native North America*, ed. Laura F. Klein and Lillian A. Ackerman (Norman: University of Oklahoma Press, 1995), 101–12; Diane Rothenberg, "The Mothers of the Nation: Seneca Resistance to Quaker Intervention," in *Women and Colonization*, ed. Mona Etienne and Eleanor Leacock (New York: J. F. Bergin Publishers, 1980), 63–87; Joan M. Jensen, "Native American Women and Agriculture" (reprint of 1977 article), in *Unequal Sisters: A Multicultural Reader in U.S. Women's History*, ed. Ellen Carol DuBois and Vicki L. Ruiz (New York: Routledge, 1991), 51–65. Readers should also consult Joy Bilharz's *The Allegany Senecas and the Kinzua Dam: Forced Relocation Through Two Generations* (Lincoln: University of Nebraska Press, 1998), and Anthony F. C. Wallace, *The Death and Rebirth of the Seneca* (New York: Alfred A. Knopf, 1969).

3. George F. Newton to John Collier, 28 Oct. 1934, #4894-1934-066, pt. 12A, Records Concerning the Wheeler-Howard Act, Box 9, RG75, National Archives, Washington, D.C.

4. U.S. Congress. House of Representatives. Committee on Indian Affairs. *Hearings on H.R. 7902*, 73rd Cong., 2d sess. (Washington: Government Printing Office, 1934), 9: 389.

5. Alice Lee Jemison to President Franklin D. Roosevelt, 20 June 1935, President Franklin D. Roosevelt MSS., OF 296, FDR Library, Hyde Park, NY.

6. U.S. Congress. House Committee on Indian Affairs. *Hearings on H.R. 7781 and Other Matters: Indian Conditions and Affairs*. 74th Cong., 1st sess. (Washington: Government Printing Office, 1935), 35–36.

7. Ibid., 48.

8. U.S. Congress. Senate. Subcommittee of the Committee on Interior and Insular Affairs. *Hearings on S. 1683, S. 1686, S. 1687: New York Indians*, 80th Cong., 2d sess. (Washington: Government Printing Office, 1948), p. 24. For Iroquois history in this era, see Laurence M. Hauptman, *The Iroquois Struggle for Survival* (Syracuse, NY: Syracuse University Press, 1986).

9. *The First American* 2 (1954): 3.

12

DELFINA CUERO

A Native Woman's Life in the Borderlands

Phillip H. Round

Borders—artificial political divides separating land, peoples, and cultures—create special challenges for those who live alongside them. The international border between Mexico and the United States, a militarized strip known as *la frontera*, or *la liña* to many who live along its two-thousand-mile length, requires of its residents complex coping strategies that extend beyond bilingual phrases and bicultural gestures. Border patrols survey the land through night vision binoculars, and barbed wire and guard posts punctuate the terrain. The border itself becomes almost a living presence in the lives of people living on either side, a psychological shadow that consigns them to what Chicana theorist Gloria Anzaldúa has called that "vague and undetermined place created by the emotional residue of an unnatural boundary."[1] For Native women, life on the frontera often means doubling the already complex roles of being "woman" and "Indian" in twentieth-century America. On the border, Native women are misrepresented and dispossessed in unique ways. Viewed as "aliens" by Anglo outsiders, their traditional movements across the sacred earth in the seasonal gathering of medicinal plants and foodstuffs are interpreted as "vagrancy" or migrancy—movements that threaten the political stability of the region, movements that must be suppressed. In the United States, they are lumped together with other "illegals" and deported back into Mexico. In Mexico they are not wanted either and are often mistreated as "indios," a people who stand in the way of progress.

There are no special green cards for the Native Americans whose homelands straddle the United States/Mexico border, and the life story of Delfina Cuero, one American Indian woman who challenged the border system and won the right to "cross over" into the United States, dramatizes how, for some Native women, life and land, storytelling and tradition, are woven into the complex history of the borderlands and the people who have traversed them for centuries. That history often takes the form of a new language and a new way of storytelling. The autobiography of Delfina Cuero describes the process by which one native woman discovered such a new language, and, through it, was reunited with her grandmother's land and traditions.

Delfina Cuero was a member of the Kumeyaay (pronounced kum ∂ ya· y) people who originally inhabited the mountain and coastal regions of what is now San Diego County and Baja California. The Kumeyaay were known in Euro-American ethnographic literature through the 1970s as the "Diegueño" and are often discussed under the more general heading of "Mission Indians," because many of their ancestors lived under the Spanish Colonial mission system in the late eighteenth and early nineteenth centuries. Throughout southern California during the period of Spanish colonization (1769–1821), traditional people who had in the past recognized each other through clan and group names in their Native tongues were grouped together under the names of the missions they lived beside—Cupeño, Luiseño, Gabrieleño. By the time California became part of Mexico (1821–1848), Europeans often knew individual Native people who lived in or near the missions by single, Spanish surnames.

Along with the translation and erasure of their Native words and names came political and economic exploitation. The Kumeyaay, Delfina Cuero's band, had early on experienced the twin forces of colonialism and Christianity. When Father Junipero Serra established the first California mission in 1769—the mission San Diego de Alcalá—he did so by taking traditional Kumeyaay lands overlooking San Diego Bay. Soon, the Spanish missionaries were seizing small groups of Kumeyaay people and forcing them to work and live at the mission, releasing them after they had "heard" the word of God, only to capture others and repeat the cycle. Thus, it is not surprising that the Kumeyaay became the most stubborn and violent opponents to the Franciscan and Dominican efforts to control Native California through the mission system. Due partly to their resistance, the Kumeyaay remained on their ancestral lands well into the twentieth century, moving across the international boundary from Alta to Baja California with the seasonal cycles.

By 1834, the Mexican government had secularized the missions of California and, in the process, turned the old religious communes into large, private haciendas run by Mexican landowners. Under this transformation, Native people like the Kumeyaay often found themselves further dispossessed of territory and forced to live as virtual serfs in the country of their ancestors. The first wave of Anglo-Americans arrived in the 1840s, and cities like San Diego grew up on the Kumeyaay's lands. In 1848, following the Mexican War, the U.S. government acquired California and established inland reservations for those Mission Indians they officially recognized as "nations." But several bands of Delfina Cuero's people, the coastal Kumeyaay, were left out of the reservation system and remained unrecognized by the American government. As a culture whose survival depended on migratory patterns tied to food resources and sacred land formations, they were too mobile and too dispersed to be confined within the rigid political definitions of an Indian tribe. With their traditional lands disappearing behind fences, and their way to the newly established reservations of eastern San Diego County blocked by politics, many Kumeyaay were compelled to live in San Diego slums or to camp in nearby hills, drifting off into Mexico when Americans encroached further onto their land and co-opted their resources. By the 1890s, many Kumeyaay men and women were more or less invisible to outsiders. They were viewed not as traditional people but as low-skilled laborers, to be hired at subsistence wages as ranch hands, miners, or domestics. Nevertheless, at special times during the year, these dispossessed bands of Kumeyaay returned to the reservations of the officially recognized Mission Indians to celebrate with them the traditional fiestas as they had done for generations.

Delfina Cuero's life story recounts the experiences of one band of Kumeyaay people in the early twentieth century and highlights the changing role of women in a traditional society beleaguered by the economic depredations of colonialism and the cultural confusion of border politics. Delfina Cuero lived in the Californian/Mexican borderland from 1900 until her death in 1972, spending most of those years migrating on foot, following the seasonal cycle of natural food harvests. Her "autobiography," a written transcription of an oral narration made in 1967 by Florence Shipek, an anthropologist and professor of American Indian history, was initially assembled to provide evidence of Cuero's U.S. citizenship in lieu of the normal documentary proof required when she found herself on the "wrong" side of the international border during an extended period of habitation in Baja California. *Delfina Cuero: Her Autobiography* is an example of a genre of American Indian literature that involves the recording of a life story by a non-Native writer.[2]

Kumeyaay life in the time of her parents and grandparents, that is, the period between the secularization of the missions in 1834 and the great influx

of American immigrants at the turn of the century, centered around semipermanent home camps, or *rancherias,* in San Diego's Mission Valley. Delfina Cuero
makes it clear in her autobiography that her people were not "Mission Indians" in the sense that Europeans used the word. Although "born in Mission
Valley," her elder relations "were not raised in the Mission. There was nobody
there anymore" (23). Delfina Cuero herself "just heard about priests; [she] never
saw one" (53). The Kumeyaay did not remain year-round in their *rancherias*
because their subsistence required a migratory cycle of hunting and gathering.
In those days, "the Indians had names for every little spot" and "each name
meant something about that place" that linked it to their migration (24).

In April and May, the Kumeyaay journeyed over the coastal range to search
the desert mountains for mescal plants. Using mesquite-wood shovels, the men
"gathered agave" and sometimes brought salt from San Diego Bay to trade with
the locals for "mesquite beans and other things from the desert" (33). In the
fall, they would trek into the mountains to collect acorns. During the rest of
the year, they stayed closer to home, spearing fish with cactus-thorn spears,
harvesting shellfish by the shore, or gathering pine nuts in the coastal pine
groves. Around their more permanent brush and reed dwellings in the valley,
they cultivated small gardens, and when the children were not helping with
the acorn and pine nut gathering, they played with mud dolls and rabbit sticks
of their own making. Within the memory of Cuero's grandparents, the Kumeyaay
went without clothing in the temperate summer months, wearing "only a
tuparaw (loincloth) for men and bark aprons for the women" (36).

For a time, the coastal Kumeyaay way of life seemed to hold its own in the
face of European colonization. Traditional ways were still regulated and ordered
as they had been in the "olden" times: "There were many . . . rules and things
we were taught and believed. There were rules so that each one knew what to do
all the time" (47). Men and women wore their facial tattoos proudly, for they
were believed to "help you go on the straight road" (40). Cuero's husband,
Sebastian Osun, had such a tattoo on his forehead, "real pretty, blue-green and
real round, like the moon and about the size of a half dollar" (39). The song cycles
of the yearly fire dance, the *kuruk,* reaffirmed the vitality of Kumeyaay culture:
"The songs that go with it have to be sung in the right order, from early evening
until dawn. There is a song for each time of the night and as the sun is rising. It
was danced at the death of a person and also to welcome a new child" (46).

By 1900, however, the lifestyle of the Kumeyaay faced a new challenge.
"White people kept moving into more and more of the places," Cuero recalls,
"and we couldn't camp around those places anymore. We went farther and
farther from San Diego, looking for places where nobody chased us away" (26).

In response to this encroachment, the Kumeyaay sought refuge in the less-populated backcountry of Baja California across the border in Mexico. Cuero's grandparents "crossed the line first" without any sense of its sociopolitical meaning: "[W]e didn't know it was a line, only that nobody chased [us] away" (26). To Delfina Cuero and her family, the *frontera* "was just a place in the whole area that had belonged to the Indians where nobody told us to move on" (54).

With this forced migration came cultural dislocation. The first things to go were the simple kitchen gardens of the base settlements: "[W]e had to move too much to plant anything. Always being told to leave, it was no use to plant" (32). Next, the Kumeyaay's life-sustaining medicinal herbs became more difficult to find: "[W]e [couldn't] go everywhere to look for them" (45). Finally, the migratory rhythms themselves ceased: "Our family went down to the beach below Ensenada and to Rosarito Beach when we couldn't get to the San Diego beaches anymore" (56).

As the travels of the Kumeyaay stretched farther and wider, so did clan relationships. Under the pressures of this enforced restlessness and the weakening of the coastal Kumeyaay's integrated network of rules and responsibilities, individuals began to abandon their extended family groups. Cuero's father deserted his family. The economic consequences of his desertion brought radical change to Cuero: "Then my mother said I had to get married so that there would be a man to hunt for us" (54). At this point that Delfina Cuero's double existence both within and without Kumeyaay tradition really began. Economic necessity forced her to marry Sebastian Osun without first having gone through the Kumeyaay initiation into womanhood. As a result, her consciousness as a Kumeyaay woman and the fate of her children became wedded to the rather fragile temporal bond of being Sebastian's wife instead of being enmeshed in a supportive network of extended kin and properly initiated women.

For a time, Delfina explained, "everything was all right; Sebastian was a good man. He worked hard. . . . He was real good to me. He took care of the children" (55). Cuero's immediate group, under the leadership of Sebastian, struggled to maintain Kumeyaay cultural order in a time of extreme dearth. Even though food was scarce, the group adhered to strict gender roles in the division of labor: "The agave gathering and roasting was men's work. Hunting game for meat and hunting for bees and honey were men's jobs also. The women hunted for wild greens, seeds, and fruit. The whole family helped with acorns and pine nuts" (57). But when Sebastian died unexpectedly, the group dissolved, and Delfina Cuero could no longer fall back on the extended Kumeyaay clan system for support of her children and herself. Although she cut her hair off in "the Indian way," she soon found that a single person couldn't sustain a hunting and gathering existence: "I had a hard time getting enough food for my children. Things got pretty bad" (60). Things got so bad, in fact, that she was forced to sacrifice her oldest son: "I finally had to sell Aureliano to a Mexican to get food" (60).

From this point on, Delfina Cuero's life reflected the pressures of a border existence quite unlike that of her grandmother, who had gathered herbs and greens, told stories, and made baskets and ollas, while her husband hunted, dug agave, and led the *kuruk* dances. Cuero described her struggle to survive: "I tried to live with several men, each one said he would take care of me but each time it was always the same. I did all the cooking, washing, ironing, and everything, all the work I had always done, but it wasn't enough. I had to cut firewood and stack it. I had to clear land and cut fence posts. I had to work like a man as well as the house and garden work, hard, heavy work. If I didn't do enough to suit him, he would beat me" (62). In stark contrast to the Kumeyaay traditions she and Sebastian had observed during their marriage, Cuero now faced a conflation of gender roles wholly alien to her Kumeyaay upbringing. Significantly, none of the men Cuero "tried to live with" was Kumeyaay. At the conclusion of her narrative, we find her almost completely absorbed into the service economy imposed on the colonized by the colonizers: "I earn my food now . . . by doing washing and ironing for the ladies on the ranches around here. There are too many people all through the mountains now for Indians to live by hunting and gathering the wild food" (64).

The events in Cuero's life chart the trajectory of a colonized people from cultural resistance to political and economic exploitation. Florence Shipek, Cuero's interviewer, emphasizes this in her introduction to the text: "This auto-biography is typical of the life stories of most of the Indians who had no place to call their own. . . . A free translation of part of their ceremonial mourning song reflects their attitude, . . . 'things may be going well for you one day, then something happens and you are destroyed. . . . Remember, it can happen to you too'" (15). Yet Delfina Cuero's life story does not merely recount the oppression of a Native population on the border. It also demonstrates her and her people's capacity for renewal and improvisation. Significantly, the role of women in Kumeyaay society became the focus of her recollection, for storytelling and womanhood serve as the empowering medicine that she needs to triumph over the oppressive weight of the Anglo-American invasion and the imposition of an international border between herself and her traditional lands.

Alongside the main narrative that details the physical deprivations Delfina Cuero had to endure, there is another, woman-centered narrative in this auto-biography, one focused on Delfina Cuero's search for the songs that energized

Kumeyaay culture during her childhood. It is as though by telling her story, Delfina Cuero hoped to reinvigorate those songs. This element of her narrative is about the revival of Kumeyaay culture through the efforts of tribal elders like herself, who kept moving, kept improvising, until they could once again return to Kumeyaay land and practice the old ways. If part of Delfina Cuero's story seems passive—the timing of her marriage is decided for her, she is compelled to sell her son, she is beaten, and she ends up doing laundry for wealthy ranchers—another facet reveals a font of female creativity that is modified, but not erased, by colonial oppression. In remembering her grandmother, Delfina recalled the creative function of traditional Kumeyaay womanhood. Her grandmother's voice emanated from the past to place Cuero's own story within a tribal context and enable her to draw on cultural practices that she had not personally experienced.[3]

Delfina Cuero's search for a song to bring her back across the border to the rancheria that was her band's semipermanent home had at its center the initiation rite of Kumeyaay girls into womanhood, a ceremony denied to Delfina herself: "My grandmother told me about what they did to girls as they were about to become women. But I'm not that old! They had already stopped doing it when I became a woman" (39). In trying to remember what her grandmother had told her of this ceremony of womanhood, Delfina Cuero was not merely searching for a personal experience that she was denied, but rather for a song cycle that centered the whole of Kumeyaay culture. Anthropologists believe that this girls' ceremony was the oldest rite practiced by the Kumeyaay and that it was one of the Kumeyaay traditions least changed by outside influence. Delfina remembered how her grandmother had emphasized its importance, many times reciting the ceremony's form:

> [T]hey dug a hole, filled it with warm sand, and kept the girl in there. They tattooed her all around her mouth and chin. They would sing about food and see if she would get hungry; to see if she could stand hunger. She wasn't allowed to eat. They danced around the top of the hole. A week I think they kept her there, I'm not sure. They didn't want the girls to get wrinkled early or to get gray, but to have good health and good babies. This helped them. I believe in it, but they didn't ask me. I don't get sick much, but I am gray and wrinkled. (39)

As outsiders to this culture, we might focus undue attention on certain preoccupations of our own: graying hair, wrinkles, and health. But Delfina Cuero's mention of these European concerns did not mean that she had assimilated them and left Kumeyaay traditions behind. A few pages later, she outlined the very practical importance the ceremony had for a twentieth-century Kumeyaay woman. When pregnant for the first time and working miles from home on her own, Delfina was suddenly stricken with a crippling pain. She recalled her first child's birth: "I started walking back home but I had to stop and rest when the pain was too much. Then the baby came, I couldn't walk any more, and I didn't know what to do. Finally an uncle came out looking for me when I didn't return. My grandmother had not realized my time was so close or she would have not let me go so far alone. They carried me back but I lost the baby" (43). The song cycle of the girls' ceremony contained important knowledge about all aspects of Kumeyaay womanhood, including information about childbirth. Without these songs, Delfina Cuero was unprepared for her ordeal. She was not alone among the Kumeyaay women of her generation: "Some of the other girls had the same trouble I did" (43).

In addition to its importance for preserving birthing knowledge, the girls' ceremony also aided the development of a mature Kumeyaay female consciousness. During the rite, the older Kumeyaay women sang to the initiate "about food to see if she could stand hunger" (39). Hunger in the ritual represented the young girl's cultural longing—hunger to be a woman, hunger to be wholly Kumeyaay. It is finally satisfied at the close of the rite when the ritually "roasted" girl is feasted and welcomed into the community as a newly born woman.

In Delfina Cuero's story, female identity also turned on her ability to stave off hunger, but the meaning of Delfina Cuero's hunger shifted as the cultural rootedness of her Kumeyaay band weakened. In the early parts of the narrative, Cuero used hunger to define the boundaries of Kumeyaay gender roles and their importance in keeping the community together: "The women had their work to do while the men worked too. Either we do this or we starve" (32). But after the band split up and Sebastian died, hunger represented Cuero's dependence upon cultural outsiders: "[W]hen the man would not let me feed my children, I would have to find someone else to work for. . . . [T]his Mexican man seemed all right. But he didn't want my children around. He didn't want to share the food with them even though I was working too" (62–63). The "Mexican man" felt no sense of community; his unwillingness to share his food with Cuero's children reflected her descent into a culture of selfish individualism.

By contrast, in the Kumeyaay girls' ceremony, hunger was depicted as communal and was alleviated by "the songs and the myths that belonged to the ceremony" (42). The songs and the myths, in a sense, "fed" the girl with the cultural sustenance she would need throughout her life. But in Delfina Cuero's twentieth-century borderlands world, songs and myths were hard to come by. When, for example, she attempted to relate a story about starfish early in the narrative, she was unable to remember it, and excused herself by saying, "There was more to it but I am not a storyteller and that is all I can remember" (29). In the past, in Kumeyaay culture, there were special people who were gifted with the ability to tell stories and they fulfilled that duty for the group (Cuero's grandfather was one). By the time Cuero was an adult, the cultural division of labor had broken down to the extent that she found herself saddled with the roles of "herb-woman," woodcutter, washerwoman, *and* storyteller.

The one story Delfina Cuero remembered and related, a trickster tale about Coyote and the crow girls, is significant:

> Then there were these two beautiful girls who were crows and who lived in a tree. An old woman was taking care of the girls and guarding them. But she went to sleep because she was too old. The coyote sneaked up and tried to climb the tree but he couldn't. Then he jumped and jumped but he couldn't reach the girls. The girls couldn't go to sleep because coyote made so much noise jumping. So the girls flew up into the sky and coyote was chasing them and crying and begged them to take him along. The younger girl asked, "Why can't we take him with us?" The older one said, "No, he can't fly." The younger replied, "Why can't we throw something down and pull him up so he can go with us?" But the older one said, "He's too bad; he would eat us." The younger girl must have fallen in love with him because she felt sorry for him. She finally threw down the end of a rope and coyote began climbing up into the sky toward the crow girls. As coyote climbed, he began talking about how he wanted to grab that girl. The older sister got upset and then mad as she heard him talking. She said, "Let's get rid of him. He'll hurt us. He's too different." The older sister cut the rope so that coyote fell and died. (41)

The grandmother figure, the spiritual center of Kumeyaay womanhood, had fallen asleep because she was too "old." Without their cultural guardian, the two crow girls ran the risk of being abused by men. At first it seems that the moral of the tale is simple. Delfina Cuero told her interviewer that the story meant "we have to watch men—there are some good men and some bad men" (41). The sleeping female elder, however, was also a reflection of Delfina Cuero's own fears about having lost touch with her grandmother's traditions. In her life, without the girls' ceremony, she had run into "some good men and some bad men," had lost a baby, and had been refused entry into her band's traditional lands.

But Delfina Cuero did not restrict the "moral" of the story to these two possible conclusions. She quickly added another, complicating element to her interpretation: "the old people did not have to tell us what the story explained at the end of the story," she said, "but I am saying what it meant to us" (42). In the old days, the people lived within the stories and knew their meanings without speaking them. In the modern world, Delfina Cuero had to verbalize their meanings in order to recapture their power. In spelling out their meaning, however, she was aware that the stories and songs assumed a new dimension. By telling Florence Shipek the story of her life, Delfina Cuero realized that she was engaged in something different from anything she or her family had ever done. While explaining what the Kumeyaay women learned in the ritual songs of initiation, she remarked, "Nobody just talked about these things ever. It was all in the songs and myths that belonged to the ceremony" (42). By calling her narration "just talk," Cuero indicated that it was a new and special kind of language, related to her new circumstances. This aspect of her autobiography reveals the many layers of historical interaction and colonial repression that make the borderlands an essential part of Delfina Cuero's life as a Native woman.

First and foremost, the borderland demanded of Delfina Cuero a political identity and a political language. Having lived in Mexico for many years without proof of U.S. citizenship, she must "just talk" her way back into the United States. The tale she related was full of comments that had less to do with ethnography than with her effort to convince a U.S. court of her legal right to live in her traditional homelands. Clearly recognizing the pragmatic value of her narrative, Cuero disrupted the flow of her story to exhort an imagined audience of powers-that-be: "I pray that something will work out so that my children and grandchildren can come back with me to where I was born" (67). Appealing to the bottom-line mentality of such an audience, she said, "I would like to come back to where I was born for good if I could. I would do anything to work to make a living" (65).

Additionally, the borderland demanded that she find new ways to reach out to her ancestors in the earth, even as that earth was being parceled out to housing developments and colonized by border guards. In order to make the Kumeyaay world her own again, she had to engage her ancestors in a dialogue about the nature of her own identity. Yet, it did not seem quite right to "just talk" to them. When she tried to do this, she was so different from them that she would never be able to regain their songs and stories. In attempting to explain who she was to outsiders as "proof" of her citizenship, she described her mother and grandmother but, in doing so, she acknowledged the fundamental difference between her experience and theirs: "I never made baskets or ollas. I never cared to do that. My grandmother could make beautiful ollas and things, also my mother, but I think I'm lazy. When I was young, I was different, I always believed in looking for plants, food and herbs, and different things. I never took time for ollas and baskets, I've always worked like a man. I've had to cut wood. . . . I guess I'm just too lazy to sit in one place" (36). "Just talking" to and about her ancestors made Cuero say uncomfortable and contradictory things. She called herself lazy and remembered at other points that her grandmother's people were "naked," that the Euro-Americans "never paid them money," and that they were "very poor then." Yet she was far from lazy. She worked all day long—cutting wood, doing laundry, and gathering plants and herbs. And her people were never "poor" in the sense that Europeans use the word—in need of pity or a handout, incapable of working hard enough to earn a living. What did she mean?

From the context of these remarks, Delfina Cuero made such comments as asides directed toward her interpreter, Rosalie Pinto Robertson, and her ethnographer, Florence Shipek. She made them in the same tone of voice and with the same self-consciousness that she made her remarks about the need to interpret the Crow Girls' story. "Talk" made her a self-conscious storyteller required to speak on the border of two cultures, using words that cut both ways. Calling herself lazy is a case in point. On one level it ironically reflected a positive appreciation of her grandmother's world. By having neglected to learn how to make baskets and ollas, Delfina could perhaps be judged as indolent from her grandmother's point of view. On another level, however, it represented her self-conscious awareness of how Indian people are viewed by non-Indians. By making her laziness a function of her migratory travels (she was, she said, too "lazy to sit in one place"), she both traded on Euro-American stereotypes about Native people's restlessness and turned them against their users. After all, the European sits in one place. Who, then, is the lazy one?

These conflicted feelings and languages did not come out of thin air. They were part and parcel of the Kumeyaay experience in the borderlands for two hundred years. To talk of money and clothing and poverty in this way was to tell the story within the story, the history of the relations between the Kumeyaay and ethnographers since their first meeting. Storytelling had become, over time, a self-conscious enterprise among the Kumeyaay, and Delfina Cuero was not the first member of the Kumeyaay to find herself talking to an ethnographer in exchange for some necessity—clothing, food, citizenship. At the turn of the century, for example, ethnographer Constance Goddard DuBois had lamented in an article for the *Journal of American Folklore* the Kumeyaay's "direful destitution" as she related the stories and songs they told her. Yet even a relatively sympathetic researcher like DuBois could not resist describing her "native informant" as a "little naked boy among the desert Indians" who was "liberally paid for [his] trouble."[4]

Delfina Cuero also was paid for her story: "The royalties from the Malki Museum Press paperback edition of her story were used for special items not covered by Old Age pension or for gifts and cash for her children" (79). And she too called her people "naked" and "poor." But her use of such words was not a judgment on herself or her people, nor were they ethnocentric slurs imposed on her narrative by an outside translator. They derived instead from the complex history embedded in the language of twentieth-century borderlands life. Delfina wove together her "talk" from traditional stories and from generations of interplay between her people and Anglos, Mexicans, farmer's wives who sought domestic laborers, Mexican men who sought spouses, and ethnographers who sought to transcribe the Kumeyaay's story for political and scientific ends. Such words were not so much signs of Delfina Cuero's confusion or of her culture's "degradation" as they were the sounds of the "lived" tempo and rhythm of Delfina Cuero's border world.

At other times there are silences in Delfina Cuero's autobiography, gaps and pauses that occured when she felt that "talk" was inappropriate or when she did not have the "pure" Kumeyaay cultural information the ethnographer wanted. At one point she reminded us that "This is what happened to me; what I was told. They may have done it differently in other places and at other times. . . . I tell only what I know" (13). And these gaps and pauses are as much a part of the border world of the Kumeyaay woman as the talk. Silence characterized the classic ethnographies of the Kumeyaay since at least the nineteenth century. Father Geronimo Boscana, writing about the Kumeyaay in 1825, noted that "A veil is cast over all their religious observances, and the mystery with which they are performed seems to perpetuate respect for them." In the twentieth century, Constance DuBois observed a similar pattern: "[T]he old chief of the Diegueños, Cinon Duro . . . has told me some . . . sacred guarded myths; but his wrath fell upon his brother Antonio . . . because he, without permission, had related to me the story."[5]

European ethnographers have tended to interpret such silences as signs of the shaman's jealous hoarding of his power, but Delfina Cuero used silence much in the same way that her grandmother's generation used fasting in the girls' ceremony—as a way to gather and sustain cultural tradition. Some things were kept from outsiders so that the Kumeyaay might have a sacred internal space for ceremony, even as outsiders chased them off the traditional land where such ceremonies physically took place. By 1968, however, when Delfina Cuero began to relate her life's story to an ethnographer, maintaining such silence was no longer always in her best interest. As Florence Shipek observed, "Delfina was willing to cooperate completely in my research because she hoped that if I knew the details of her life I might be able to find some document which would prove that she came from the San Diego area, enabling her to return to the United States permanently with her children and grandchildren" (15). Delfina Cuero's cooperation required that she break the very proprieties that had fostered silences in the ethnographic record for centuries. "In the course of this research," Shipek pointed out, Delfina Cuero was "asked to break one more custom, one which was difficult and mentally painful to break: a taboo on the discussion of, and the naming of, deceased relatives and friends" (12).

Delfina Cuero's autobiography moves from talk to silence in a halting rhythm that echoes the confusions that result from living on the border. When, at the end of her narrative, Delfina Cuero offered up a "prayer" for deliverance from Mexico and her "undocumented" identity, we become aware of the incredible pressure that the border exerted on her speech: "I keep praying to God that before I am too old to work for my living I can come back where I belong and be among the few relatives I still have alive, I pray that something will work out so that my children and grandchildren can come back with me to where I was born" (67). How are we to read this plea from a Native woman who wants to return to the land of her ancestors? As the supplication of a "Christianized Indian"? Or as a prayer of resistance?

Delfina Cuero herself considered this prayer to be yet another form of "just talk," that new language she had learned: "Nobody ever told me about God, that I can remember. But I thank God all the time, especially for the plants. . . . I don't know anything about priests or church, this is just talking to God myself and asking God's help" (53). Even prayers in the borderlands contain many layers of language intertwined in the supplicant's history—Kumeyaay, Spanish Catholic, colonial, Mexican, American. Delfina Cuero's prayer shuttled back and forth between Kumeyaay and European words and selves. In this one sentence, Delfina Cuero revealed that she is not Christianized, for she never had to be "told" about God. She affirmed, instead, her ongoing and active performance of spiritual celebration and "song," even in the absence of those songs that she could no longer remember from the women's ritual and her grandfather's curing rites. Significantly, the "prayer"—often viewed in the Christian tradition as a "moment of silence"—became a moment in which public and private, reticence and celebration, intersected. It combined both tradition and innovation. Delfina prayed for deliverance from government-imposed exile and gave thanks for the plants of the borderlands. Finally, by insisting that "this is just talking to God myself," she drew attention to her own empowerment; even in her "poor" and alien state, she did not need an outsider to tell her how to sing spiritual songs.

One final narrative strand in the autobiography of Delfina Cuero connects Kumeyaay border life past and present with its author's quest for the songs that might reunite her with the land of her grandmother. Woven into the talk and the silences of her life story is a dialogue with ethnographic literature itself. Kumeyaay people have been answering outsiders' questions for two hundred years, and their answers have been simplified and disregarded, twisted and ignored. In 1906, Constance Goddard DuBois made the following comments on her methods of transcribing what Kumeyaay people told her: "It only remains, in recopying, to put into slightly better form the English of my interpreter, being extremely careful never to introduce the slightest change in idea. For instance, where Sant says, 'It looked ugly,' I write, 'It was an ugly sight.' Whenever it seems expedient, however, I use the exact words of my interpreter, my constant endeavor being towards simplicity, and always towards the truth." In this way, not only were the Kumeyaay's ideas altered, but their shapes and rhythms as well. DuBois added: "[T]he old men are extremely intelligent in . . . carrying out the idea which I enforce, that a pause must be made after each sentence or two for translation and transcription. Nothing is left to memory, but all is written down as nearly as possible word for word."[6]

With the help of Mrs. Rosalie Pinto Robertson, Florence Shipek tried to break this cycle of interference and paternalism by "attempt[ing] to make the words and ideas adhere as closely as possible to Delfina's original expressions" (17). But even Shipek's presentation differs substantially from the few extant transcriptions of other Kumeyaay speakers.

A direct transcription of a Kumeyaay man's speech made by a linguist in 1954 gives us a glimpse of how Delfina Cuero's "talk" might have sounded. When asked to describe in Kumeyaay what he saw when presented with a stick figure representation of a "single male foreground, pointing at tree, background," Ramon Ames responded: "As far as I can see he seems to be walking. I wonder where he's going. I don't know, but it seems to me, he's standing somewhere. Going. But as far as I can see, he seems to have no eyes. It seems to me that he has no hair. I wonder if you people know . . . I wonder if any of you know what he is doing."[7] Ramon Ames's last question is a good one, and it is this sort of reflexive response which seems to be imbedded in Delfina Cuero's own moments of "talk." But perhaps even more significant is his emphasis on *going*. It reflects that element in native storytelling that often gets repressed by European linear narration. In order to make Native people's stories "less repetitive," ethnographers have often erased the circling and the echoing that is central to many such tales.

Ramon Ames's insistence on *going*—putting the linguist's stick figure into motion—offers the reader of *Delfina Cuero: Her Autobiography* a way of linking the history of Kumeyaay food gathering, forced migration, U.S. immigration ideology, and the performative agency of Delfina Cuero herself to a place called the borderlands. In a sense, Ames's verb-based discourse produces a circling narrative whose patterns parallel the circuitous social and historical migrations that the Kumeyaay traveled in twentieth century. Ames's own story, when parsed out from the purely linguistic data gathering in which ethnographer Alfred Hayes was engaged, focuses on generational conflict and the assimilation of the young to Anglo-American cultural ways, the difficulties of speaking a "new" language, and the shrinking of Kumeyaay lands in much the same way that Delfina Cuero's narrative does.

Speech on these dispossessing borderlands has become for the Kumeyaay, in the words of Ramon Ames, "a new language we've got," and Delfina Cuero's autobiography dramatizes how life for Native women in the borderlands produces "talk" and "silences" that reflect the history of her people's interaction and struggle with the forces of colonization and dispossession.[8] The oscillation we find in her narrative between the songs and myths of the Kumeyaay tradition and the narrative "talk" of her contemporary subject position describes a series of difficult *crossings*—from spiritual hunger to physical hunger, from Mexico to the United States, from girl to woman. But these crossings are never contradictions, never abandonments, of Kumeyaay womanhood. Her "talk," though modern and not part of the traditional song cycles, is not an immigration from her homeland, but rather a *migration*, circling back finally to her grandmother's stories and her grandmother's land.

The historical and social horizon of this "talk" is to be found in the United States–Mexican border, a political and economic barrier transformed by "talk" into a positive space of improvisational storytelling. Delfina Cuero is herself an *atravesada*, "one who crosses," whose story of the destruction and reconstruction of a Kumeyaay woman's consciousness demonstrates how borderlands history persists in the stories told by Kumeyaay, Cupeño, Mohave, Cahuilla, Luiseño, and other peoples whose lives and voices each day traverse the *frontera* of desert and ocean, city and country, Mexico and California. To hear it, we must allow the very mobility American society equates with illegal immigrants and unwanted "vagrants" to speak. We must hear what Ramon Ames called the *going*.

When we listen to this undercurrent of song in the autobiography of Delfina Cuero, we hear cultural improvisations directed against a U.S. immigration ideology in which she can appear only as the "illegal alien." Time and again in her narration she broke free from such narrative bondage, even as she documented real injustice, to give voice to a playful, questing consciousness: "Even now, as old as I am, some days I'll be going along and I'll see a puddle and bend down and make a face or animal's head in the mud. Just model in the clay" (36). Her creative collaboration with Shipek and Robertson yielded a story whose meanings spill over the closed readings such political assumptions engender. Heard in its migratory cadences, Cuero's talk resists the unidirectional narrative flow of Euro-American myths that nostalgically lament the passing of the Indians and simplistically represent the Mexican border as an uncontested line separating "us" and "them."

Following the publication of her own narrative, Cuero became even more immersed in the confusions and ironies of a postindustrial America. She was feted at an author's party in Los Angeles by her publisher; her son Aurelio was murdered on the streets of Tecate for his paycheck; and her other boy, Santos, was mistakenly diagnosed as schizophrenic and forcibly hospitalized. Upon the resolution of her immigration status, she was taken under the wing of Kumeyaay tribal elders many years her junior. Back at her reservation home, she pecked holes in the surrounding rocky hillsides to once again grind acorns in the traditional way. No longer starving, she told her interviewer, "I still live on my Indian food when I can get it" (30). When asked to do so by anthropologists, Delfina would return to her former gathering spots, pick medicinal herbs and plants, and recite their Kumeyaay names.

As Delfina Cuero's autobiography demonstrates, an American Indian life story performed in the borderlands has special resonance that does not translate into a generalized "Indian" autobiography. In its own crossings of consciousness and borders, Delfina Cuero's narrative reminds us "that one 'becomes a woman' in ways that are much more complex than in a simple opposition to men," for the active agency of Native American women's discourse in the borderlands is constituted by a multiplicity of relations—to tradition, to the land, to community and family, to women elders, to song, to narrative, and to "the line" itself.[9] Within each relation, the postcolonial Native woman encounters borders of all kinds. In coming to voice, however, she may transform them from absolute limits to infinite depths and manifold perspectives.

NOTES

1. *Borderlands/La Frontera: The New Mestiza* (San Francisco: Spinsters/Aunt Lute, 1987), 3.

2. (Ballena Press, 1991). Page numbers for quotations appear in the text. Arnold Krupat analyzed this genre in *For Those Who Come After* (Berkeley: University of California Press, 1985), 31.

3. This is what the American Indian theorist Gerald Vizenor would call "tribal pres-ence." *Manifest Manners: Postindian Warriors of Survivance* (Hanover: Wesleyan University Press, 1994), 21.

4. "Mythology of the Mission Indians," *Journal of American Folklore* 19 (1906): 145.

5. DuBois, "Religious Ceremonies and Myths of the Mission Indians" *American Anthropologist*, n.s. 7 (1906): 621.

6. DuBois, "Mythology," 146.

7. Alfred S. Hayes, "Field Procedures While Working with the Diegueño," *International Journal of American Linguistics* (1954), 186.

8. Ibid., 187.

9. Norma Alarcón, "The Theoretical Subjects of *This Bridge Called My Back* and Anglo-American Feminism," in *Making Face, Making Soul/Hacienda Caras Creative and Critical Perspectives by Women of Color* (San Francisco: Aunt Lute, 1990), 360.

13

ANNA MAE PICTOU-AQUASH

An American Indian Activist

Devon A. Mihesuah

I am the one who fought for you
And I know I'd do it all again.
I would never blame any one of you
If there was nothing you could do.
But remember what went into my name when I died for you.
And I'd do it again in a heartbeat.
I'm Anna Mae Pictou.[1]

Numerous American Indian women have been involved in the activities of the American Indian Movement since its inception in the mid-1960s, but men, including Dennis Banks, Russell Means, Leonard Peltier, Vernon and Clyde Bellecourt, John Trudell, and Leonard Crow Dog, have garnered most of the attention. The media and scholars have largely ignored the role of women in the movement. Only recently, in a few articles and the books *Lakota Woman* (1990) and *Ohikita Woman* (1993), have female participants in AIM, the Wounded Knee occupation, and other Native activist organizations been heard.

The life of Anna Mae Pictou-Aquash demonstrates what it means to be a modern Native woman aggressively fighting racial, cultural, and gender oppression. She and other activist American Indian women also illustrate that there are a variety of definitions of "feminism" even among women of the same cultural, racial, and class groups. Anna Mae is particularly notable because she sought to create a fair world for all American Indians and to empower Native women. Additionally, Anna Mae has emerged as a martyr for Native women and male freedom fighters, a symbol both of the courage of Native women as well as the possible fate of outspoken individuals who displease their government and members of their own organizations.[2]

Anna Mae was born on March 27, 1945, the third child of Mary Ellen Pictou and Francis Levi, on the poverty-ridden reserve of Shubenacadie in Nova Scotia, Canada. Shortly after Levi abandoned his family in 1949, Mary Ellen married Noel Sapier, and they moved the family to Pictou's Landing, a northern area of the reservation where Anna Mae learned about her tribe's history. Like most other members of the Mi'kmaq tribe, Anna Mae's family lived in poverty. When she was eight, she developed tuberculosis of the eye and lungs. When she recovered, she began attending school at an off-reserve institution. Though Anna Mae maintained an A average, blatant racism and negative stereotyping of Indians left her despondent, and she dropped out.

In 1956 Anna Mae's stepfather died of cancer. Her mother soon married a man on another reserve, and Anna Mae, Mary, and her brother Francis moved in with their married sister Rebecca. They struggled through their young adulthood without electricity, plumbing, or a regular source of food except for clams and fish. Anna Mae labored at low-paying jobs such as potato and berry harvesting. In 1962 she decided to move to Boston with another Mi'kmaq, Jake Maloney. She found work in a factory, and by 1965, she and Jake had two daughters, Denise and Deborah. Although they were fairly successful in their Boston life, they missed Nova Scotia, and several times they moved back and forth between Canada and Boston.

Anna Mae was not satisfied with her life as a suburbanite, although she enjoyed learning karate, the martial art her husband later taught as his career. She yearned for the company of other Indians, so she became involved in organizing an Indian community center that eventually became the Boston Indian Council, an establishment designed to support Natives who had moved from reservations to the intimidating city. Maloney was not interested in Anna Mae's activities, nor was he faithful. After she discovered his affair with a white woman, they separated.

Anna Mae was not the only frustrated Native to emerge from the 1950s. Indians living in cities and on reservations had a difficult time: they faced poverty, racism, and identity confusion. Many drank to cope with stress; others vented their frustrations in less legal ways. Throughout the 1960s, many incarcerated American Indians were angry young men with histories of crime and identity crises. Ojibwes Clyde Bellecourt and Eddie Banai, who were jailed in

Minnesota for robbery, believed that if Indians were organized they could address the serious issues facing their people. They coordinated regular discussions with Native inmates in order to familiarize themselves with their tribal cultures. After Bellecourt's release in 1964, he and other Minneapolis Indians, including Dennis Banks, an Anishinabi who had attended an Indian boarding school, served in the Air Force, and been convicted for burglary, helped to form Concerned Indian Americans. Dissatisfied with the acronym CIA, the group changed its name to American Indian Movement (AIM).[3]

AIM's first goals were to help Natives obtain better living conditions and to create street patrols to monitor police for excessive use of force. Meanwhile, "Red Power" demonstrations for Native rights and "fish-ins," fishing in violation of state regulations, took place on the west coast and in New York State. AIM obtained considerable financial support from churches and community action groups and organized a "survival school" in Minneapolis where Indian children could simultaneously learn about white society and their tribal cultures. The movement adopted the upside-down American flag, an internationally recognized sign of distress, as its symbol, which angered Native veterans.

While working at the Boston Indian Council, twenty-five-year-old Anna Mae attended her first AIM activity, a protest of Thanksgiving for which Indians boarded the Mayflower II, a replica of the ship that brought Pilgrims to Plymouth. Soon after, she moved to Bar Harbor, Maine, to work in the Teaching and Research in Bicultural Education School Project (TRIBES), a career she enjoyed. When lack of funding closed the school in 1972, she and her daughters moved back to Boston. She enrolled in the Wheelock College New Careers program and obtained a satisfying job as a teacher's aide in an all-black child care center. Despite her lack of formal education, Brandeis University offered Anna Mae a scholarship, but by that time, she was thoroughly dedicated to American Indian causes and declined it.

Back in Boston, Anna Mae met an Ontario Ojibwa artist, Nogeeshik Aquash, who moved in with her and her daughters. Anna Mae and Nogeeshik participated in the first part of AIM's "March on Washington," also known as the "Trail of Broken Treaties," a protest designed to call attention to the federal government's disregard of rights guaranteed by treaties.[4] AIM members eventually occupied and partially destroyed the Bureau of Indian Affairs (BIA) building, a move that garnered AIM the dubious reputation as a violent organization.

While AIM appealed to many Indians across the country, it also repelled many traditional Indians who viewed AIM members as young, glory-seeking Indians, many of whom grew up in urban areas and had little knowledge of tribal culture. Non-Indians labeled it a group led by ex-cons and communists who espoused an antiwhite attitude. Disagreements among its leaders appeared almost immediately, and fractures in the movement continue today, a circumstance that is not surprising given the diversity of Native America. Nevertheless, AIM continued to grow. Many American Indians, frustrated with their lives and with a federal government that appeared uninterested in their problems, were enthused by AIM. Like Anna Mae, they perceived AIM as an organization that promised not only to alert Americans to the issues Indians faced but also to solve them. Association with AIM became a source of identity and pride.[5]

In January 1973, a white man fatally stabbed Wesley Bad Heart Bull, a young Lakota from Pine Ridge reservation, and South Dakota officials charged him only with involuntary manslaughter. Incensed AIM members and supporters burned down the courthouse in Custer. AIM's presence heightened tension on nearby Pine Ridge reservation where many Oglala Sioux opposed their tribal chairman, Richard Wilson. They claimed he was a "one-man council," a nepotist, and a "dictator" who controlled the tribal government.[6] When Wilson realized that tribal members had appealed to AIM for help, he banned the movement from the reservation. However, on Tuesday, February 27, 1973, urged on by Pine Ridge residents (mainly traditional Oglala women), about 200 AIM members took control of the hamlet of Wounded Knee. Dick Wilson asked the U.S. government for assistance, and within hours, armed federal marshals sealed off the town. AIM fortified its position. The government responded with FBI agents, U.S. Army "advisors," and military weapons. Exchanging gunfire with outsiders, accepting food drops from daring pilots, and watching negotiations falter, Indians held their location inside a church for seventy-one days.

Debates over the purpose of the Wounded Knee takeover raged across the reservation. Many residents of Pine Ridge were grateful to see AIM challenge what they believed to be an overbearing, despotic tribal government. Others opposed AIM's presence and argued that most of those involved in the takeover were neither from South Dakota nor knowledgeable of their own tribal cultures, much less of Lakota culture. They conceded that some of the AIMers truly wanted to help, but they criticized others, especially the leadership, as purely attention seekers.

When Anna Mae and Nogeeshik learned of the takeover, she resigned from her job at the General Motors plant in Massachusetts. Leaving her two children in the care of her sister Mary, she and Nogeeshik went to South Dakota, where they secretly transported food and medical supplies through the government barricades. Anna Mae performed mostly domestic chores like cooking and cleaning at Wounded Knee, and she assisted in the delivery of Pedro, the baby of Mary Brave Bird, who later married and divorced spiritual leader Leonard

Crow Dog. The day after the birth, caught up in the excitement of Wounded Knee, she and Nogeeshik made a personal choice to marry in a traditional Lakota ceremony conducted by Wallace Black Elk.

Although the male AIM leadership at Wounded Knee depended on women to cook and clean for them, the men preferred that the women stay in the background. They did not seem impressed with the "masculine" roles many women played in the takeover and defense of Wounded Knee. Anna Mae, for example, walked nightly patrols and dug bunkers. In addition to being physically fit, she was thoughtful, organized, and self-confident. She often spoke of pursuing her ambition to write a book, "A People's History of the Land," the Natives' versions of their tribes' histories and cultures. Anna Mae was not likely to accept a subservient role for long. According to her sister Mary Lafford, she adopted the mannerisms of those around her: "After a while she showed men themselves and they didn't like it."[7] In addition to her ideas about how a more egalitarian leadership structure should be organized, Anna Mae's aspirations, emotional strength, intellect, and martial arts background intimidated some men, and she lost support from those who were most insecure.

Many women belonged to AIM, but men always dominated the organization. At Wounded Knee men negotiated with government officials, and media coverage ignored the women's participation during the takeover. This is not surprising considering that neither of the stereotypes non-Indians held of Native women—"squaw drudge" or "princess"—possesses leadership abilities. The press focused on the flamboyant AIM individuals, most notably Russell Means, a mixed-blood Oglala who had previously worked as an accountant and ballroom dance instructor. His dress of braids, beads, and jewelry, combined with his angry rhetoric, catered to the press's stereotypical image of the Plains Indian warrior. He appeared to gain momentum with every interview and photograph, causing one of his confidants to remark that "the press created Russell Means."[8]

Inside the barricades, seemingly separated from the vocal, attention-getting males and away from the limelight of the overbearing press, women worked at washing and patching clothes, scrubbing dishes, and tending to the sick and injured. White women activists, some of whom were in contact with the women at Wounded Knee, criticized them for accepting roles they considered inferior and subservient. While the Native women performed most of the physical labor, most of them did not regard their roles as less important than those of men. They justified their "invisible" work by pointing out that men and women had specific tasks that were equally essential to tribal survival.

Feminism of the 1970s, especially, dwelled upon women as victims of patriarchal control with little thought to the heterogeneity among women, particularly to those of color who also had to contend with racial oppression. For many Native women, a concern about community and tribal survival took precedence over individual rights. In 1975, Seneca activist Laura Waterman Wittstock attempted to explain to feminists the Native perspective: "No group can impart power on another group. Setting women aside as a group of underprivileged human beings and then trying to figure out ways to impart power to them ignores custom, culture, and in the instance of American Indians, national sovereignty."[9] Many white feminists and some Native women urged Native women, presumably subjugated by Indian men, to fight for gender equality. Other Native women, however, argued that while they often were oppressed because of their gender, they were primarily disempowered because of their race. Eradication of racist oppression was, to many Native women, more important than ending sexist oppression.

Native women acknowledged that the government and the press would listen to the men, not them, and they understood the practicality of allowing the men to speak and negotiate for the group. Women possessed the emotional strength and knowledge to take matters into their own hands at Wounded Knee, but who outside the tribe would listen to them? Who would take them seriously? The female participants at Wounded Knee, like the women of the Iroquois and other tribes in colonial times, were aware that male Euro-Americans did not want to negotiate with women despite the power Native women possessed. At least five of the thirteen Oglalas involved in negotiations with the government after the Wounded Knee takeover were traditional women who had a deep knowledge of and commitment to their tribal cultures. While these women allowed the men to take center stage, they did not approve of Native men adopting the European ideology that females are subservient to males.

After the seige ended at Wounded Knee, the Aquashes returned to Boston to continue their activism. When they could not obtain funding to open a survival school there, they moved to Ottawa where Anna Mae organized a successful Native fashion show at the National Arts Centre in 1974. Always resourceful in locating funds for AIM, Anna Mae revitalized the "ribbon shirt," originally created by northeastern tribes to spruce up the ordinary clothes provided by missionaries. She intended to sell them, but the seamstresses she employed gave all the shirts as presents to spouses and boyfriends. In addition to her fundraising, Anna Mae engaged in enough activism for the FBI to keep her under observation. In particular, she participated in the Menominees' takeover of the Alexian Brothers Catholic Monastery in Wisconsin.

While Anna Mae was at Wounded Knee, her ex-husband took custody of their children, an arrangement to which Anna Mae did not object until the girls decided to live with their father permanently. Although she knew that Maloney could provide a better material life for their daughters, their decision still grieved her, and she sought consolation in her work for AIM. She traveled extensively, forged support groups, raised funds, and ferried messages. She set up AIM's West Coast branch, a move that signaled not only AIM's national influence but also Anna Mae's prominence in the movement.

In 1974, Anna Mae and Nogeeshik separated after months of his verbal and attempted physical abuse, usually brought on by his drinking. Among Lakotas, being married by the pipe, like Anna Mae was, is sacred, and the expectation of couples married in this fashion is that they cannot divorce; those who do are accused of "playing with the pipe," that is, committing a sacrilege. Yet abuse of Native women by men (and sometimes the other way around) is so commonplace that one partner often will break the sacred trust. Although she was not Lakota, Anna Mae respected the meaning of the pipe, and she felt guilt over breaking her vows. Guilt-ridden by this failed marriage, Anna Mae turned to alcohol, which often produced angry outbursts. This behavior only added to her sense of failure since she and fellow activist Leonard Peltier had taken a strong stand against drinking after Wounded Knee and often chided AIM leaders about imbibing.

After the siege at Wounded Knee, Russell Means, Dennis Banks, and others were indicted for their roles in the takeover, and for years afterward they faced a variety of charges.[10] "We broke even," says John Trudell about Wounded Knee.[11] Nevertheless, men and women across the country experienced a surge of interest in their cultures. Men began growing their hair and wearing clothing like the AIM leaders. "City Indians became new reborn Indians," said resident Milo Yellow Hair about the Indians who flocked to Pine Ridge in search of their Indian heritage. "We were like the library that never got used."[12] The AIM leaders also directed America's attention to problems contemporary Indians faced and illustrated that Indians were not merely relics of the past. Chapters sprang up across the country, and the organization became important enough for the FBI to begin planting informers—Indians and non-Indians alike—in its midst. But Wounded Knee changed little for Indians in South Dakota.

Poverty, crime, and health problems still raged on Pine Ridge, and in 1975 a "reign of terror" began against AIM and its supporters on the Pine Ridge reservation. Members of Wilson's political faction beat, shot, and terrorized residents on almost a daily basis. By the end of the year, at least 47 Indians were dead, most under mysterious circumstances. FBI intrusions, imprisonments, violent unsolved deaths, and discoveries of infiltrators into the organization resulted in collective paranoia. AIM members and residents of Pine Ridge found it difficult to trust anyone—including each other—and even unlikely persons were revealed as FBI informers. Douglass Durham, for example, worked as Dennis Banks's personal bodyguard for over a year. He was privy to AIM's plans and worked in several AIM offices across the country. While Anna Mae and Durham were working at the St. Paul AIM office during the Banks and Means trials, Anna Mae observed both his abuse of women and his dyed black hair. She suspected Durham might be an informer, and in February of 1975, her suspicions were confirmed, exacerbating the paranoia.[13] Not surprisingly, the prominent AIM leader Anna Mae Pictou-Aquash, who had worked with Durham, also came under suspicion by many AIM leaders and members.

An intimate relationship with the organization's leader, Dennis Banks, compounded Anna Mae's difficulties and garnered her the nickname "Dennis's West Coast Woman." Banks was married to a friend of Anna Mae, Kamook, a young Oglala woman who was pregnant with Banks's child.[14] Revelation of Anna Mae's relationship with Banks devastated Kamook, their friends, and Anna Mae. Because of rumors of her being a FBI informer, her exposed affair, and her membership in West Coast AIM and not Dakota AIM, Anna Mae endured ethnocentrism at the hands of other Native women. She had already been snubbed at Wounded Knee for being a Canadian Native by Lakota AIM women known as the "Pie Patrol." Anna Mae gave them "a piece of her mind," according to Mary Crow Dog, but ostracism by women with whom she had wanted to work must have cut deep.[15]

So, too, did the accusations by AIM's spiritual leader, Leonard Crow Dog, that she was an FBI informer. At the Farmington, New Mexico, AIM National Convention, Dino Butler, Leonard Peltier, and Bob Robideau interrogated her, some say at the behest of Vernon Bellecourt. Peltier commented years later that he did not really believe she was an informer, but "She was involved in a lot of stuff, and she could have done a lot of damage if she was an informer."[16]

Dismayed and saddened by her colleagues' suspicions, Anna Mae almost returned to Nova Scotia, but she instead decided to stay in South Dakota in order to help elderly Oglala women. Many of these women knew Anna Mae's experiences in Canada were like their own, and they accepted her. According to Roselyn Jumping Bull, Anna Mae once told her, "After I realized how you people live I didn't want none of the things I had before. I left everything because I wanted to show you how I love you people and want to help you." Jumping Bull explained shortly after Anna Mae's death, "None of the other girls ever talk like that—she's the only one."[17]

Anna Mae had learned about her tribe's culture while she was young, and unlike the AIM leadership and many of its members who had grown up in urban areas, Anna Mae had lived most of her life, except for several years in Boston, in a tribal environment. She spoke her tribal language, knew her tribe's history and customs, and understood the traditional strength of Mi'kmaq women. It must have been unsettling for her to live in the harsh reality that included not only racism against Indians by whites but also misogyny among many AIM men and acceptance of the men's behavior by many of the Native women with whom she worked. Anna Mae chose to work with AIM rather than her own people because she believed that AIM could address a range of Native grievances and serve not only displaced and confused Natives but also people like her who were secure in their tribal and ethnic identities.

The "reign of terror" that had induced paranoia soon reached Anna Mae personally. On the morning of June 26, 1975, two FBI agents, Ronald Williams and Jack Coler, arrived on the Jumping Bull property with a subpoena for teenager Jimmy Eagle, who was accused of stealing boots. Shots rang out from the ranch house, and shortly afterward, the two agents and a young Oglala man, Joseph Killsright Stuntz, were dead. Armed agents quickly arrived at the Jumping Bull property, and under orders from their leader, Norman Zigrossi, the team swept the reservation with M-16s, helicopters, and dogs. They interrogated anyone they pleased without warrants. Angry that they could not locate the culprits, the FBI created a list of individuals who they believed knew the killer's identity, and Anna Mae's name was included. In September, while Indians were camped at the property of Al Running and at Leonard Crow Dog's Paradise, dozens of armed agents raided the properties, destroying many sacred cultural items in the process of searching for suspects in the killings of the FBI agents. Anna Mae was one of those arrested at Crow Dog's.

After being transported to Pierre, Anna Mae was interrogated for over six hours about the deaths. She insisted that she was in Iowa at the time, but agent David Price persisted, telling her that if she cooperated, she would be given a new identity and a place to live. He also warned her that if she did not cooperate and tell them who the killers were, he would "see her dead within the year." She replied, "You can either shoot me or put me in jail. That's what you're going to do to me anyway." She was released on bail and promptly fled underground.

In November 1975, Anna Mae, along with Dennis Banks and Leonard Peltier, was sought on a fugitive warrant, and on the evening of November 14, two vehicles (one owned by Marlon Brando) were stopped by a state trooper in Oregon. Anna Mae was arrested, handcuffed, shackled to the pregnant Kamook Banks, and extradited to South Dakota where she faced charges of transporting and possessing dangerous weapons. Because she had not been indicted on earlier charges, the judge released her on bail and she went underground once more.

Darrell Dean "Dino" Butler and Robert "Bob" Robideau also were arrested that fall and stood trial in June 1976 for the murders at Pine Ridge. They were acquitted. Also a suspect in the shooting, Peltier fled to Canada to avoid arrest. Because of false testimony given by Myrtle Poor Bear, who claimed to have seen Peltier kill the two agents, Peltier was extradited to the United States and was convicted of murder. Peltier remains in prison.[18]

While she was in hiding, Anna Mae called her sisters in Nova Scotia. Speaking Mi'kmaq in case of wiretaps, she told them that she expected to be shot sooner or later. If anything did happen to her, she wanted Mary to raise her two daughters. She was thirty years old, and it was the last time her family spoke to her.

On the unusually warm winter afternoon of February 24, 1976, in the northeast corner of the Pine Ridge reservation in South Dakota, a small American Indian woman lay curled, apparently sleeping, at the bottom of an embankment on the property of cattle rancher Roger Amiotte. Far from the closest town, Wanblee, she was inadequately dressed for the cold winter night in a ski jacket and blue jeans. Her attire did not matter, however, because she had been dead for at least two months.

Amiotte immediately called the Oglala tribal police, who responded in twenty minutes. Within hours, so did a large number of deputies and four FBI agents, several of whom were a hundred miles away when they got word of the discovered body. Amiotte wondered, "Why all these authorities?" Bodies were frequently found across the reservation during the turbulent years of unrest between the FBI and American Indians, and no other deceased Native had drawn this kind of attention.

The woman was taken to the Pine Ridge hospital where, after a cursory autopsy, the resident pathologist at the nearby Scottsbluff, Nebraska, hospital ruled that she had died of exposure. Instead of fingerprinting her, he severed her hands at the wrist and, at the behest of the FBI, sent the extremities to Washington, D.C., for identification. Physicians at the Pine Ridge hospital were puzzled at the pathologist's conclusion since they had seen a bloody flow from the base of the dead woman's skull consistent with traumatic injury. Nevertheless, without waiting for identification or announcing that a woman's body was in the morgue available for identification by possible family members, officials named the woman "Jane Doe" and buried her in a local Catholic cemetery.

The day after the burial, word came from Washington that the hands belonged to Anna Mae Pictou-Aquash. On March 5, Anna Mae's sisters in Canada were notified of her death. Her older sister, Mary Lafford, doubted the coroner's conclusion that Anna Mae had died of exposure and demanded, through AIM attorney Bruce Ellison, that she be exhumed and that another autopsy be performed. This time, a Minnesota pathologist quickly discovered that Anna Mae had been shot in the base of the skull at point-blank range with a .32 handgun. He also concluded that Anna Mae had been raped. He was surprised that the cause of death had not been noticed during the first autopsy. So was the U.S. Civil Rights Commission, whose report referred to the oversight as incredible.[19]

On the cold, snowy day of March 14, 1976, Anna Mae was reburied on land belonging to Wallace Little forever next to the grave of Joe Killsright Stuntz, the Oglala man who was killed during the shoot-out between Indians and FBI agents. Her grave was prepared by young Oglala women, one of whom lay in the grave to determine if it was long enough. They adorned the Mi'kmaq woman's mutilated body with moccasins, a ribbon shirt, jeans, and a jacket with the AIM crest and upside-down American flag, and then they wrapped her in a star quilt. Instead of placing her in the government-issued coffin, the men assisting in preparations smashed it to bits. A pregnant woman gathered sage, and six youths served as pallbearers. No male AIM leader attended the burial, nor did her ex-lovers or ex-husbands. Russell Means and his brother Ted, along with several AIM members, drove past her funeral on the way to a basketball game a few miles away. After her mourners departed, black, red, yellow, and white streamers attached to poles signifying the sacred directions danced in the wind. Wind blew hard and bitter, the way it responds, elders say, after a murder victim has been removed from the grave.

Paula Gunn Allen's truism, "You cannot be political without being spiritual," applies to Anna Mae Pictou-Aquash more than most activists.[20] Throughout the last months of her life, Anna Mae spoke often about her premonitions of her death. Shortly after publication of *Voices from Wounded Knee*, which included a wedding picture of Anna Mae and Nogeeshik, Anna Mae took to heart what one of the elders saw in the photograph: that she had no future and would die soon. Later, Anna Mae confided to friend Bernie Nichols that she had dreamed she flew to the Spirit World in the form of a bird.[21] Prior to her trial in Pierre, Anna Mae commented to Nilak Butler (wife of Dino) that after all the fingerprints the FBI had taken of her, "the only way I could get away with anything, with all the fingerprints they took, would be to have my hands cut off."[22]

Intense debate over who killed Anna Mae emerged soon after her burial. FBI director Clarence Kelley stated that he was satisfied that the FBI had nothing to do with her death, while another agent active in the 1970s events, Zigrossi, suggested that the AIM leadership had ordered her death because it believed she was an informer working for the FBI. Her former lover, Dennis Banks, fearful that if that was true, "it would crush our movement," launched a half-hearted investigation of events that turned up little. AIM leader John Trudell, who lost his wife and three children in a mysterious trailer home fire twelve hours after he gave an anti-FBI speech in Washington D.C., argued that the FBI ordered Anna Mae's death in order to avenge the death of their two agents. "I think getting Anna Mae and Joe Stunz made it two-to-two," he said.[23] Nogeeshik Aquash, still involved in the struggle for Native rights, tried to find his ex-wife's killers. After years of collecting information about AIM and the FBI through the Freedom of Information Act, Nogeeshik, wheelchair-bound following a car wreck, was killed in a suspicious fire that destroyed his Sault Ste. Marie home along with his documentation.

Despite cursory probes and exculpatory pronouncements, little real investigation into Anna Mae's murder took place for years, and the last days of her life are unclear. In the early 1990s Robert A. Pictou-Branscombe, a highly decorated Mi'kmaq combat Marine veteran, began pursuing information about his cousin. In the early 1990s, he concluded that in very early December 1975, she was questioned persistently by AIM members about being an informer. Then she was taken forcibly to South Dakota where she was executed. Theda Nelson Clark, Arlo Looking Cloud, and teenager John Boy Patton, seeking approval from and acceptance by AIM leaders, were involved in the killing.[24] From 1994 to 1998, reporters from *News from Indian Country*, a Wisconsin-based newspaper, interviewed a variety of people, including journalists, AIM members, and residents of Pine Ridge. It concluded that the FBI, using tactics of COINTELPRO, the bureau's counterintelligence program, "bad jacketed," or purposely created the illusion of Anna Mae as an informer for the FBI in order to confuse AIM. One AIM member accused Trudell of instigating her execution, while others thought that the Bellecourt brothers and Means played a role in her death. After all, they reasoned, Means had not been supportive of Anna Mae's efforts for AIM.[25] In March 1999, Detective Abe Alonzo of the Denver, Colorado, police department, received permission to investigate Anna Mae's death. By June, Alonzo had narrowed the field to the same culprits as had Pictou-Branscombe.[26] In an October 1999 press conference, Pictou-Branscombe accused the AIM leadership of conspiring to have his cousin murdered. One month later on November 3, Russell Means announced in an emotionally charged statement in Denver that Vernon Bellecourt had ordered Anna Mae's execution in a phone call to which other AIM leaders were privy.[27]

Hostility toward Anna Mae Pictou-Aquash stemmed from many sources. The FBI probably did plant false rumors that Anna Mae and others were informers. But there are other reasons for the profound distrust and acrimony that led to her death. AIM members might have experienced the "siege mentality" common to combatants during times of war. Extraordinary circumstances produced heightened sensitivity and even irrationality that sometimes was directed toward those who did not seem to fit in. Anna Mae was an "outsider," a Canadian Indian, whose strong personality attracted attention to that status. The rumor that Peltier confided to her the identity of the FBI killers and her knowledge of AIM's "secrets" made her a potentially dangerous person. Furthermore, many AIM members, including some of the AIM women, were jealous of Anna Mae's strong female character and her position within the AIM hierarchy. Whatever the mix of charged emotions, tragedy resulted.

Anna Mae had confronted many of the same difficulties as other Native women. American Indian women must find ways to meet the demands of all their worlds: self, family, community, tribe, state, and country. Often they are pressured to keep the old ways, while at the same time learning non-Native ways to support their families. Native women, both inside and outside the academy, speak of the interconnectedness of female, male, tribal, and racial oppression, and like Anna Mae, they strive for liberation of all. They may sometimes struggle for gender rights, but gender is inexorably tied to race and tribe. There are Native women who call themselves "feminists" and who fight only for individual rights, but they often have no tribal connection.

The reality is that most Native women—whether full blood or mixed-blood, living on or off tribal lands, activist or indifferent—are concerned about both racial and gender oppression. Despite rhetoric about white feminism having no meaning for Native women, not all Native women reject every aspect of white feminism, and they are no less "Indian" for their beliefs. When they identify themselves as "feminists," they often mean they are "Native Activists," concerned with more than just female marginalization. Indeed, they fight for fishing, land, water, and treaty rights, and at the same time, they have no desire to be labeled inferior by anyone because they are women. They fight for racial liberation in order to transcend the effects of colonialism that may cause tribal men to behave abusively in the first place, and this appears to have been one of Anna Mae's goals.

Many Native women aspire to the traditionally powerful social, political, economic, and religious roles they held in their tribes historically. However, they cannot reclaim their cultures by themselves. Women might be aware of their traditional and potential power, but men often try to ignore it. Most of the AIM male leaders admitted that they knew little about their cultures until they joined AIM, and although they were taught about the traditional roles of women, their behavior did not always reveal enthusiasm for tribal stories that featured powerful women.

"There is a curious contradiction in Sioux society," wrote Mary Crow Dog. "The men pay great lip service to the status women hold in the tribe. Their rhetoric on the subject is beautiful. . . . they always stood up for our rights— against outsiders!" But the reality within the compound at Wounded Knee differed: "We did the shit work, scrubbing dishes or making sleeping bags out of old jackets." Mary Crow Dog also lamented the chauvinism among the ranks of Lakota AIM men, including her one-time husband, medicine man Leonard Crow Dog. She expressed irritation at the Native and white women "groupies" who gladly served as "wives" for the AIM leadership: in addition to providing sex, they cooked, cleaned, sewed, and braided hair for prominent men. She also disapproved of the men's behavior, but, like many other Native women, she rationalized men's conduct as a result of colonialism.[28]

To be fair, by no means have all Native men absorbed the patriarchal mindset that colonialism brought to the New World. Women speak glowingly of AIM male members who treated women with respect and honor. Traditional men and those Native men attempting to follow traditions by placing women in egalitarian roles display little ego and have no desire to place themselves in dominant positions.

AIM male leaders of the 1970s and 1980s attempted to revive the Plains "warrior" role of the past by stepping forward as aggressive leaders, but they failed to advocate a struggle against the bonds of colonial oppression and embrace gender equality. Russell Means in his autobiography, for example, commented on the women at Wounded Knee: "Taking the glory was not on their agenda. Understanding the female-male balance, they felt no need to be anointed publicly with leadership."[29] That might be true, but Means was not about to allow females publicity.[30] The few women Means wrote about were members of his family or women elders. He did not mention Anna Mae despite her leadership role in AIM. He also revealed his feelings about women to author Peter Mathiessen in a diatribe over FBI informer Douglass Durham: "Durham was a gofer, a nothing! He was like a woman, worse than a woman; we used to give him pocket money, send him out for coffee!"[31] Means rationalized his attitude: "If our older women knew and respected their role, Indian men of my generation didn't. We had been robbed of our heritage through the brutality experienced by our parents and passed on to us all."[32] Other Native men, however, do not approve of excusing bad behavior by blaming colonialism for dysfunctional gender roles. "That's a sorry argument," one man said after a discussion with me about this essay. "We have to take responsibility for our own actions."

Anna Mae was not the only woman who dealt with the misogyny of AIM men. In 1990 Laguna Pueblo writer Paula Gunn Allen revealed one reason some Indian women preferred not to work closely with male AIM leaders:

> They were out drinkin' all the time, they were fuckin' their way across the United States, they were leaving a lot of uncared for babies behind, not to mention young women. Dreadful things. Finally, these three women called them in and they said in no uncertain terms, "We'll show you who the real warriors are here. We are! You think you're so big. You haven't done nothing and you can't do nothing without us." Every Indian knows that. You want something done, call a woman. They all know that. The men know it, the women know it. But the situation is such, that when the white world wants things Indian, a spiritual leader for example, you know who they call. They call the men.[33]

Unfortunately, many Native men struggled for racial equality, but their aggressive behavior, often made worse by excessive drinking, destroyed the male-female balance essential to their cultures. In private correspondence with me, a critic of one prominent AIM leader contended that the man defeated the purpose of fighting for tribal rights and sovereignty: "He is quick to intimidate the weak, especially females, and both verbally and physically abuses them."

Native women have much to lose by publicly discussing the dysfunctional gender roles within their tribes. Like African American women, American Indian women keep their secrets close and often fight for group rights more stridently than gender rights. Wittstock explained: "Any who believe that giving up cultural and racial customs in exchange for enhanced individual rights and privileges play into the end-game—the dominant societies will increase in strength, the non-white communities will lose power increasingly."[34]

American Indian women continued the struggle for Native rights throughout the 1970s and 1980s. In 1974 Lakota women organized W.A.R.N.—Women of All Red Nations—in order to deal with a variety of social issues important to Native females: education, health care, sterilization, treaty rights, and political incarceration of Native people.[35] Women also have formed societies to deal with the problem of abuse, which is so prevalent within tribes today. On the Lakota reservation at Rosebud, for example, there is the White Buffalo Woman Society and at Pine Ridge the Sacred Shawl Society. Even in death, Anna Mae Pictou-Aquash has become a part of this movement. Dennis Banks acknowledged her pervasive influence in response to an interviewer's question about the last time he saw Anna Mae: "I see Annie Mae today in every brave wom[a]n. She represented the troubles going on in the Indian community for centuries, and I've often felt that women such as these are the real warriors."[36] In May 1999, the international, nonprofit A.N.N.A. Foundation was incorporated in Arizona by Anna Mae's family in order to continue what she started: to "preserve the Native languages, cultures, and traditions of the American Indian people." A.N.N.A. Foundation offers support to a variety of programs and to individuals who are pursuing university degrees or careers in art and entertainment, health and wellness, and drug and alcohol rehabilitation.[37]

Anna Mae lived up to the expectations she set forth for herself in a letter to her sister Rebecca in the last month of her life: "My efforts to raise the consciousness of whites who are so against Indians in the States were bound to be stopped by the FBI sooner or later. . . . But I'm not going to stop fighting until I die, and I hope I'm a good example of a human being and my tribe."[38] No matter where they struggle, Native women such as Anna Mae Pictou-Aquash, who often have not been the most visible or vocal of Native activists, have proved through their actions, beliefs, and strength that they were, and still are, the foundations of their Nations.

NOTES

This essay is dedicated to the family of Anna Mae. Thanks to Robert A. Pictou-Branscombe for the lengthy conversations about his cousin; to Harald Prins for his editorial comments and information on Mi'kmaqs; to Elizabeth Castle for discussions about Native activism; and to Anna Mae's daughters, Denise Maloney-Pictou and Deborah Maloney-Pictou, for conversations about their mother.

1. Excerpt from song, "I'd Do It Again in a Heartbeat." Music and lyrics by Shannon M. Collins, Executive Director of the A.N.N.A. Foundation. Used with permission.

2. This essay is merely a brief overview of an extremely complicated topic. Information came from numerous sources; some are listed here. It is difficult, however, to ascertain with certainty the origin of some statements and events because many of the works used are journalistic in nature and do not include references. Furthermore, they often closely paraphrase each other. I primarily have cited only those statements that appear to be unique to this essay. For information on Anna Mae specifically, see Joanna Brand's *The Life and Death of Anna Mae Aquash* (Toronto: Lorimer and Co., 1978, 1993); David Weir and Lowell Bergman, "The Killing of Anna Mae Aquash," *Rolling Stone* (April 7, 1977): 51–55; Shirley Hill Witt, "Brave Hearted Woman: The Struggle at Wounded Knee," *Civil Rights Digest* 8 (1976): 38–45; and Devon A. Mihesuah, "Interview with Denise Maloney-Pictou and Deborah Maloney-Pictou," *American Indian Quarterly* 24 (2000):

forthcoming. Several web sites are devoted to Aquash's life and the intrigue surrounding her death. See *www.dickshovel.com/annalay.html* and *www.dickshovel.com/annaarch.html*, as well as numerous interconnected pages that feature original material and reprinted excerpts from previously published material on Anna Mae. The most comprehensive volume on the Mi'kmaqs, which the tribe has endorsed, is Harald E. L. Prins, *The Mi'kmaq: Resistance, Accommodation, and Cultural Survival* (Fort Worth: Harcourt Brace College Publishers, 1996).

3. Numerous books chronicle the activities of AIM and the events leading up to and following the occupation of Wounded Knee. Among the most notable are Robert Anderson, Joanna Brown, Jonny Lerner, and Barbara Lou Shafer, *Voices from Wounded Knee, 1973: In the Words of the Participants* (New York: *Akwesasne Notes*, 1974); Mary Brave Bird, *Ohitika Woman* (New York: Harper Collins, 1992); Mary Crow Dog, *Lakota Woman* (New York: Harper Collins, 1990); Peter Mathiessen, *In the Spirit of Crazy Horse* (New York: Viking Press, 1983); Robert Warrior and Paul Chaat Smith, *Like a Hurricane: The American Indian Movement from Alcatraz to Wounded Knee* (New York: New Press, 1996); Rex Wyler, *Blood of the Land: The Government and Corporate War Against the American Indian Movement* (New York: Random House, 1982). Particular care must be taken in reading the Crow Dog and Brave Bird books, as many scholars and activists have argued that both were heavily edited by the white male coauthor. Also see Bella Stumbo, "A World Apart," *Los Angeles Times Magazine* June 15, 1986, pp. 10–21; Gerald Vizenor, "Dennis of Wounded Knee" *American Indian Quarterly* (Spring 1983): 51–65; "Penthouse Interview: Russell Means," *Penthouse* (April 1981): 136–38, 188–91, 194; "Penthouse Interview: Vernon Bellecourt: He Is the Symbol of the Most Militant Indian Group Since Geronimo," *Penthouse* (July 1973): 58–60, 62–64, 122–32.

4. Vine Deloria, Jr., *Behind the Trail of Broken Treaties: An Indian Declaration of Independence* (Austin: University of Texas Press, 1985).

5. Devon A. Mihesuah, "American Indian Identities: Issues of Individual Choices and Development," *American Indian Culture and Research Journal* 22.2 (1998): 193–226; Joanne Nagel, *American Indian Ethnic Renewal: Red Power and the Resurgence of Identity and Culture* (Oxford, 1996); Rachel A. Bonney, "The Role of AIM Leaders in Indian Nationalism," *American Indian Quarterly* 3.3 (1977): 209–224.

6. For opposing viewpoints on Wilson's tenure as chairman, see *Indian Country Today*'s issue "Looking Back at Wounded Knee," 12.35 (February 25, 1993).

7. Brand, *Life and Death*, 117.

8. Personal correspondence, from entry in diary, 29 Jan. 1986.

9. "On Women's Rights for Native Peoples," *Akwesasne Notes* 7.4 (Early Autumn 1975): 39.

10. John William Sayer, *Ghost Dancing the Law: The Wounded Knee Trials* (Cambridge: Harvard University Press, 1997).

11. Quoted from Robert Redford's 1991 movie documentary, "Incident at Oglala: The Leonard Peltier Story."

12. Quoted from PBS video, "In the Spirit of Crazy Horse."

13. "Anatomy of an Informer," *Akwesasne Notes* 7.2 (Early Summer 1975): 14–16; "Anatomy of an Informer, Part 2," *Akwesasne Notes* 7.5 (Early Winter 1975): 10–13.

14. By 1975, Banks had fathered 15 children with multiple mothers. "The *Black Scholar* Interviews: Dennis Banks." *Black Scholar* (June 1976): 28–36.

15. To illustrate the intrigue surrounding some aspects of this case, a web site offering a reprint of the "Anna Mae Aquash Time Line" compiled by *News From Indian Country* March 18, 1998, states that the "Pie Patrol" was comprised of women active in AIM: Madonna Gilbert, Thelma Rios-Conroy, and Lorelei Decora Means. In *Lakota Woman*, Mary Crow Dog describes the Patrol as "loud-mouth city women, very media conscious, hugging the limelight" (138); yet, curiously, in her second book, *Ohikita Woman*, she describes these same women as those she felt "particularly close to" at "the Knee" (194, 200–201).

16. Matthiessen, *In the Spirit of Crazy Horse*, 147.

17. Brand, *Life and Death*, 133, 136; Weir and Bergman, "The Killing of Anna Mae Aquash," 54.

18. See "Incident at Oglala" for chronicle of events. See also Leonard Peltier and Harvey Arden, *Prison Writings: My Life is My Sun Dance, by Leonard Peltier, US Prisoner 89637-132* (New York: St. Martin's Press, 1999).

19. Letter from U.S. Commission on Civil Rights, Shirley Hill Witt, Regional Director, and William F. Muldrow, Equal Opportunity Specialist, to John A. Buggs, March 31, 1976.

20. Judith Anne Antell, "American Indian Women Activists," Ph.D. dissertation, University of California, Berkeley (1990), 158.

21. See movie, "Brave Hearted Woman," produced by Lan Brookes Ritz in 1979.

22. Matthiessen, *In the Spirit of Crazy Horse*, 270.

23. Weir and Bergman, "The Killing of Anna Mae Aquash," 54.

24. See HYPERLINK *http://www.diskshovel.com/bra2.html*.

25. Ibid.

26. *Indian Country Today*, March 29–April 5, 1999, A4; "Justice at Last for Anna Mae?" *Toronto Sun*, 13 June 1999, C6.

27. Jamie Monastyrski, "Aquash Family Accuses AIM of Her Murder," *Indian Country Today*, Oct. 4–11, 1999; Personal communication with Shannon M. Collins, 3 Nov. 1999. The news conference was also reported by the Associated Press and at *http://members.aol.com/Apictou/pictou-branscombe.html*.

28. Crow Dog, *Lakota Woman*, 66, 69, 78, 138.

29. Russell Means and Marvin J. Wolf, *Where White Men Fear to Tread* (New York: St. Martin's Press, 1995), 265.

30. Indeed, he said during his 1974 trial that one way to express manhood was through activism. See *Ghost Dancing the Law*, 91.

31. Matthiessen, *In the Spirit of Crazy Horse*, 125.

32. Means and Wolf, *Where White Men Fear to Tread*, 265.

33. Antell, "American Indian Woman Activists," 170–71.

34. "On Women's Rights for Native Peoples," 39.

35. Marla Powers, *Oglala Women: Myth, Ritual, and Reality* (Chicago: University of Chicago Press, 1986), 126, 150; Winona LaDuke, "Words from Indigenous Women's

Network Meeting," *Akwesasne Notes* 17.6 (Early Winter 1985): 8–9; "Women of All Red Nations (W.A.R.N.)" *Akwesasne Notes* 10.5 (Winter 1978): 15.

36. Quoted in documentary, "Brave Hearted Woman."

37. The A.N.N.A. Foundation, Inc., web address is *http://hometown.aol.com/ANNAinc/Foundation.html*.

38. Weir and Bergman, "The Killing of Anna Mae Aquash," 53.

14

ADA DEER
Champion of Tribal Sovereignty

Nancy Oestreich Lurie

In 1953, Congress adopted House Concurrent Resolution 108, which called for the "termination" of Indian reservations and federal jurisdiction over the tribes as quickly as possible. Termination was designed to dissolve reservations and, in combination with the euphemistically named Voluntary Relocation Program, disperse Indian people irrevocably into the nation's urban centers.[1] The government and general public always had expected Indians to simply vanish as a people, and though their numbers dwindled steadily throughout the nineteenth century, tribal remnants seemed unable to fulfill their supposedly inevitable destiny of becoming one with the dominant society. The proponents of termination saw it as finally closing the books on unfinished business. The first tribe to be terminated under HCR 108 was the Menominee of northeastern Wisconsin. A Menominee woman, Ada Deer, was in the forefront of the struggle that began in the late 1960s to bring about the repeal of her tribe's termination. The Menominees' victory opened the way for the restoration of federal jurisdiction to other terminated tribes, and Ada's experience battling for her own tribe led her to become an advocate for all Native people.

Ada Deer was born on August 7, 1935, at the hospital in Keshena, Wisconsin, the administrative center of the Menominee Reservation. She was the first of nine children, five of whom survived infancy, born to Constance Stockton Wood and Joseph Deer. Her father was Menominee and her mother a non-Indian from a wealthy Philadelphia family. Constance rejected the genteel expectations of her class that her twin sister, Adah, had embraced. She studied nursing and worked first among the poor in Appalachia and then with the Indian Service, where, after a stint at the Rosebud Sioux Reservation, she found employment at the tribal hospital on the Menominee Reservation. The marriage started romantically enough, on a farmstead with livestock in a rustic log cabin that Connie and Joe built themselves, but it was marked increasingly by domestic strife and arguments over money. Though a nonconformist in many ways and fiercely dedicated to Menominee rights, Connie was still the product of a white Protestant upbringing that valued frugality and hard work. Joe disliked farming, much preferring to hunt, fish, and relax with his drinking companions. Following long established custom among Menominee men, he worked for wages at the mill. Though born into a traditional family, he was reluctant to impart his knowledge of tribal culture to his children or teach them Menominee, his own first language. He thought that the less they knew about being Indian the more likely they were to escape the suffering he had endured in a Catholic boarding school, where he struggled to finish the eighth grade in a system that deprecated Native culture.

When Ada was small and her brother, Joe, Jr., was a toddler, her mother's father and her Aunt Adah appeared unexpectedly on the reservation to persuade Ada's mother to leave her husband and children and come back East with them. She refused, but the incident made a profound impression on Ada. Her grandfather, whom she would never see again, slammed the door of his big, expensive car and shouted as he drove off, "All right, Constance. Stay out here in the backwoods with your little half breeds."[2] While Ada embraced her mother's sense of determination and the value she placed on education, she found her personal identity with her father's people, among whom she grew up. Childhood encounters with racism only served to strengthen her pride as an Indian and a Menominee.

Although the Menominees were not wealthy when HCR 108 was passed, they were considerably better off than the vast majority of tribes and had bright prospects for the future because their reservation had not been divided and diminished, like most reservations, by the General Allotment Act of 1887. Their reservation of some 230,000 heavily wooded acres of both hard- and softwoods, established by treaties in 1854 and 1858, was the foundation of a tribal forestry industry. At a time when lumber barons in northern Wisconsin were clearcutting vast forests, the Menominees developed the practice of cutting selectively for sustained yield. In 1908, at tribal behest, Wisconsin Senator Robert La Follette, Sr., engineered legislation to establish a lumber mill at the reservation town of Neopit. In time, the tribe developed its own nonprofit utility companies and took over support of a Catholic-run hospital and two schools. The only federal funding the Menominees received was a small amount for a government school that less than a quarter of the children attended. The forest industry even paid for the Bureau of Indian Affairs' (BIA's) administration of the reservation. Anyone who wanted to work could find employment, and people expected to be self-supporting. Although this meant an inefficiently large labor force by corporate standards, the lumber business still generated annual "stumpage" profits of a few hundred dollars for each tribal member. Interest-bearing savings also accumulated for the tribe as a whole.

The major problem for the Menominees, as was true on other reservations, was the heavy administrative hand of the BIA. Although Menominee people were employed at various levels in the tribal business from lumberjacks to mill hands and white-collar clerical personnel, all upper-level management positions were controlled by the Indian Bureau and held by non-Menominees. To gain greater leverage in their own affairs, particularly in negotiating contracts affecting their lumber enterprise, in 1928 the Menominees adopted a tribal constitution and by-laws with an elected ten-member Advisory Council that dealt with the local BIA agent and staff. The General Council made up of all adult members of the tribe had veto power over the Advisory Council. Tribal politics tended to be dominated by a small number of families who got elected to the Advisory Council because they had the education and facility in English to deal with the bureau, although they were not fully trusted by the rank and file. Unable to exercise power directly, the people manipulated power with protracted discussion at General Council meetings, a process that outsiders often regarded as factionalism but in reality was a traditional strategy for negotiating from a position of weakness. In this way, the majority managed to prevent implementation of measures they opposed even if they did not necessarily get what they really wanted. Menominee leaders often counted on this tactic to help them resist BIA dictates. In 1934, when the Indian Reorganization Act offered a format for constitutional government to tribes across the country, the Menominees retained their existing government but utilized the Collier program to expand their advisory powers to review budgetary matters.

On the eve of World War II, when Ada was six, the family—now including her sister Ferial—moved from the Menominee Reservation to Milwaukee where there were better economic opportunities and where her brother Robert was born. Ada and Joe, Jr., were the only Indian children in the public school they attended. The class bullies picked on them until they figured out a strategy of taking on their tormentors one at a time, and then they gave as good as they got. Despite the city conveniences of electricity and running water, however, the Deers missed the reservation, and after the war began, they moved back to their old home where Ada's youngest sibling, Constance, or "Connie Junior," was born. Dissatisfied with the government and parochial schools on the reservation, Ada's mother persuaded the bureau and local white authorities to let her children attend a public school in the town of Shawano ten miles away. Again, the Deer children encountered anti-Indian attitudes among their classmates, but the encouragement of teachers who recognized Ada's intellectual ability overshadowed the hostility. She later recalled, "I was lucky. My teachers took an interest in me. Other Indians were not so lucky. About twenty-five of us entered high school together. Only seven graduated. Some were dropouts. Others were 'kickouts.' Most weren't given a fair chance."[3] It was more than luck; it also was being her mother's daughter. Besides recognizing Ada's scholarly ability, her teachers could relate to Ada's spunky, outgoing personality. Like many non-Indians, the teachers found highly disconcerting the quiet, expressionless demeanor some Indian students employed to cope with unfamiliar situations and interpreted it as hostility or stupidity.

Even with her mother's encouragement, however, it was not easy for Ada to keep up with her schoolwork given the rigors of living in a cabin without modern conveniences and sharing limited space with four younger siblings whom she was expected to help bring up. Although Ada usually made good grades without much effort, she learned persistence and self-discipline on the tough subjects that she took to qualify for college. She not only demonstrated considerable academic ability, she also developed social skills and particularly enjoyed school dances. One summer she was chosen to attend a youth leadership camp. In her senior year she won the school's Original Oration Contest, was editor of her class yearbook, and was appointed to the Youth Advisory Board of the Governor's Commission on Human Rights.

When she graduated from high school in the spring of 1953, Ada had little sense of how deeply the atmosphere in Congress threatened Indian people. Life seemed to be full of promise, not just for the Menominees in general but for Ada in particular. Constance had entered her daughter's photograph, taken in an "Indian" outfit, in a publicity contest to find the "six most beautiful Indian girls" for an appearance in a B grade Hollywood western, "The Battle of Rogue River." Ada won a bit part, took her first plane ride, and had her initial taste of life in the public eye.[4] She did not pursue stardom in Hollywood, but events began to unfold that ultimately brought Ada and the Menominees more publicity than they ever imagined.

For most of Ada's life, the Menominees had been involved in a suit against the BIA. Exercising the power they had acquired in 1934 under the Indian Reorganization Act to review their account books, the Menominees uncovered substantial evidence of BIA mismanagement in marketing timber blown down in a tornado on the reservation. Rather than harvesting the timber immediately, the BIA let it rot in order to avoid depressing timber prices for white-owned lumber companies. The case dragged on for seventeen years until, in 1951, the U.S. Court of Claims handed down a judgment that netted the tribe $7.6 million. Added to their existing savings, the tribe had nearly $10 million in working capital. A majority of Menominees voted to use more than half of the judgment money for $1,500 per capita payments to the approximately 3,300 Menominees as compensation for lost income. Most agreed that some of the remaining money should go to improving the hospital and other facilities and exploring economic diversification to meet the demands of a growing population with rising economic expectations. Release of per capitas had to be approved by Congress, which added a termination rider to the tribe's request. The proposed legislation was dropped because of Menominee opposition to the rider, thus staving off termination for a while but also withholding the tribe's per capita payments.

Proponents of termination had long eyed the Menominees as good experimental material since the tribe appeared to have sufficient capital to go it alone. In the view of Senator Arthur V. Watkins (R.-Utah), the primary architect of termination, they already were well along the way to assimilation. He thought that all Menominees were trying to emulate the highly acculturated, English-speaking leadership. Instead, these leaders formed only one of several long established, coexisting subsets of the population who had adopted different strategies in relation to the larger society in order to survive as Menominees.[5] Watkins was so eager to push termination that in June of 1953, before the Senate even voted on HCR 108, he made a special trip to the Menominee Reservation to address a General Council meeting.[6] Employing threats, chicanery, and deception, he procured the tribe's ostensible agreement to termination.

The turnout was light at the meeting because people did not even want to discuss the matter, but the few in attendance constituted the 5 percent quorum that had been adopted as a temporary expedient during World War II so that tribal business could be conducted while many adults were away in military service or defense work. Watkins demanded an immediate response, cutting short the kind of lengthy discussion typical of General Councils. He made clear that Congress was determined to terminate the Menominees whether they liked it or not, and he implied that a favorable vote would at least give the Menominees some say regarding the terms of the legislation. He also promised the release of their per capitas. A single motion covered the request for their per capitas and an agreement to "the principle of termination." There were 169 votes for the motion; five opposed. A few days later, when people had had time to discuss the situation, they called another General Council attended by nearly 200 people who voted unanimously against the motion, even if it meant foregoing their per capitas.[7]

Congress refused to recognize this second vote, ignored petitions signed by many more Menominees opposing termination, and passed the Menominee Termination Act on June 18, 1954. It was to take effect in 1958 to allow time to develop a plan to convey the Menominees' land from federal to state jurisdiction and develop a structure to manage their assets and business affairs. Complications in creating a workable plan and Menominee protests that the tribe was not ready to be terminated led to delays until 1961 when Congress decreed that, ready or not, termination would take effect.

Ada, who enrolled in the University of Wisconsin at Madison in the fall of 1953, was not particularly aware of tribal politics. Few Menominees, in fact, knew what was going on in Washington, D.C., where the planning committee, composed of a few government-appointed Menominee representatives but dominated by lawyers and legislators, worked in isolation from the tribe. It would also be some time before the legislation made a discernible difference in the lives of most Menominees. Meanwhile, Ada, inspired by her mother, decided to enter the medical field and become a doctor, but she found herself drawn to the humanities and social sciences. As a member of the Youth Advisory Board of the Governor's Human Rights Commission, she expanded her knowledge of Indian affairs and honed her skills in public speaking. By her senior year, Ada had decided that a career in social work was ideal for her academic interests and natural inclinations. When she graduated, Ada became the first Menominee to earn a Bachelor's degree at the University of Wisconsin.[8]

While Ada was in college, a bitter schism developed on the reservation. All Menominees, whatever their social status, opposed termination, which they denounced as an unjust and capricious policy experiment that treated them as "government guinea pigs." Opinion divided sharply, however, as to the best course of action in regard to termination. Ada's mother was a highly vocal supporter of the faction that believed termination was designed explicitly to rob the Menominees of their valuable land and timber and to destroy the Menominee tribe. These people sought to prevent termination from ever taking effect. Others felt it was futile to oppose Uncle Sam and wanted a termination plan that would protect their assets and salvage some degree of tribal integrity despite losing federal recognition and their rights as Indians. Predictably, the old guard leadership, which still dominated the reservation institutions that the people depended on, took the latter position and used the threat of economic retaliation to silence criticism and dissent. In 1957, Constance Deer was summarily fired from her job as a nurse at the reservation hospital for her opposition. Refusing to be intimidated, she became even more outspoken. She scraped together the money to go to Washington to lobby Congress for Menominee rights, but her arguments against termination had little effect. Back home, Connie expected Ada, who was to graduate that spring, to return to the reservation and do something about the situation there.

Ada wanted to make a difference in Indian affairs and to appease her mother, but she knew that she needed more education and practical experience in order to really help. She therefore immediately enrolled in Columbia University's Graduate School of Social Work because of its reputation as the top-ranked program in the country. However, Ada quickly discovered that her academic mentors neither knew nor cared to be informed about American Indian problems. She had a hard time developing a program of course work and field placements that would prepare her for the career she wanted in community organization rather than conventional casework or psychiatric social work.

After a year at Columbia, she was exhausted and broke. Tribal educational funding that had helped defray some of her undergraduate expenses had been an early casualty of the dire fiscal effects of termination. She spent the next two years working with African American youth programs in the Bedford-Stuyvesant area and then resumed her studies with the aid of graduate fellowships. Her difficulties with advisors who just could not comprehend her goals as an Indian person persisted. "In many ways," she recalled, "Columbia had been an unpleasant experience," but she found some compensation in the excitement of living in New York and the people she met there.[9] In 1961 Ada became the first American Indian to complete a Master's degree at Columbia and the first member of her tribe to earn a Master's degree.

Ada was eager to return to the Midwest to work with Indian people. She could not find work on the Menominee Reservation where her mother's activism had alienated those who controlled employment. She accepted the position of program director at the Waite Neighborhood House in Minneapolis, one of the few urban agencies in the country with an Indian program. The following year, she had an opportunity to meet Philleo Nash, whose appointment as commissioner of Indian affairs by John F. Kennedy marked a rejection of the postwar Indian policy and promotion of respect for Indian rights and tribal self-determination. Nash, who held a Ph.D. in anthropology, was impressed with Ada's depth of understanding of the problems created by relocation and she, in turn, was impressed with his approachability, expertise, and compassion as an administrator. Nash hinted that the BIA needed people like Ada, and two years later she was offered a job as community services coordinator in the bureau's Minneapolis area office. Although interested in learning about the BIA from the inside, Ada wondered if she would be discouraged from speaking candidly on Indian affairs. She was relieved to find that she had complete freedom in her program of leadership training for tribal self-determination and in her outreach work to educate the white community about Indian problems. By 1964, Ada's effectiveness prompted Nash to give her paid leave for six months with instructions to "go wherever you want and meet whomever you want . . . to learn as much as you can about Indian affairs." During this period, she traveled widely among Indian communities and learned about their concerns. For Ada, "It was like packing twenty-five years experience and education into half a year."[10]

Unfortunately, by the time Ada returned to Minneapolis, there had been a massive turnover in the Indian Bureau. After Kennedy's death, the Johnson administration looked for quick fixes to Indian problems and overruled Nash's arguments for patience. Though his superiors professed concern for Indian rights, they were not inclined to support him against senators whose white constituents took precedence over Indians. Disheartened by the undermining of Indian confidence in the bureau that he had worked so hard to establish, Nash resigned, and many of his handpicked personnel were replaced or reassigned.[11]

Ada's old job in Minneapolis had been abolished, and she was put to work as an employment counselor with no voice in program development and no recognition of her broad knowledge of Indian affairs. She quit the bureau and found a job with an Indian project under the auspices of the University of Minnesota. It proved unsatisfactory, as did her subsequent position as a school social worker with the Minneapolis Board of Education, which assigned her to a school with few Indian students. In any event, Ada was anxious to return to Wisconsin because of the Menominees' growing difficulties with termination. She was delighted when the University of Wisconsin-Stevens Point offered her the directorship of the campus Upward Bound project. She also had responsibility for developing other programs to prepare Indian students for college and to help them complete their degrees. Besides affording the opportunity to work with Indian students, Stevens Point was less than two hours drive from the former reservation, now Menominee County.

Ada found a dismal situation when she returned home. Although termination had been touted as freeing Indians from second-class citizenship, the terminated Menominee people were more restricted, kept in greater ignorance, and less able to operate on their own behalf than had been the case under the most repressive regimes of the Indian Bureau in times past. How could this have happened?

The termination plan developed between 1954 and 1961 was enormously complex, so complex that the Menominees understood neither its details nor its implications.[12] Briefly, it was designed to transfer the tax-free reservation land from the jurisdiction of the United States to the jurisdiction of the State of Wisconsin as county land subject to taxation and to convey the Menominees' tribally held assets from federal to private corporate management. The Menominees, given only the limited choice between having the reservation divided among three neighboring counties or becoming a new county on a ten-year trial basis, opted for the latter in order to keep their sense of tribal identity and former reservation land base intact. Termination removed the BIA infrastructure for which the tribe had paid. The new county did not have school buses or buildings, police cars or jails, a courthouse, hospital facilities, or road maintenance equipment. Therefore, Menominees had to contract for services with neighboring Shawano County, where a great deal of anti-Indian prejudice prevailed. The arrangement was particularly unfortunate since Menominee County people could not vote in Shawano County for officials in control of such sensitive community concerns as public education and law enforcement.

Under the termination plan, the tribe's assets and responsibility for their management were conveyed to a corporation, Menominee Enterprises, Inc. (MEI). Each Menominee enrolled as of 1954 received a certificate representing 100 nonnegotiable shares of voting stock and a $3,000 bond paying 4 percent annual interest to mature in the year 2000. The Menominee tribal roll was closed with the passage of the Termination Act in 1954—a kind of genocide by accident of date of birth. It was not unusual for older siblings in one family to be legally Menominee, that is, enrolled certificate holders, while their younger brothers and sisters were not.

The structure of MEI appeared to give a majority voice to the Menominees. Seven of the twelve members of the board of directors had to be Menominees and so did four of the seven members of the MEI Common Stock and Voting Trust that elected the board of directors. However, the body of the Menominee people, the Menominee certificate holders, were two levels removed from the board that made decisions. Furthermore, the structure was rigged so that many of the Menominee elected officers were people likely to go along with the views of white businessmen who served on the board of directors or voting trust. The Menominee certificate holders who elected the members of the voting trust that elected the board had very little power. If the structure of the MEI seems complicated, bear in mind that it was not presented this clearly to the Menominees when termination took effect. The Menominees soon began to feel the effects of termination, but only legal expertise and research ultimately laid bare the corporate structure for general comprehension.

According to the termination plan, the MEI Assistance Trust held the certificates of minors and adult incompetents. As designated by the plan, a non-Menominee officer of the First Wisconsin Trust Company voted those certificates as a block. Minors were people under the age of twenty-one, which meant that Menominee parents or guardians did not have charge of their children's or wards' assets. A couple might vote for Candidate A, for example, only to realize that their minor children's shares were voted for Candidate B, favored by the officer voting the shares of the assistance trust. Further abuse came from rulings on the competency of adults to vote their own shares. In 1954 a BIA employee determined the competency of individuals, and her criteria included whether a person spoke English and conformed to the norms of non-Indian society. For example, Ernest Neconish, a respected, bilingual elder who cast one of five votes against termination in 1953 because he understood Watkins' terms, always observed traditional tribal protocol on formal occasions and spoke through an interpreter. On that basis, the employee declared him incompetent and empowered the assistance trust to vote his shares.

As they lost the authority to control their assets, the Menominees began to see their economic situation deteriorate. The Menominees' systematic impoverishment during the 1960s stemmed from three unwarranted assumptions on which the termination plan was based. The first was that the Menominees were "ready" for termination because they had a nest egg of nearly $10 million. In fact, more than half of this sum was already dispersed in per capita payments as part of the termination legislation of 1954. Some $2 million more had to be spent on per capitas to rectify a BIA bookkeeping error in stumpage underpayments that occurred prior to termination. Most astonishing, the government was so beguiled by the myth of rich Menominees that the Menominees were required to pay a substantial amount of the cost (including high-priced legal counsel) to produce the termination plan they had not wanted in the first place. This does not exhaust the list of ill-advised expenditures that left the Menominees with a $350,000 operating deficit at the outset of termination in 1961. The second assumption—shared by many members of the business community, lawyers, government officials, and Indian politicians conditioned to accept the views of their white associates—was that Indians were by nature incompetent to recognize their own best interests and should be left in the dark as much as possible. Finally and most disheartening was the widely accepted view that the Menominees had brought their problems on themselves and had no reason to complain because they had voted for termination in order to exchange their tribal birthright for a mess of per capitas.

The Menominees had no access to their own financial resources, controlled by MEI, to oppose the injustices they faced. Termination had abolished tribal government and turned their reservation into a county in little more than name. MEI, in effect, had become the Menominees' government and, as owner of all the pretermination tribal assets, the county's only taxpayer. Wisconsin did not want to be stuck with a dependent county, and so the state jacked up the tax assessment in Menominee County accordingly. Instead of the old General Councils where the Menominees discussed what was going on, they now had shareholders' meetings conducted by condescending officials. While they saw familiar faces from the old tribal Advisory Council on the board of directors, there also were white men claiming to be their leaders. Slick reports to shareholders with colored illustrations and incomprehensible graphs proclaimed how well the corporation was doing, but any Menominee could see things were going downhill.

Faced with debt, an overwhelming tax burden, a lumber mill the bureau had allowed to deteriorate, and empty coffers, MEI sold the tribe's utility companies, closed the hospital, and reduced the mill's labor force. These economizing measures severely lowered the standard of living, especially the health of the community, and raised the unemployment rate. MEI encouraged shareholders to buy their homesites in the county and gave them a discount if they applied their bonds to the purchase price. This scheme lessened the corporation's tax burden by shifting property to individual Menominees and allowed it to retire bonds early with no outlay of cash or interest payments. With layoffs of mill workers, however, people who accepted this offer often found that they could not pay their new taxes and stood in danger of losing their land.

What ultimately precipitated united action against MEI was the board's total incomprehension of the depth of tribal feeling shared by all the Menominees in regard to their land, woods, and waters. Always desperate for revenue, MEI had leased a stretch of the Wolf River, the county's main waterway, to the state of Wisconsin for a public campground. It also leased lots on some small lakes and along the Wolf River where whites built summer homes. MEI then quietly sold these plots outright to increase the number of county taxpayers. This was a limited expedient, however, because much of the county not covered by productive forests was swampy wetland. In 1967 MEI entered into a "50/50" partnership with a major midwestern land developer to build dams to make artificial lakes that would affect more than 5,000 acres of county land and create 2,500 parcels of expensive, taxable real estate.

The timing of the land development partnership—often called Legend Lake for the first in a projected chain of lakes—happened to coincide with new opportunities for the Menominees to strike back. In 1966, a federally funded agency, Wisconsin Judicare, was established to assist indigent clients in northern Wisconsin. Some Menominees turned to the director, Joseph Preloznik, to help stop the Lakes project. Besides revealing MEI's deceptions about the project, Preloznik discovered that the Wisconsin Department of Natural Resources had winked at the developer's failure to obtain permits for dams that threatened ecological degradation even beyond the project area. He also learned that Legend Lake was but the most recent skein in termination's incredible tangle of goof-ups, cover-ups, and obfuscation that he needed to unsnarl and explain in layman's terms so that the Menominees could make informed decisions about the courses of action available to them.

In addition to access to long-needed legal assistance, the Menominees benefited from the experiences of their own people who had relocated to urban areas. Not dependent on MEI-controlled jobs and resources, they were able to challenge the old leadership and the white power structure. The December 1969 shareholders meeting in Keshena signaled the new order. Ada's sister Connie, now a student at the University of Wisconsin in Madison, questioned MEI's financial report. Told that she could find the detailed figures at the corporation's office, she went there, but officials turned her away with the excuse that they were too complex for her to understand. The rebuff roused Ada and other Menominees to action.

By early 1970, Connie, Ada, and Preloznik had joined forces to inform the Menominee people who lived in Chicago and Milwaukee about the situation on their former reservation. The meetings evolved into Determination of Rights and Unity of Menominee Shareholders (DRUMS), with Jim White and Lloyd Powless as leaders of the local chapters in these cities. In early July, DRUMS held an informational meeting at the Keshena school gym. Predictably, MEI labeled DRUMS "outside agitators" and, to discourage attendance, deputized twenty-five mill hands, who lined up menacingly along the back wall. Nevertheless, the room was soon packed. Apart from some initial heckling of DRUMS speakers and a minor fracas between the MEI "guards" and a media person outside the building, the meeting was peaceful. It was a real eye-opener for county residents. George Kenote, a Menominee and chair of the voting trust, spoke for MEI, but his patronizing double-talk was no match for lawyer Preloznik and well-informed DRUMS members. A Menominee County chapter of DRUMS soon formed and launched a monthly DRUMS newspaper.

Although MEI tried not to publicize the fact, in December of 1970 the Menominees had the opportunity to abolish the voting trust that included the assistance trust, which had exercised such extraordinary power in Menominee affairs. Every ten years for thirty years after termination began, the shareholders could decide by majority vote whether or not to continue the trust, but its continuation was virtually assured because the trust itself controlled the votes of minors and incompetents, nearly 20 percent of the total in 1970. Since DRUMS had organized so recently and time was short, Preloznik obtained a court order to delay the vote until the following April in order to mount a proxy fight. Although the MEI management described proxies as "gang voting," they were sufficiently shaken to expand the trust from four to seven members to allow the Menominees more representation. Because of deaths and inheritance, the shares were no longer all allocated in blocs of 100 per Menominee (some had even passed out of Menominee hands), so DRUMS devoted an enormous amount of volunteer leg- and paperwork to locate the scattered shareholders and persuade them to sign proxies for DRUMS to vote their shares. In the April balloting, the majority of shares voted favored discontinuing the trust, but not all of the shares were voted. Therefore, DRUMS lost on a technicality that required 51 percent of the *total* number of shares be cast against the trust, a percentage greater than DRUMS had amassed. Despite this disappointment, the proxy fight demonstrated the power of unified effort, and if DRUMS could not abolish the voting trust, the proxies could help to take it over. In a special election, Ada and another DRUMS activist won positions on the trust.

DRUMS took the offensive. In 1971, Preloznik initiated litigation against MEI and the land developer. At the same time, DRUMS held protest demonstrations, picketing at the land sales office in the country, at posh restaurants around the state where MEI treated potential purchasers of Legend Lake property to steak dinners, and at the First Wisconsin Trust Company in Milwaukee. In August, DRUMS became formally incorporated with White as national president and Powless as vice president. During the first two weeks of October DRUMS conducted a well-planned and highly publicized march of 221 miles from Keshena to the state capitol in Madison to enlist the support of Governor Patrick Lucey, who continued to hope for a reconciliation between MEI and DRUMS. Besides efforts to improve conditions in the county, DRUMS was now fully committed to the daunting goal of a Congressional act overturning termination. By the end of 1971, Preloznik had contacted the Native American Rights Fund (NARF), which helped him draft legislation with regular input from the Menominee people.

ADA threw herself into DRUMS's work. While White united the Menominee people in mass public expressions of their opposition to MEI and termination itself, Ada appealed to the American public to right this great wrong. Drawing on a national network developed during college and graduate school, through her various jobs, and in her travels, she rallied housewives, students, philanthropists, university professors, and people prominent in Indian affairs to give their time, effort, and money to support DRUMS's endeavors. In many ways, Ada became the public face of DRUMS.

When regular elections for new voting trust positions were held in November, DRUMS and MEI each submitted slates of candidates, and Governor Lucey tried to push a compromise slate. The DRUMS candidates, including Ada, won, and she became chair of the voting trust. The result was that DRUMS took over MEI, and so MEI became dedicated to the repeal of termination. At the behest of MEI, Ada went to Washington to lobby Congress. As the action moved increasingly to Washington, however, DRUMS began showing signs of internal dissension, and its members polarized between White and Ada. Ironically, DRUMS's success destroyed MEI's utility as a symbol of all the wrongs of termination. After chasing down proxies, picketing, and protesting, the rank and file wanted immediate results. But only Congress could abolish termination, and even if DRUMS achieved that goal, the effects of more than a decade of termination could not be undone overnight.

Intent on carrying the fight to repeal termination to the halls of Congress, Ada tended to underestimate the growing rift in DRUMS and the lengths to which their opponents eventually would go to discredit them. With the Nixon administration having officially denounced the termination policy, Ada knew DRUMS could count on Republican support but, like all politically astute Indian leaders, she knew of the perils for any minority to put all its eggs in one political basket. In 1972 she attended the Democratic convention to promote an Indian rights plank in the party platform. The Menominees' Congressional delegation—all Democrats—were solidly behind the Menominees, and they had begun working on legislation, based on drafts supplied by Judicare and NARF, to repeal termination. But passage was far from assured. When the act was first introduced in 1972, Congress recessed before it even came up for a vote. In Wisconsin, rumors flew that the failure was Ada's fault and that she had "sold out."

When Ada began visiting offices on Capitol Hill, some people recognized her name but not her face. Ada's disarming response to people who remembered her mother was, "Same family, same cause, different generation!" No one had paid much attention to "Ma Deer," but Ada's lobbying brought out major dailies such as the *Washington Post* and the *New York Times* in support of the Menominee cause. Although Ada tried to stress the essential role of DRUMS and all Menominees in bringing the struggle this far, the media could not resist focusing on the dynamic, articulate, photogenic Indian woman. These assets in dealing with the white world, however, were a liability among those who already resented and distrusted her outspoken, "un-Indian" take-charge style. With the limelight shifting to Ada, Jim White resigned from DRUMS and called for it to disband.

Reintroduced in 1973, the Menominee Restoration Act passed overwhelmingly in the House on October 16 and in the Senate on December 7. The bill required the immediate election of a nine-member Restoration Committee as the interim government. This committee would develop a constitution, oversee the opening and updating of the tribal roll, and dismantle and restructure the corporation. Ada's election as chair of the committee, in effect making her the head of the restored Menominee tribe, demonstrated that she still had the confidence of a majority of her people. Nevertheless, as the committee members struggled to create a constitution, critics charged them with dragging their feet and ignored their attempts to keep the Menominees informed through open meetings and printed materials.

Although deeply aware of intratribal dissension, the committee and many Menominees were taken off guard on January 1, 1975, when a new group of young militants calling themselves the Menominee Warrior Society (not a traditional Menominee institution) occupied a vacant mansion owned by the Roman Catholic order of Alexian Brothers in the town of Gresham several miles from the reservation. They claimed the building for the Menominee tribe to use as a hospital. Inspired by Alcatraz, Wounded Knee, and other pan-Indian takeovers of government property in the 1960s and early 1970s, the Warriors had not participated in DRUMS's systematic campaign against termination.

The Restoration Committee, fatigued by the long struggle to repeal termination and their work to restore stability to the reservation, responded in exasperation that the building was not on Menominee land and would be a white elephant to renovate, especially when their plans were well underway for a health facility on the reservation. Ada and her supporters also were annoyed that the press, along with prominent figures in the fields of entertainment and civil rights, who had remained indifferent and even negative toward DRUMS during its first years, rushed to Gresham to lionize the "Warriors." Even the governor ignored the Restoration Committee, the Menominees' federally designated government at the time, and appointed an arbitrator to treat solely with the Warriors and Alexian Brothers. The Warriors revealed their real objective in their demand that Restoration Committee members be removed from office. Despite a ringing battle cry of "Deed [to the property] or Death," the occupation gradually fizzled out, with some Warriors doing time for vandalism, but the incident further delayed the committee's work and exacerbated growing violence on the reservation, including arson and murder, that lasted for several years.

With the approval of the new tribal constitution in 1976, Ada resigned from the Restoration Committee, satisfied that the Menominee were properly launched for the future, and the next year, she accepted a position as a lecturer in the School of Social Work at the University of Wisconsin in Madison. Another year passed before the Menominees held elections and the new government became fully operative. Ada had sought representation of all the Menominees so that no individual or faction would become indefinitely entrenched in power, and the Menominees seem to have realized her goal. Over the years, membership in the Legislature has included Jim White (who took back the family surname, Washinawatok, changed to White in his grandfather's generation), many of Ada's long-time supporters, her brother Robert, old-line MEI officers, a former Warrior Society member, and younger people newly involved in tribal affairs. The Menominees have made steady progress since the postrestoration turmoil in lumbering, new tribal enterprises, health, education, welfare, and programs to perpetuate the tribal language and traditions.

Although Ada's identity remained firmly rooted in her tribe, she sought to use her experiences with Menominee termination to promote Native rights more broadly. In 1977, she completed a two-year congressional appointment to the American Indian Policy Review Commission, a massive investigative effort by a team of distinguished Indian people in response to a decade of grievances expressed in Indian activism across the country. The commission produced a multivolume report on the state of Indian affairs and policy recommendations.

Recognizing that the Menominee tragedy stemmed largely from their lack of political power or influence, Ada sought to become more involved in state and national politics. A registered Democrat since 1969, she ran unsuccessfully for the office of secretary of state of Wisconsin in 1978 and 1984. In 1981–82, she was tapped to serve on a commission established by the Democratic Party to address the issues of underrepresented constituents and the rights of women and minorities. Continuing her involvement with the party, in 1984 she served as a delegate at large at the Democratic National Convention, and in 1992 she won the Democratic primary in Wisconsin's Second District to become the first Indian woman to run for Congress. "Me Nominee," Ada proclaimed with her irrepressible humor when the results were announced. She lost in the general election to a Republican newscaster, who was more adept in the challenging give-and-take with the media. Many political observers attributed her defeat to her resolute refusal of contributions from Political Action Committees (PACs), a decision that gave her opponent, who accepted PAC money, an edge in campaign funding. This decision reflected her commitment, deepened by the Menominee struggle against MEI, to making political institutions responsive to individual citizens rather than to well-heeled special interest groups.

Given her vast experience and the contacts she made while lobbying for the Menominees in Washington, Ada was a natural choice for assistant secretary of the interior for Indian affairs (formerly called commissioner of Indian affairs) when President Clinton took office in 1993. She was not the first Indian to hold the job, but she was the first woman. Responding to congressional hearings with grace and aplomb, she received an unprecedented standing ovation upon her confirmation. She saw her appointment as redounding to the honor of the Menominee tribe rather than simply a personal achievement. Consequently, she chose to be sworn in on the reservation by Menominee tribal judge Sarah Skubitz at the "Woodland Bowl," the traditional tribal powwow grounds, where some 5,000 people gathered for the occasion.

Ada's experience in the Menominee restoration battle made her acutely sensitive to the vulnerability of Native people throughout the United States. One of the issues with which she had to deal as head of the BIA was Indian gaming. First bingo and then casino-style gambling had begun to provide substantial revenue to some tribes. Complaining of violation of state sovereignty and special privileges for Indians, states and non-Indian gaming interests challenged tribal sovereignty in the courts. Generally, the courts upheld tribal sovereignty, and Indian gaming proliferated during Ada's tenure. In 1997 Congress established the National Indian Gaming Commission as a regulatory body. The future of Indian gaming seemed in part to rest on the commission's ability to reconcile opponents, promote responsible gaming, and prevent the involvement of organized crime. Although she already headed the BIA, Ada agreed to serve as acting chair of the commission until a regular appointment was made, and she divided her time for a number of exhausting months between two full-time jobs.

Ada's support for gaming—and the sovereignty it embodied—was not the only way in which she supported tribal self-determination across the country. Aware that the Alaska Native Claims Act of 1971, touted as benefiting Native people, bore some frightening parallels to the Menominee Termination Act, Ada unhesitatingly approved federal recognition and protection of tribal sovereignty for the 224 Alaskan Native villages. Acknowledging that many long-term problems in the BIA remained to be dealt with, she accomplished the specific goals that had prompted her to accept the position in the first place, and in 1997, she resigned to return to Madison and academic life. In January 2000, she was appointed head of the university's Indian Studies program.

Ada Deer's leadership dramatically changed the lives of all Menominees, both male and female. A non-Indian mother, a college education, and even long residence away from the Menominee reservation made her no less a Menominee. Taking the skills she learned from her mother and honed in the non-Indian world, Ada confronted the leadership of her tribe, powerful political and economic interests in Wisconsin, and ultimately the Congress of the United States to defend the rights of her people. She then took her commitment to democracy, self-determination, and tribal sovereignty to the BIA. Her ability to use the leadership and organizational styles of the non-Indian world helped the Menominees win a significant victory in the twentieth century, and her example provides genuine hope for the rights of all Native people in the twenty-first.

NOTES

Besides published sources cited, a great deal of the information on the drive to repeal the Menominee Termination Act and restore the reservation is based on my firsthand observations as an Action Anthropologist recruited by Ada, who knew me from various Indian conferences we both had attended. This account also is enriched by interviews with Ada conducted in the course of her visits with me since the summer of 1999.

1. For information on termination, see Donald L. Fixico, *Termination and Relocation: Federal Indian Policy, 1945–1960* (Albuquerque: University of New Mexico Press, 1986), and Gary Orfield, *A Study of the Termination Policy* (Denver, CO: National Congress of American Indians, 1965). For a broader study of land loss and other effects of allotment, see Kirke Kickingbird and Karen Ducheneaux, *One Hundred Million Acres* (New York: Macmillan, 1973).

2. Ada Deer, *Speaking Out* (Chicago: Childrens Press, 1970), 16.

3. Ibid., 32.

4. Ibid., 39.

5. Louise Spindler, "Menominee," in *Handbook of North American Indians*, vol. 15: *Northeast* (Washington, D.C.: Smithsonian Institution, 1978), 722.

6. Arthur V. Watkins, "Termination of Federal Supervision: The Removal of Restrictions over Indian Property and Person," *The Annals of the American Academy of Political and Social Science* 311 (1957): 55.

7. Deborah Shames, ed., *Freedom with Reservation: The Menominee Struggle to Save Their Land and People* (Washington: National Committee to Save the Menominee People and Forests, 1972), 7–9.

8. Deer, 38–42.

9. Ibid., 47.

10. Ibid., 52–53.

11. James Officer, "Philleo Nash: Anthropologist and Administrator," in *Applied Anthropologist and Public Servant: The Life and Work of Philleo Nash*, ed. R. Landman and K. Halpern, National Association for the Practice of Anthropology, *Bulletin* 7 (1988): 11–15.

12. For additional information, see Nancy Oestreich Lurie, "Menominee Termination: From Reservation to Colony," *Human Organization* 31 (1972): 257–70; Lurie, "To Save the Menominee People and Forests," in *Approaches to Algonquian Archaeology*, ed. M. Hanna and B. Kooyman (Calgary: Archaeological Association of the University of Calgary, 1982), 243–52; Lurie, "Menominee Termination," in *An Anthology of Western Great Lakes Indian History*, ed. Donald L. Fixico (Milwaukee: University of Wisconsin-Milwaukee, 1987), 243–52; and Nicholas Perloff, *Menominee Drums: Tribal Termination and Restoration* (Norman: University of Oklahoma Press, 1982).

FURTHER READING

In Anthropology, History, and Literature

Albers, Patricia, and Beatrice Medicine, eds. *The Hidden Half: Studies of Plains Indian Women*. Washington, DC: University Press of America, 1983.

Albers, Patricia, and Willaim James. "Illusion and Illumination: Visual Images of American Indian Women in the West." In *The Women's West*, Ed. Susan Armitage and Elizabeth Jameson. Norman: University of Oklahoma Press, 1987. Pp. 35–50.

Allen, Paula Gunn. *Spider Woman's Granddaughters: Traditional Tales and Contemporary Writing by Native American Women*. Boston: Beacon Press, 1989.

———. *The Sacred Hoop: Recovering the Feminine in American Indian Traditions*. Boston: Beacon Press, 1986.

Anderson, Karen L. *Chain Her By One Foot: The Subjugation of Women in Seventeenth-Century New France*. New York: Routledge, 1991.

Anderson, Karen. *Changing Woman; A History of Racial Ethnic Women in Modern America*. New York: Oxford University Press, 1996.

Awiakta, Marilou. *Selu: Seeking the Corn Mother's Wisdom*. Golden, CO: Fulcrum Publishing, 1993.

Bahr, Diana Myers. *From Mission to Metropolis: Cupeno Indian Women in Los Angeles*. Norman: University of Oklahoma Press, 1993.

Bataille, Gretchen M. *American Indian Women: A Guide to Research*. New York: Garland, 1991.

———. *Native American Women: A Biographical Dictionary*. New York:Garland, 1993.

Bataille, Gretchen M., and Kathleen Mullen Sands. *American Indian Women: Telling Their Lives*. Lincoln: University of Nebraska Press, 1984.

Bell, Betty Louise. *Faces in the Moon*. Norman: University of Oklahoma Press, 1994.

Benedek, Emily. *Beyond the Four Corners of the World: A Navajo Woman's Journey*. New York: Knopf, 1995.

Bernstein, Alison. "A Mixed Record: The Political Enfranchisement of American Indian Women During the Indian New Deal." *Journal of the West* 23 (1984): 13–20.

Blackwood, Evelyn. "Sexuality and Gender in Certain Native American Tribes: The Case of Cross-Gender Females." *Signs* 10 (1984):27–42.

Bonvillain, Nancy. "Gender Relations in Native North America." *American Indian Culture and Research Journal* 13 (1989): 1–28.

Boyer, Ruth McDonald, and Narcissus Duffy Gayton. *Apache Mothers and Daughters: Four Generations of a Family*. Norman: University of Oklahoma Press, 1992.

Brand, Joanna. *The Life and Death of Anna Mae Aquash*. Toronto: Lorimer & Co., 1978.

Braund, Kathryn E. Holland. "Guardians of Tradition and Handmaidens to Change: Women's Roles in Creek Economic and Social Life during the Eighteenth Century." *American Indian Quarterly* 14 (1990): 239–58.

Brave Bird, Mary. *Ohitika Woman*. New York: Harper Collins, 1992.

Brown, Jennifer S. H. *Strangers in Blood: Fur Trade Families in Indian Country*. Vancouver: University of British Columbia Press, 1980.

Brown, Judith K. "Economic Organization and the Position of Women Among the Iroquois," *Ethnohistory* 17 (1970): 151–67.

Buffalohead, Priscilla A. "Farmers, Warriors, Traders: A Fresh look at Ojibway Women." *Minnestota History* 48: (1983): 236–44.

Campbell, Maria. *Halfbreed*. Lincoln: University of Nebraska Press, 1982.

Carson, James Taylor. "From Corn Mothers to Cotton Spinners, Continuity in Choctaw Women's Economic Life, A.D. 950–1830." In *Women of the American South: A Multicultural Reader*, Ed. Christie Farnham. New York: New York University Press, 1997.

Chuchryk, Patricia. *Women of the First Nations*. Winnipeg: University of Manitoba Press, 1994.

Coleman, Michael. "American Indian School Pupils as Cultural Brokers: Cherokee Girls at Brainerd, 1828–1829." In *Between Indian and White Worlds: The Cultural Broker*, Ed. Margaret Connell Szasz. Norman: University of Oklahoma Press, 1994. Pp. 122–36.

Conte, Christine. "Ladies, Livestock, Land, and Lucre: Women's Networks and Social Status on the Western Navajo Reservation." *American Indian Quarterly* 6 (1982): 105–24.

Crow Dog, Mary. *Lakota Woman*. New York: Harper Collins, 1990.

Deloria, Ella. *Waterlily*. Lincoln: University of Nebraska Press, 1988.

Demos, John. *The Tried and True: Native American Women Confronting Colonization*. Oxford: Oxford University Press, 1995.

Devens, Carol. *Countering Colonization: Native American Women and Great Lakes Missions, 1630–1900*. Berkeley: University of California Press, 1992.

Emmericah, Lisa. "'Right in the Midst of My Own People': Native American Women and the Field Matron Program." *American Indian Quarterly* 15 (1991): 201–16.

Erdrich, Louise. *Love Medicine*. New York: Holt, Rinehart & Winton, 1984.

Giglio, Virginia. *Southern Cheyenne Women's Songs*. Norman: University of Oklahoma Press, 1994.

Glancy, Diane. *Pushing the Bear: A Novel of the Trail of Tears*. New York: Harcourt Brace, 1996.

Gonzalez, Ellice B. "An Ethnohistorical Analysis of Micmac Male and Female Economic Roles." *Ethnohistory* 29 (1982): 117–29.

Green, Rayna. "The Pocahontas Perplex: The Image of Indian Women in American Culture." *Massachusetts Review* 16 (1975): 703–704.

———. *Native American Women: A Contextual Bibliography*. Bloomington: Indiana University Press, 1984.

———. *That's What She Said: Contemporary Fiction and Poetry by Native American Women*. Bloomington: Indiana University Press, 1984.

———. *Women In American Indian Society*. New York: Chelsea House, 1992.

Hale, Janet Campbell. *The Jailing of Cecelia Capture*. New York: Random House, 1985.

Harjo, Joy. *She Had Some Horses*. New York: Thunder's Mouth Press, 1983.

Harjo, Joy, and Gloria Bird, eds. *Reinventing the Enemy's Language: Contemporary Native Women's Writings of North America*. New York: W. W. Norton, 1997.

Hill, Sarah. *Weaving New Worlds: Southeastern Cherokee Women and Their Basketry*. Chapel Hill: University of North Carolina Press, 1997.

Hogan, Linda. *Mean Spirit: A Novel*. New York: Atheneum, 1990.

Hopkins, Sarah Winnemucca. *Life Among the Piutes: Their Wrongs and Claims*. Reno: University of Nevada Press, 1994.

Horne, Esther Burnett, and Sally McBeth. *Essie's Story: the Life and Legacy of a Shoshone School Teacher*. Lincoln: University of Nebraska Press, 1998.

Hungry Wolfe, Beverly. *The Ways of My Grandmothers*. New York: Morrow, 1981.

Jacobs, Margaret D. *Engendered Encounters: Feminism and Pueblo Cultures, 1879–1934*. Lincoln: University of Nebraska Press, 1999.

Jensen, Joan. "Native American Women and Agriculture: A Seneca Case Study." *Sex Roles: A Journal of Research* 3 (1977): 423–42.

Johnson, E. Pauline. *The Moccasin Maker*. Norman: University of Oklahoma Press, 1998.

Kidwell, Clara Sue. "Indian Women as Cultural Mediators." *Ethnohistory* 39(1992): 97–107.

Klein, Laura F., and Lillian A. Ackerman, eds. *Women and Power in Native North America*. Norman: University of Oklahoma Press, 1995.

Lamphere, Louise. "Historical and Regional Variability in Navajo Women's Roles." *Journal of Anthropological Research* 45 (1989): 431–56.

Landes, Ruth. *The Ojibwa Woman*. New York: Norton, 1971.

Landsman, Gail. "The 'Other' as Political Symbol: Images of Indians in the Woman Suffrage Movement." *Ethnohistory* 39 (1992): 247–84.

Leacock, Eleanor Burke. "Women in an Egalitarian Society: the Montagnai-Naskapi of Canada." In *Myths of Male Dominance: Collected Articles of Women Cross-Culturally*, Ed. Eleanor Burke Leacock. New York: Monthly Review Press, 1981.

Linderman, Frank B. *Pretty Shield: Medicine Woman of the Crows*. Lincoln: University of Nebraska Press, 1972.

Little Coyote, Bertha, and Virginia Giglio. *Leaving Everything Behind: The Songs and Memories of a Cheyenne Woman*. Norman: University of Oklahoma Press, 1997.

Lurie, Nancy. *Mountain Wolf Woman, Sister of Crashing Thunder: A Winnebago Indian*. Ann Arbor: University of Michigan Press, 1961.

Mankiller, Wilma, and Michael Wallis. *Mankiller: A Chief and Her People*. New York: St. Martin's Press, 1993.

McBride, Bunny. *Molly Spotted Elk: A Penobscot in Paris*. Norman: University of Oklahoma Press, 1995.

———. *Women of the Dawn*. Lincoln: University of Nebraska Press, 1999.

McCartney, Martha W. "Cockacoeske, Queen of Pamunkey: Diplomat and Suzeraine." In *Powhatan's Mantle: Indians in the Colonial Southeast*. Ed. Peter H. Wood, Gregory A. Waselkov, and M. Thomas Hatley. Lincoln: University of Nebraska Press. Pp. 173–95.

Mihesuah, Devon. *Cultivating the Rosebuds: The Education of Women at the Cherokee Female Seminary*. Urbana: University of Illinois Press, 1993.

Namias, June. *White Captives: Gender and Ethnicity on the American Frontier*. Chapel Hill: University of North Carolina Press, 1993.

Niethammer, Carolyn. *Daughters of the Earth: The Lives and Ledgends of American Indian Women*. New York: Collier Books, 1977.

Osburn, Katherine M. B. *Southern Ute Women: Autonomy and Assimilation on the Reservation, 1887–1934*. Albuquerque: University of New Mexico Press, 1998.

Perdue, Theda. *Cherokee Women: Gender and Culture Change, 1700–1830*. Lincoln: University of Nebraska Press, 1998.

Peters, Virginia Bergman. *Women of the Earth Lodges: Tribal Life on the Plains*. North Haven, CT: Archon Books, 1995.

Peterson-del Mar, David. "Intermarriage and Agency: A Chinookan Case Study." *Ethnohistory* 42 (1995): 1–30.

Pool, Carolyn Garrett. "Reservation Policy and the Economic Position of Wichita Women." *Great Plains Quarterly* 8 (1988): 158–71.

Powers, Marla. *Oglala Women: Myth, Ritual, and Reality*. Chicago: University of Chicago Press, 1986.

Reyer, Carolyn, Beatrice Medicine, and Debra Lynn White Plume, eds. *Cante Ohitika Win (Brave Hearted Women): Images of Lakota Women from the Pine Ridge Reservation, South Dakota*. Vermillion: University of South Dakota Press, 1991.

Roessel, Ruth. *Women in Navajo Society*. Rough Rock, AZ: Navajo Resource Center, 1981.

Schlegel, Alice. "Male and Female in Hopi Thought and Action." In *Sexual Stratification: A Cross-Cultural View*, Ed. Alice Schlegel. New York: Columbia University Press, 1977. Pp. 245–69.

Shipek, Florence. *Delfina Cuero: Her Autobiography*. Menlo Park, CA: Ballena Press, 1991.

Shoemaker, Nancy. *Negotiators of Change:Historical Perspectives on Native American Women*. New York: Routledge, 1995.

———. "From Longhouse to Loghouse: Household Structure Among the Senecas in 1900." *American Indian Quarterly* 15 (1991): 329–38.

———. "The Rise or Fall of Iroquois Women," *Journal of Women's History* 2 (1991): 39–57.

Silko, Leslie Marmon. *Ceremony*. New York: Viking Press, 1977.

Sneve, Virginia Driving Hawk. *Completing the Circle*. Lincoln: University of Nebraska Press, 1995.

Spector, Janet D. *What This Awl Means: Feminist Archaeology at a Wahpeton Dakota Village*. St. Paul: Minnesota Historical Society Press, 1993.

Spindler, Louise S. *Menominee Women and Culture Change*. American Anthropological Association, Memoir 91, 1962.

St. Pierre, Mark. *Madonna Swan: A Lakota Woman's Story, As Told Through Mark St. Pierre*. Norman: University of Oklahoma Press. 1991.

Stockel Henrietta. *Women of the Apache Nation: Voices of Truth*. Reno: University of Nevada Press, 1991.

Szasz, Margaret Connell. "'Poor Richard' Meets the Native American: Schooling for Young Indian Women in Eighteenth-Century Connecticut." *Pacific Historical Review* 49 (1980): 215–35.

Tong, Benson. *Susan La Flesche Picotte, M.D.: Omaha Indian Leader and Reformer*. Norman: University of Oklahoma Press, 1999.

Tooker, Elisabeth. "Women in Iroquois Society." In *Extending the Rafters: Interdisciplinary Approaches to Iroquoian Studies*, Ed. Michael K. Foster, Jack Campisi, Marianne Mithun. Albany: State University of New York Press, 1984. Pp. 109–23.

Trennert, Robert A. "Educating Young Indian Girls at Nonreservation Boarding Schools, 1878–1920." *Western Historical Quarterly* 13 (1982): 271–90.

Van Kirk, Sylvia. *Many Tender Ties: Women in Fur Trade Society, 1670–1870*. Norman: University of Oklahoma Press, 1980.

Wall, Steve, ed. *Wisdom's Daughters: Conversations with Women Elders of Native America*. New York: Harper Collins, 1993.

Welch, Deborah. "American Indian Women: Reaching Beyond the Myth." In *New Directions in American Indian History*, Ed. Colin Calloway. Norman: University of Oklahoma Press, 1988. Pp. 31–48.

Woodsum, Jo Ann. "Gender and Sexuality in Native American Societies: A Bibliography." *American Indian Quarterly* 19 (1995): 527–54.

Wright, Mary C. "Economic Development and Native American Women in the Early Nineteenth Century." *American Quarterly* 33 (1981): 525–36.

Youst, Lionel. *She's Tricky Like a Coyote: Annie Miner Peterson, an Oregon Coast Indian Woman*. Norman: University of Oklahoma Press, 1997.

Young, M. Jane. "Women, Reproduction, and Religion in Western Puebloan Society." *Journal of American Folklore* 100 (1987): 436–45.

Young, Mary E. "Women, Civilization, and the Indian Question." In *Clio Was a Woman: Studies in the History of American Women*. Ed. Mabel E. Deutrich and Virginia C. Purdy. Washington, DC: Howard University Press, 1980: 98–110.

INDEX